PUBLIC–PRIVATE PARTNERSHIP MONITOR

PAPUA NEW GUINEA

DECEMBER 2020

ASIAN DEVELOPMENT BANK

6 ADB Avenue, Mandaluyong City, 1550 Metro Manila, Philippines
Tel +63 2 8632 4444; Fax +63 2 8636 2444
www.adb.org

Printed in the Philippines

ISBN 978-92-9262-112-4 (print); 978-92-9262-113-1 (electronic); 978-92-9262-114-8 (ebook)
Publication Stock No. SGP210068-2
DOI: http://dx.doi.org/10.22617/SGP210068-2

Notes:
In this publication, "$" refers to United States dollars.
ADB recognizes "China" as the People's Republic of China.

On the cover: In Papua New Guinea, public–private partnership projects in various sectors have led to sustainable economic growth and development (photos by Gerhard Joren/ADB).

Cover design by Claudette Rodrigo.

Contents

Tables and Figures

Tables

Figures

Foreword

We are pleased to present the *Public–Private Partnership Monitor*, a detailed review of the current state of the public–private partnership (PPP) enabling environment in selected countries in Asia and the Pacific.

Availability of adequate infrastructure is a measure of a country's ability to sustain its economic growth. For economies across Asia and the Pacific, provision of basic infrastructure services, including water, health, energy, transportation, and communications, is an important public sector activity. As demand for infrastructure has increased faster than government budgets, the public sector has increasingly considered partnership with the private sector as an alternate modality for financing infrastructure.

The Asian Development Bank (ADB) estimates that Asia and the Pacific must spend $1.7 trillion a year on infrastructure until 2030 to maintain growth, meet social needs, and respond to the effects of climate change. That amount is expected to go up. The traditional sources of finance for infrastructure—the government's budgetary allocations—have not been enough to meet the demand. Prior to the coronavirus disease (COVID-19) pandemic, ADB estimated an annual infrastructure gap of $204 billion to be filled through private sector investment. That amount is also now expected to increase.

For the private sector, investment in infrastructure, whether through PPPs or otherwise, represents an investment avenue competing with various other investment options available. In order to compete, and to crowd in private capital into infrastructure, governments need to provide a conducive environment to adequately establish and protect the rights of the private sector, and the necessary support to ensure every asset brought to market provides returns that are commensurate with the risks.

The PPP Monitor provides the investor community with business intelligence on the enabling environment, policies, priority sectors, and deals to facilitate informed investment decisions. For ADB developing member countries (DMCs), the PPP Monitor serves as a diagnostic tool to identify gaps in their legal, regulatory, and institutional framework. ADB and other international development agencies can also benefit from the PPP Monitor as it could be useful in initiating dialogues to assess a country's readiness to tap PPPs as a means to develop and sustain its infrastructure.

Building on the success of the previous editions of the PPP Monitor, the new PPP Monitor is now being brought online to widen its reach. More countries will be continually added in the PPP Monitor and it is expected to become a primary knowledge base for assessing a country's PPP environment for the government and the business community. The PPP Monitor features an interactive online version which allows users to compare and contrast the key PPP parameters and features across the DMCs. The online version of the PPP Monitor may be accessed at www.pppmonitor.adb.org.

The PPP Monitor has been upgraded to provide a "one-stop" information source, derived from a consolidation of (i) the previous PPP Monitor; (ii) leading PPP databases of multilateral development banks like the World Bank and the International Finance Corporation (IFC) and organizations like the Economist Intelligence Unit (EIU) [Infrascope] and the Global Infrastructure Hub (GI Hub) [InfraCompass]; (iii) reports of a country's PPP unit; (iv) a country's legal framework; and (v) consultations with leading technical experts and legal firms as well as financial institutions.

The PPP Monitor includes more than 500 qualitative and quantitative indicators to profile the national PPP environment, the sector-specific PPP landscape (for eight identified infrastructure sectors), and the PPP landscape for local government projects. The COVID-19 pandemic has pushed social infrastructure into the forefront of policy and planning; hence, where possible, this PPP Monitor takes a bigger focus on social and municipal aspects like health, education, and affordable housing.

The PPP market in most of ADB DMCs is still at an emerging/developing stage, and continuous regulatory reforms and institutional strengthening are required to facilitate further private sector investment in infrastructure and to create a sustainable pipeline of bankable projects. Through the PPP Monitor, ADB continues to provide support for DMCs in addressing various infrastructure and PPP-related challenges, in developing sustainable infrastructure projects, and in delivering efficient and effective public services through PPPs. ADB also helps DMCs improve their investment climates, formulate sound market regulations, and build robust legal and institutional frameworks to encourage private sector participation in infrastructure through PPPs.

We hope that this PPP Monitor will pave the way for continued dialogue between the public and private sectors and stimulate the adoption of PPPs in Asia and the Pacific region.

Yoji Morishita
Head, Office of Public–Private Partnership
Asian Development Bank

Acknowledgments

The *Public–Private Partnership Monitor: Country Profile—Papua New Guinea* was prepared by the Asian Development Bank (ADB) Office of Public–Private Partnership (OPPP), in close coordination with the Papua New Guinea (PNG) Resident Mission.

Sanjay Grover, public–private partnership (PPP) specialist of the PPP Thematic Group Secretariat, led the preparation of the PPP Monitor. He also developed and streamlined the analytical framework for capturing the national, sectoral, and municipal PPP landscape presented in this report.

Yoji Morishita, head of the OPPP, and Srinivas Sampath, chief of the PPP Thematic Group, provided guidance and support in developing the PPP Monitor.

The PPP Monitor uses data published by the governments of ADB DMCs—on their official websites and in reports, publications, laws, and regulations—as well as data published by other multilateral development agencies and included in industry publications and databases such as those of the World Bank, Organisation for Economic Co-operation and Development (OECD), World Economic Forum, International Monetary Fund (IMF), Inframation Group, IJGlobal, Economist Intelligence Unit (Infrascope Index), Global Infrastructure Hub, TheGlobalEconomy.com, Bloomberg, S&P Global, Trading Economics, and PPP Knowledge Lab.

ADB has partnered with the CRISIL Infrastructure Advisory and Panapps Inc. The CRISIL Infrastructure Advisory shared its expertise and provided inputs in developing the PPP Monitor for PNG while the Panapps Inc. has published this report online.

Ricardo McKlmon, Jezreel Pabia Uy, and Carmelia Godoy managed the contributors internal and external to ADB. With guidance from Papua New Guinea Resident Mission country director David Hill and country economist Ed Faber, Henri Devys and Rosemary Ong from OPPP reviewed the publication and provided quality control.

Several others provided help and support—Cyrel San Gabriel edited the report, Asiatype Inc. and Levi Rodolfo Lusterio performed typesetting and proofreading respectively, and Claudette Rodrigo designed the cover. April-Marie Gallega and Ayun Sundari of the Knowledge Support Division of the ADB Department of Communications provided guidance and assistance in the publication process.

Definition of Terms

Term	Definition
Public–private partnership (PPP)	Contractual arrangement between public (national, state, provincial, or local) and private entities through which the skills, assets, and/or financial resources of each of the public and private sectors are allocated in a complementary manner, thereby sharing the risks and rewards, to seek to provide optimal service delivery and good value to citizens. In a PPP, the public sector retains the ultimate responsibility for service delivery, although the private sector provides the service for an extended time. Within Asian Development Bank operations, all contracts such as performance-based contracts (management and service contracts), lease–operate–transfer, build–own–operate–transfer, design–build–finance–operate, variants, and concessions are considered as various forms of PPP. Excluded are: • contracts involving turnkey design and construction as part of public procurement (engineering, procurement, and construction contracts); • simple service contracts that are not linked to performance standards (those that are more aligned with outsourcing to private contractor staff to operate public assets); • construction contracts with extended warranties and/or maintenance provisions of, for example, up to 5 years post completion (wherein performance risk-sharing is minimal as the assets are new and need only basic maintenance); and • all privatization and divestures.
Affermage or lease contracts	Under a lease contract, the private sector developer is responsible for the service in its entirety and undertakes obligations relating to quality and service standards. Except for new and replacement investments, which remain the responsibility of the government contracting agency, the operator provides the service at his expense and risk. The duration of the leasing contract is typically 10 years and may be renewed up to 20 years. Responsibility for service provision is transferred from the public sector to the private sector and the financial risk for operation and maintenance is borne entirely by the private sector operator. In particular, the operator is responsible for losses and for unpaid consumers' debts. Leases do not involve any sale of assets to the private sector.
Availability-/performance-based payments	Method of investment recovery in PPP projects, when payments to the private party are made by the government contracting agency over the lifetime of a PPP contract in return for making infrastructure or services available for use at acceptable and contractually agreed performance standards.
Best and final offer (BAFO)	An incentive mechanism provided by the government contracting agency to the private sector developer initiating a PPP project through the unsolicited proposal route (USP proponent) to be automatically shortlisted for the final bidding round and provide its best and final offer to match the other bidders' best offer.
Build–lease–transfer	A PPP type whereby a private sector developer is authorized to finance and construct an infrastructure or development facility, and upon its completion hands it over to the government contracting agency on a lease arrangement for a fixed period after which ownership of the facility is automatically transferred to the government contracting agency.

continued on next page

continued from previous page

Term	Definition
Build–operate–transfer	Build–operate–transfer (BOT) and similar arrangements are a specialized concession in which a private firm or consortium finances and develops a new infrastructure project or a major component according to performance standards set by the government. Under BOTs, the private sector developer provides the capital required to build a new facility. Importantly, the private operator now owns the assets for a period set by contract—sufficient to give the developer time to recover investment costs through user charges.
Build–own–operate	A PPP type whereby a private sector developer is authorized to finance, construct, own, operate, and maintain an infrastructure or development facility from which the private sector developer is allowed to recover its total investment, operating and maintenance costs plus a reasonable return thereon by collecting tolls, fees, rentals or other charges from facility users. Under this PPP type, the private sector developer which owns the assets of the facility may assign its operation and maintenance to a facility operator.
Build–transfer	A PPP type under which the private sector developer undertakes the financing and construction of a given infrastructure or development facility, and after its completion hands it over to the government contracting agency, which pays the private sector developer on an agreed schedule its total investments expended on the project, plus a reasonable rate of return thereon. This arrangement may be employed in the construction of any infrastructure or development project, including critical facilities which, for security or strategic reasons, must be operated directly by the government contracting agency.
Commercial close	Indicates the signing of the PPP contract between the government contract agency and the identified private sector developer. Usually occurs after the terms and conditions of the draft PPP contract are negotiated and agreed between the government contracting agency and the identified private sector developer.
Competitive bidding	A process under which the bidders submit information detailing their qualifications and detailed technical and financial proposals, which are evaluated according to defined criteria—often in a multi-stage process—to select a preferred bidder. Competitive bidding may also include competitive negotiations and license schemes.
Concession	A PPP type which makes the concessionaire (established by the selected private sector developer) responsible for the full delivery of services in a specified area, including operation, maintenance, collection, management, and construction and rehabilitation of the system. Importantly, the private sector developer is responsible for all capital investment. Although the concessionaire is responsible for providing the assets, such assets are publicly owned even during the concession period. The public sector is responsible for establishing performance standards and ensuring that the concessionaire meets them. In essence, the public sector's role shifts from being the service provider to regulating the price and quality of service.
Currency conversion swap fee	A premium which is paid by the borrower to settle on a swap in which the parties sell currencies to each other subject to an agreement to repurchase the same currency in the same amount, at the same exchange rate, and on a fixed date in the future.
Direct agreement	An agreement normally made between the concessionaire (established by the private sector developer), the government contracting agency, and the lenders. The agreement usually gives the lenders step-in rights to take over the operation of the key PPP contracts.
Direct negotiations	A type of PPP procurement under which the PPP contract is awarded on the basis of a direct agreement with a private sector developer without going through the competitive bidding process.
Dispute resolution	A process to resolve any dispute between the government contracting agency and the private sector developer as agreed in the PPP contract. The possible dispute resolution mechanisms in a PPP contract could include resolution through: • discussion between both parties, • dispute resolution board, • expert determination, • mediation or conciliation, or • arbitration.

continued on next page

continued from previous page

Term	Definition
Environmental impact assessment	A process of evaluating the likely environmental impacts of a proposed project or development, taking into account interrelated socioeconomic, cultural, and human health impacts, both beneficial and adverse.
Feed-in tariff (FIT)	A policy mechanism designed to accelerate investment in renewable energy technologies by offering long-term purchase agreements for the sale of renewable energy electricity.
Financial close	An event whereby (i) a legally binding commitment of equity holders and/or debt financiers exists to provide or mobilize funding for the full cost of the project, and (ii) the conditions for funding have been met and the first tranche of funding is mobilized. If this information is not available, construction start date is used as an estimated financial closure date.
Financial equilibrium	A mechanism in a PPP agreement for dealing with changes, when changes in specified conditions and circumstances trigger compensating changes to the terms of the agreement. Some civil law jurisdictions emphasize economic or financial equilibrium provisions that entitle a partner to changes in the key financial terms of the contract to compensate for certain types of exogenous events that may otherwise impact returns. The partner is protected as the economic balance of the contract must be maintained and adequate compensation paid for damages suffered. Unexpected changes that merit financial equilibrium may arise from force majeure (major natural disasters or civil disturbances), government action, and unforeseen changes in economic conditions.
Force majeure	An event that is reasonably beyond the reasonable control of the affected party as a result of which such party's performance of its obligations under the PPP contract is prevented or rendered impossible. Force majeure events may include • war, civil war, armed conflict or terrorism; • nuclear, chemical, or biological contamination unless the source or the cause of the contamination is the result of the actions of or breach by the concessionaire or its subcontractors; • pressure waves caused by devices travelling at supersonic speeds, which directly causes either party (the "Affected Party") to be unable to comply with all or a material part of its obligations under the contract; or • any other similar events that are beyond reasonable control of the affected party, and prevent or render impossible the performance by such party of its obligations under the PPP contract.
Government contracting agency	The ministry, department, or agency that enters into a PPP contract with the private sector and is responsible for ensuring that the relevant public assets or services are provided.
Government guarantee	Agreements under which the government agrees to bear some or all risks of a PPP project. It is a secondary obligation which legally binds the government to take on an obligation if a specified event occurs. A government guarantee constitutes a contingent liability, for which there is uncertainty as to whether the government may be required to make payments, and if so, how much and when it will be required to pay. In practice, government guarantees are used when debt providers are unwilling to lend to a private party in a PPP because of concerns over credit risk and potential loan losses. Government guarantees can also be used to benefit equity investors in a PPP company when they require protection against the investment risks they bear.
Government pay (Off-take)	Represents the payment made by the government contracting agency to the concessionaire (established by the private sector developer) for the infrastructure assets provided and services delivered through a PPP project. These payments could be: • usage-based—for example, shadow tolls or output-based subsidies; • based on availability—that is, conditional on the availability of an asset or service to the specified quality; and • upfront subsidies based on achieving certain agreed milestones.

continued on next page

continued from previous page

Term	Definition
Gross-cost contract	A type of PPP contract arrangement in the railway sector under which all revenues (from fares and other sources) are transferred to the government contracting agency, and the risks absorbed by the developer are confined to those associated with the cost of operations.
Hybrid arrangement	A method of investment recovery in PPP projects when payments to the private party are made as a combination of user charges and availability payments over the lifetime of a PPP contract, in return for making infrastructure or services available for use at acceptable and contractually agreed performance standards.
Independent power producer (IPP) scheme	A scheme whereby a producer of electrical energy, which is not a public utility, makes electric energy available for sale to utilities or the general public. A scheme whereby a producer of electrical energy, which is a private entity, owns and/or operates facilities to generate electricity and then sells it to a utility, central government buyer, or end users. The IPP invests in generation technologies and recovers their cost from the sale of the electricity.
Institutional arbitration	An arbitration process in which a specialized institution intervenes and takes on the role of administering the arbitration process between the government contracting agency and the private sector developer for a PPP project-related dispute. This institution would have its own set of rules which would provide a framework for the arbitration, and its own form of administration to assist in the process.
Interest rate swap fee	A premium paid by the borrower for a hedging contract to convert a floating interest rate into a fixed rate. The two parties agree to exchange interest rate payments based on a notional principal amount, with typically one paying a fixed rate and the other generally paying a floating rate.
Joint venture	An alternative to full privatization in which the infrastructure is co-owned and operated by the public sector and private operators. Under a joint venture, the public and private sector partners can either form a new company or assume joint ownership of an existing company through a sale of shares to one or several private investors. The company may also be listed on the stock exchange.
Lender's step-in rights	Lender's rights in project-financed arrangements to "step in" to the project company's position in the contract to take control of the infrastructure project where the project company is not performing.
Management contract	A PPP type which expands the services to be contracted out to include some or all of the management and operation of the public service (i.e., utility, hospital, port authority). Although ultimate obligation for service provision remains in the public sector, daily management control and authority is assigned to the private partner or contractor. In most cases, the private partner provides working capital but no financing for investment.
Material adverse government action	An action by the government which directly and materially affects the private party of a PPP project in performing its obligations under the relevant PPP contract, and which would reasonably be expected to result in a material adverse effect.
Net-cost contract	A type of PPP contract arrangement in the railway sector under which all revenues (from fares and other sources) are retained by the developer, and traffic and revenue risks are absorbed either fully or as per a contractually agreed portion.
Nominal interest rate	The nominal interest rate is the interest rate applicable to a borrowing before taking inflation adjustment into account. In certain cases, nominal interest rate also refers to the advertised or stated interest rate on a borrowing, without taking into account any fees or compounding of interest. Nominal interest rate = Real interest rate + Inflation rate
Nonrecourse/ limited recourse project financing	The financing of the development or exploitation of a right, natural resource, or other assets where the bulk of the financing is to be provided by way of debt, and is to be repaid principally out of the assets being financed and their revenues.

continued on next page

continued from previous page

Term	Definition
Output-based aid (OBA)	Refers to development aid strategies that link the delivery of public services in developing countries to targeted performance-related subsidies. OBA provides a way in which international financial institutions can directly structure their financing to benefit poor people, even when the service provider is a private company. OBA is the use of explicit, performance-based subsidies funded by the donor agencies to complement or replace user fees. It involves the contracting out of basic service provision to a third party—such as private companies, nongovernment organizations, community-based organizations, and even public service providers—with subsidy payment tied to the delivery of specified outputs. This means that targeted and valuable subsidies to disadvantaged populations are funded through donor funds. The private partner, meanwhile, can only recover this funding by achieving specific performance outcomes.
Project bond financing	An alternative source of financing infrastructure project by placing bonds.
Project development	Indicates the stage of the PPP project lifecycle including PPP project identification, preparation, structuring, and procurement up to commercial close between the government contracting agency and the private sector developer.
Project development fund (PDF)	A fund dedicated to reimbursing the cost of feasibility studies, transaction advisors, and other costs of project development, to encourage contracting agencies to use high-quality transaction advisors and best practice. PDFs provide the specialized resources needed to conduct studies, to design and structure a PPP, and then to procure the PPP.
Real interest rate	The real interest rate is the interest rate applicable to a borrowing that takes inflation rate into account. Real interest rate = Nominal interest rate – Inflation rate
Regulatory framework	A framework encompassing all laws, regulations, policies, binding guidelines or instructions, other legal texts of general application, judicial decisions, and administrative rulings governing or setting precedent in connection with PPPs. In this context, the term "policies" refers to other government-issued documents, which are binding on all stakeholders, are enforced in a manner similar to laws and regulations, and provide detailed instructions for the implementation of PPPs.
Rehabilitate–operate–transfer	A PPP type whereby an existing facility is handed over to the private sector developer to refurbish, operate and maintain for a franchise period, at the expiry of which the legal title to the facility is turned over to the government contracting agency.
Risk allocation matrix	Matrix indicating the allocation of the consequences of each risk to one of the parties in the PPP contract, or agreeing to deal with the risk through a specified mechanism which may involve sharing the risk.
Service contract	A PPP type under which the government contracting agency hires a private company or entity to carry out one or more specified tasks or services for a period, typically 1–3 years. The government contracting agency remains the primary provider of the infrastructure service and contracts out only portions of its operation to the private partner. The private partner must perform the service at the agreed cost and must typically meet performance standards set by the government contracting agency. Government contracting agencies generally use competitive bidding procedures to award service contracts, which tend to work well given the limited period and narrowly defined nature of these contracts.
Social impact assessment	Includes the processes of analyzing, monitoring, and managing the intended and unintended social consequences—both positive and negative—of planned interventions (policies, programs, plans, projects) and any social change processes invoked by those interventions. Its primary purpose is to bring about a more sustainable and equitable biophysical and human environment.
Social infrastructure	Covers social services, including hospitals, schools and universities, prisons, housing, and courts.

continued on next page

continued from previous page

Term	Definition
State-owned enterprise (SOE)	A company or enterprise owned by the government or in which the government has a controlling stake.
Swiss challenge	A process in public procurement when a government contracting agency that has received an unsolicited bid for a project publishes details of the bid and invites third parties to match or exceed it.
Tax holiday	A government incentive program that offers tax reduction or elimination to projects and/ or businesses. In the context of a PPP project, tax holidays are provided to exempt the concessionaire from making any tax payments during the initial demand ramp up period to make the project financially viable.
Unsolicited bid	A proposal made by a private party to undertake a PPP project. It is submitted at the initiative of the private party, rather than in response to a request from the government contracting agency.
User charges	A method of investment recovery in PPP projects when payments to the private party are fully derived from tariffs paid by users or off-takers over the lifetime of a PPP contract, in return for making infrastructure or services available for use at acceptable and contractually agreed performance standards.
Viability gap funding	A scheme wherein the projects with low financial viability are given grants (or other financial support from the government) up to a stipulated percentage of the project cost, making them financially viable as PPPs.

Abbreviations

ADB	-	Asian Development Bank
BOO	-	build–own–operate
BOT	-	build–operate–transfer
BPNG	-	Bank of Papua New Guinea
CADIP	-	Civil Aviation Development Investment Program
CASA	-	Civil Aviation Safety Authority
CIF	-	cost, insurance, and freight
CPI	-	consumer price index
DOT	-	Department of Transport
DPE	-	Department of Petroleum and Energy
DPLGA	-	Department of Provincial and Local Government Affairs
GDP	-	gross domestic product
GEMS	-	General Enterprise Management Services
ICCC	-	Independent Consumer and Competition Commission
ICT	-	information and communication technology
IPBC	-	Independent Public Business Corporation
IPP	-	independent power producer
LLG	-	local-level government
MTDP	-	medium-term development plan
MTDS	-	medium-term development strategy
MTEF	-	medium-term expenditure framework
MTFS	-	medium-term fiscal strategy
NAC	-	National Airports Corporation
NEC	-	National Executive Council
NEFC	-	National Economic and Fiscal Commission

NEP	-	National Education Plan
NHC	-	National Housing Corporation
NHP	-	National Health Plan
NICTA	-	National Information and Communications Technology Authority
PEFA	-	public expenditure and financial accountability
PFMS	-	public financial management system
PNG	-	Papua New Guinea
PNGASL	-	Papua New Guinea Air Services Ltd.
PNGDSP	-	Papua New Guinea Development Strategic Plan
PNGPCL	-	Papua New Guinea Ports Corporation Limited
PPA	-	power purchase agreement
PPL	-	PNG Power Limited
PPP	-	public–private partnership
ROT	-	rehabilitate–operate–transfer
SOE	-	state-owned enterprise
VFM	-	value for money
VGF	-	viability gap funding
WASH	-	water, sanitation, and hygiene

Guide to Understanding the Public–Private Partnership Monitor

The *Public–Private Partnership Monitor* (PPP Monitor), a flagship publication of the Asian Development Bank (ADB), profiles the current state of the PPP enabling environment in ADB's developing member countries (DMCs) in Asia and the Pacific. The PPP Monitor features, for the first time, a data-driven, interactive online version, which allows users to compare and contrast the key PPP parameters and features across the featured DMCs. While the featured countries are a small sample, more countries will be continually added in the PPP Monitor, which is expected to become a knowledge base for assessing a country's PPP environment for the government and the business community. The new PPP Monitor builds on the success of the first and second editions of the PPP Monitor.

The PPP Monitor provides a snapshot of the overall PPP landscape in the country. This downloadable guide also assesses more than 500 qualitative and quantitative indicators that have been structured per topic—the national PPP landscape, the sector-specific PPP landscape (for eight identified infrastructure sectors and a separate section for other sectors), and the PPP landscape for local government projects. The PPP Monitor also captures the critical macroeconomic and infrastructure sector indicators (including the *Ease of Doing Business* scores) from globally accepted sources.

Each of the topics and associated subtopics presented below are characterized by qualitative and quantitative indicators. Qualitative indicators take the form of a question to which "Yes," "No," "Not Applicable," or "Unavailable" answers can be given. Quantitative indicators are represented in the form of numbers, ratios, investment value, and duration.

For each of the developing member countries covered, the information and data are organized along the following topic clusters:

Overview

Topic	Subtopics
Overview	• Overview of the PPP legal and regulatory framework • Number of PPP projects reaching financial close from 1990 until the end of 2019 across sectors • Total investment made in PPPs from 1990 to 2019 across sectors • Features of past PPP projects including the number of PPPs procured through various modes • Number of PPP projects under preparation and procurement • Number of PPP projects supported by government • Payment mechanism for PPPs • Foreign sponsor participation in PPPs from 1990 to 2019 • Major sponsors active in the infrastructure sector in the country • Challenges associated with the PPP landscape in the country

National Public–Private Partnership Landscape Indicators

To profile the national PPP landscape, the indicators are grouped into three major categories: national PPP enabling framework, government support for PPP projects, and maturity of the PPP market.

Topic	Subtopics
National PPP legal and regulatory framework	Details on the legal and regulatory framework applicable to PPPs and its evolution since the introduction of PPPs in the country Details on the other supporting laws and regulations governing PPPs in the country
PPP types	Details on the PPP types allowed to be used as per PPP legal and regulatory framework. In case the PPP legal and regulatory framework does not specify the PPP types, this section provides the details on the specific PPP types which have been adopted for various PPP projects at various stages of the PPP lifecycle.
Eligible sectors	Details on various infrastructure sectors for which projects could be procured through the PPP route as per the PPP legal and regulatory framework
PPP institutional framework	Details on the PPP institutional framework including the availability of a PPP Unit, the functions of the PPP Unit, the principal public entities associated with PPPs and their respective functions, and the details of the public entities responsible for PPP project identification, appraisal, approval, oversight, and monitoring
Entities responsible for PPP project identification, approval, and oversight	
Entities responsible for PPP project monitoring	
The PPP process	Details on the various stages of the PPP process including PPP project identification, preparation, structuring, procurement, and management as per the PPP legal and regulatory framework in the country
PPP standard operating procedures, toolkits, templates, and model bidding documents	Details on the standard operating procedures, and standard templates or model bidding documents available for PPPs (if any) Details on the key clauses in a PPP agreement based on the review of select PPP Agreements already executed, and/ or the review of the PPP legal and regulatory framework
Lender's security rights	Rights of a lender including the charge of project assets
Termination and compensation	Definition on whether the private player is eligible for compensation in case of PPP project termination due to various reasons
Unsolicited PPP proposals	Details on possibility of submission of unsolicited PPP proposals, and their treatment, including potential advantages provided to the unsolicited PPP proposal proponent at the PPP procurement stage
Foreign investor participation restrictions	Definition on whether there are any statutory restrictions on foreign equity investments and ownership in PPP projects
Dispute resolution	Definition of the dispute resolution process and the mechanisms available in the country
Environmental and social issues	Details on whether the legal and regulatory framework governing PPPs stipulates a mechanism for managing the environmental and social impact of a PPP project, including the potential environmental and social issues which could be caused by a PPP project

continued on next page

continued from previous page

Topic	Subtopics
Land rights	Definition of the various mechanisms through which landownership and/or land use rights could be provided to the private partner in respect of the project site for a PPP project Details on land records and registration which could be provided to the private partner
Government financial support for PPP projects	Details on the various mechanisms of government financial support available to make PPP projects financially viable Salient features of government financial support mechanisms available
Project development funding support	Details on the various sources through which funding could be availed for the development activities (preparation, structuring, and procurement) of a PPP project Details on stages of the PPP project development during which such funding could be availed and utilized, including payments to transaction advisors
PPP project statistics	Details on the key PPP statistics in the country such as the availability of (i) a PPP database showing distribution of PPP projects across sectors and across various stages of the PPP lifecycle, and (ii) a national PPP project pipeline and its alignment with the National Infrastructure Plan for the country
Sources of PPP financing	Details on the sources of financing for PPP projects in the country Details on typical key financing terms for various sources of financing, banks active in project finance for the last 24 months, active PPP project sponsors in the country for the last 24 months, availability of derivatives market, and availability of credit rating agencies in the country

Sector-Specific Public–Private Partnership Landscape Indicators

To profile the sector-specific PPP landscape, the indicators are grouped into 5 major categories: (i) sector-specific PPP contracting agencies, (ii) sector laws and regulations, (iii) sector master plan (including sector-specific PPP pipeline), (iv) features of the past PPP projects in the sector, and (v) sector-specific challenges for PPPs. The sectors which do not appear consistently across the featured countries are covered under the "Other Sectors" category in the sector-specific PPP landscape.

Topic	Subtopics
Contracting agencies in the sector	Details on which government agencies could act as the contracting agencies for a PPP project
Sector laws and regulations	Details on the applicable sector laws and regulations for PPP projects, including the sector regulators and their respective functions.
Foreign investment restrictions in the sector	Details on the maximum allowed foreign equity investment in greenfield PPP projects in the sector
Standard contracts in the sector	Specification on whether standard contracts are available for PPP projects in the sector

continued on next page

continued from previous page

Topic	Subtopics
Sector master plan	Details on the master plan and/or roadmap adopted for infrastructure development in the sector by the national government and the corresponding line ministry Details on the pipeline of PPP projects for the sector aligned with this sector master plan and/or roadmap Details on the PPP projects under preparation and procurement in the sector
Features of past PPP projects	Features of the past PPP projects based on supporting indicators in terms of the number and value (where applicable) of PPP projects for each supporting indicator
Tariffs applicable to the sector	Details on the indicative tariffs applicable in the sector based on the examples of select PPP or other projects operational in the sector
Typical risk allocation for PPP projects in the sector	Details on the typical risk allocation between the government contracting agency and the private partner based on examples of select PPP projects which have achieved commercial close
Financing details for PPP projects in the sector	Typical financing details based on past PPP projects on the lines of the supporting indicators
Challenges associated with PPPs in the sector	Details on the PPP-related and sector-specific challenges faced by PPP projects in the sector
Typical sector-specific infrastructure indicators for the country	Details on select sector-specific infrastructure indicators for the country

Local Government Public–Private Partnership Landscape

To profile the PPP landscape for local government projects, the indicators are grouped into seven major categories: (i) local governance system, (ii) infrastructure development plans for local governments, (iii) sectors in which local governments can implement PPPs, (iv) revenue sources for local governments, (v) borrowings by local governments, (vi) budgetary allocation to local governments, and (vii) credit rating of local governments.

Topic	Subtopics
Key indicators related to local governments in the country	Details on the local governments using select key indicators on (i) the number and levels of local governments, (ii) the typical expenditure profile and heads, (iii) the typical revenue profile and heads, (iv) the typical debt profile and heads, and (v) grants and transfers from the higher levels of government
Local governance system	Details on the local governance system in the country, including the various levels of local governments; their roles, responsibilities, and functions; and the devolution of powers from the higher levels of government to the various levels of local governments
Infrastructure development plan for local governments	Details on the infrastructure development plans prepared by the local governments based on their capital investment projects in the pipeline, and the coverage of such infrastructure development plans
PPP enabling framework for local governments	Details on the PPP enabling framework applicable to local government PPP projects, including PPP legal and regulatory framework, PPP policy framework, and PPP institutional framework

continued on next page

continued from previous page

Topic	Subtopics
Eligible sectors for PPPs for local governments	Details on the eligible sectors in which PPPs could be undertaken by the local government as government contracting agency
Revenues for local governments	Details on the typical sources of revenue for local governments
Borrowings by local governments	Details on the typical sources of debt financing available for local governments, the purpose for which borrowed funds could be used, the terms of such borrowings, and the borrowing exposure of select local governments
Budgetary allocation to local governments	Details on the budgetary allocations and transfers to the local governments from the higher levels of government
Credit rating of local governments	Details on the precedence of local governments being rated by credit rating agencies in the country, and the details of credit ratings obtained by select local governments in the past
Case study on a local government PPP	A case of a PPP project undertaken by a local government in the past covering details on project background, project assets, PPP structure for the project, risk allocation among the parties for the project, project finance and project revenue details, and key learnings from the PPP project

Critical Macroeconomic and Infrastructure Sector Indicators

This section captures the critical macroeconomic and infrastructure sector indicators (including the *Ease of Doing Business* scores) from globally accepted sources.

Topic	Subtopics
Critical macroeconomic and infrastructure sector indicators	Details of the select key macroeconomic and infrastructure indicators for the country
Ease of Doing Business	Details on the various *Ease of Doing Business* parameters for the country based on the World Bank's *Ease of Doing Business* publication

Time Periods

The research was carried out in 2020 with the aim of reflecting the status as of the end of 2019. Therefore, some indicator data may have changed between the said period and the publication date of this report.

In country-level and sector-level sections, quantitative data in relation to the number of projects reflect the cumulative number of projects over the periods 1990–2017, 1990–2018, and 1990–2019. Otherwise, the data represent the status at each individual year.

Currency Equivalents

(As of 6 August 2020)

Currency unit – kina (K)
K1.00 = $0.289002
$1.00 = K3.46

I. Overview

Until 2008, public–private partnerships (PPPs) in Papua New Guinea were implemented on an ad hoc basis without a formal PPP enabling framework in place. In 2008, the Government of Papua New Guinea endorsed the National PPP Policy which provided the principles and the policy framework for PPPs in Papua New Guinea. The National PPP Policy defines PPPs and provides the scope, objective, and principles of the policy. It outlines the institutional framework for governance and accountability in delivering PPPs. It also details the various stages and the process for a PPP project, including development, procurement, implementation and contract management, and termination.[1]

Based on the National PPP Policy, the National Executive Council approved the Public–Private Partnership Act (PPP Act) in 2014 to provide the legal basis for identifying, preparing, procuring, implementing, and managing PPP projects in Papua New Guinea. The PPP Act provides for the procurement and delivery of infrastructure facilities and services through PPP arrangements, and gives power to certain public bodies to enter into such arrangements.[2] The PPP Act was passed by the Parliament of Papua New Guinea in September 2014 and gazetted in January 2018. However, the government has not implemented the PPP Act yet, as there are amendments to further strengthen it. These amendments are yet to be circulated for comments and inputs from the public.

The PPP Act provides for the establishment of the PPP Centre, a statutory agency to be established to implement the PPP Act and monitor its enforcement. Arrangements with the PPP Centre are guided by the National PPP Policy and the PPP Act. The PPP Centre would be set up as a "specialist" adviser to the National Executive Council and would be directly accessible by line agencies.[3] The PPP Centre would determine whether a PPP is the most appropriate mode of developing a project, using methods such as value for money assessments based on whole-of-lifecycle costs and public sector comparator benchmarking analysis. The PPP Centre would support line agencies (at the national, provincial, and district levels) through various stages of project preparation and procurement. It is envisaged that projects submitted to the PPP Centre will be pre-approved by the National Executive Council (the cabinet) through inclusion in the proposed National PPP Infrastructure Pipeline (an allocation in the national budget) or by cabinet decision. A PPP Steering Group would serve as the supervisory committee of the PPP Centre. The PPP Centre would not be set up as a decision-making body. Instead, it would coordinate and implement the decisions made by the PPP Steering Group and the National Executive Council (NEC).

The PPP Act also provides for the establishment of the PPP Steering Group, which would include the heads of the Department of Treasury and the Department of National Planning and Monitoring, and the PPP Forum.

---

1 Government of Papua New Guinea, Department of Treasury. 2014. *National PPP Policy 2014*. Port Moresby. https://www.treasury.gov.pg/html/misc/Special%20Projects/PPP/PNG%20National%20PPP%20Policy%202014.pdf.

2 The Economist Intelligence Unit. Papua New Guinea. https://infrascope.eiu.com/.

3 S. Kuman. 2018. New Formal Framework to Help Develop Infrastructure within PNG. *Allens Insights & News*. 26 February. https://www.allens.com.au/insights-news/insights/2018/02/new-formal-framework-to-help-develop-infrastructure-within/#Footnotes.

Given that the prescribed bodies under the PPP Act are yet to be established and set up, the procurement process under the PPP Act have not yet been enforced or implemented. As of April 2018, these administrative bodies were not yet in place.[4] In the 2018 National Budget presentation, it was mentioned that some of the activities envisaged in 2018 include

- developing a roadmap that would assist the government in identifying and implementing a pipeline of projects under PPP arrangements;
- ensuring that relevant PPP projects are selected, developed, delivered, and managed in a structured, transparent, and efficient manner; and
- facilitating the procurement for all PPP projects (footnote 3).

The PPP Act excludes mining, gas, and petroleum projects, and all associated development agreements or projects undertaken as part of the government's tax credit scheme. Infrastructure procurement projects involving a Relevant Public Body,[5] wherein the value of which exceeds the referral threshold, would automatically qualify for PPP arrangements under the PPP Act. The referral threshold value would be set in the PPP Act regulations. However, there is a general indication that the referral threshold value of a project will be K50 million.[6]

Though the PPP Act and the PPP regulations are yet to be implemented, in sectors which are already regulated by independent or universal regulators such as the Independent Consumer and Competition Commission (ICCC), including telecommunications, water, and power, the PPP agreements must also be in compliance with the ICCC regulations. All PPP transactions within sectors that are currently regulated by the ICCC would need to comply with the terms of the individual concession agreements related to the project as well as any umbrella regulations set by the ICCC related to the industry (footnote 1).

There have been various PPP projects developed in Papua New Guinea. The first two PPP projects had reached financial closure long before the introduction of any of Papua New Guinea's PPP Policy and the recent commencement of Papua New Guinea's PPP Act. These are the Port Moresby Diesel-Fired Plant in 1996 and the PNG Water Limited potable water treatment plant in 1997. Both projects involve state-owned enterprises (SOEs) and foreign investors. In 2011, Papua New Guinea's ICCC awarded a build-own-operate contract and a value-added services license for 15 years to Bemobile Limited, a PNG limited-liability company, to strengthen the country's backbone infrastructure for telecommunications and to reduce its reliance on the legacy infrastructure of Telikom PNG (the state-owned telecom service provider). The objective was to upgrade and expand the existing telecommunications network in Papua New Guinea to increase national geographic and population coverage. There are also several proposed PPP projects including PPL – Ramu II Hydroelectric Power Plant project, Lae port expansion project, and the Port Moresby (Jacksons) International Airport development, which are at various stages of preparation. In late 2017, a PPP contract was signed for Lae port expansion project. In November 2019, the Port Moresby Power Station was commissioned.

From 1990 to 2019, six projects have already reached financial closure.[7] Figure 1 presents the projects that have achieved financial closure during the said period.

---

4 *Post-Courier*. 2018. PPP Act in Operation. 18 April. https://postcourier.com.pg/ppp-act-operation/.

5 As per the PPP Act, a Relevant Public Body is defined as (i) the Independent State of Papua New Guinea; (ii) local or provincial governments; or (iii) a statutory body established by an Act which is not a provincial or local-level government entity or an entity in relation to which the State controls the composition of the board, controls more than 50% of the voting power in the company, or holds more than 50% of the issued share capital in the company.

6 World Bank. Benchmarking Infrastructure Development. https://bpp.worldbank.org/; footnote 3.

7 World Bank. Infrastructure Finance, PPPs and Guarantees. Country Snapshots. Papua New Guinea. https://ppi.worldbank.org/en/snapshots/country/papua-new-guinea (accessed 30 June 2020).

Figure 1: Public–Private Partnership Projects That Achieved Financial Closure, 1990–2019

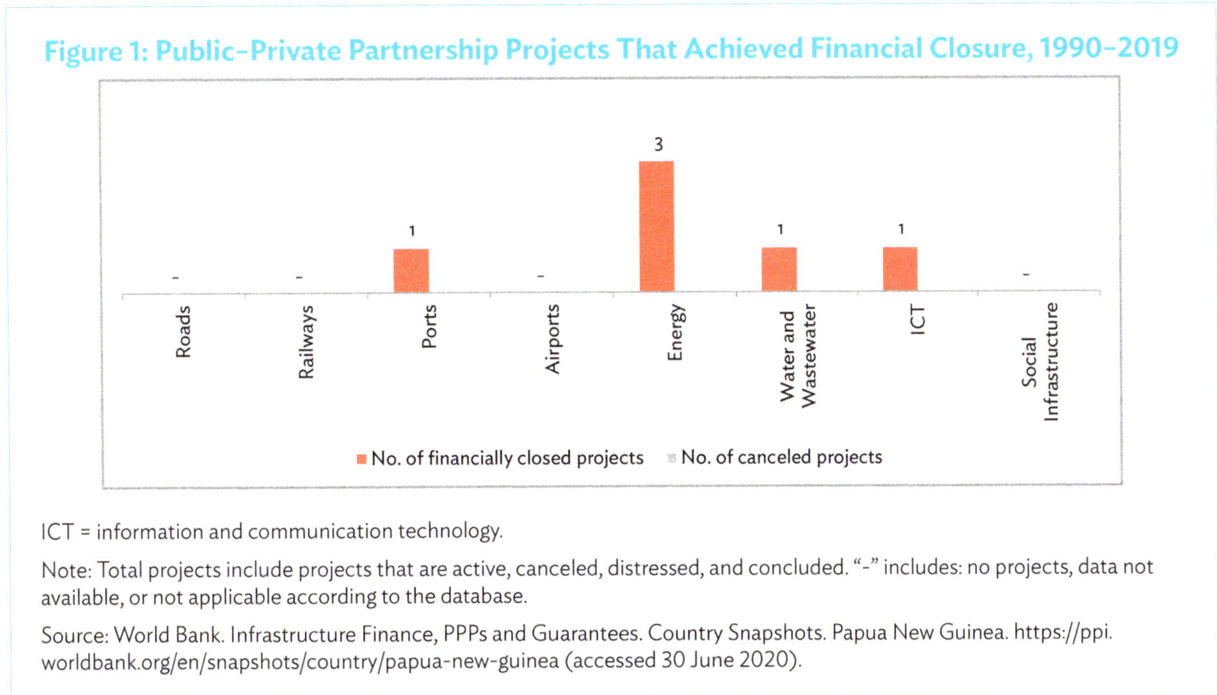

ICT = information and communication technology.

Note: Total projects include projects that are active, canceled, distressed, and concluded. "-" includes: no projects, data not available, or not applicable according to the database.

Source: World Bank. Infrastructure Finance, PPPs and Guarantees. Country Snapshots. Papua New Guinea. https://ppi.worldbank.org/en/snapshots/country/papua-new-guinea (accessed 30 June 2020).

Figure 2 presents the status of various PPP projects in Papua New Guinea that were awarded to private players.

Figure 2: Status of Public–Private Partnership Projects across Sectors

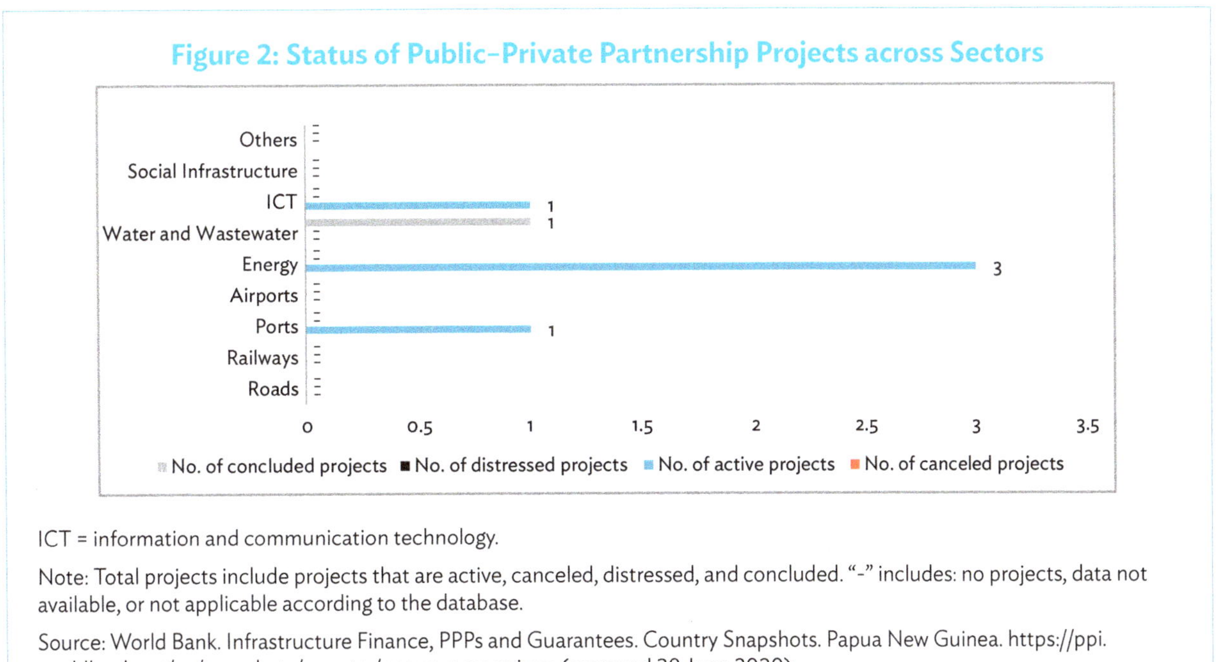

ICT = information and communication technology.

Note: Total projects include projects that are active, canceled, distressed, and concluded. "-" includes: no projects, data not available, or not applicable according to the database.

Source: World Bank. Infrastructure Finance, PPPs and Guarantees. Country Snapshots. Papua New Guinea. https://ppi.worldbank.org/en/snapshots/country/papua-new-guinea (accessed 30 June 2020).

In the energy sector, the investment was $362 million (K1252.59 million as of June 2020), followed by that in the water and wastewater sector at $71 million (K245.67 million as of June 2020). Figure 3 shows the total investment in each sector from 1990 to 2019, and the average size of a PPP project in each of these sectors.

Figure 3: Investment in Public–Private Partnership Projects by Sector, 1990–2019
($ million)

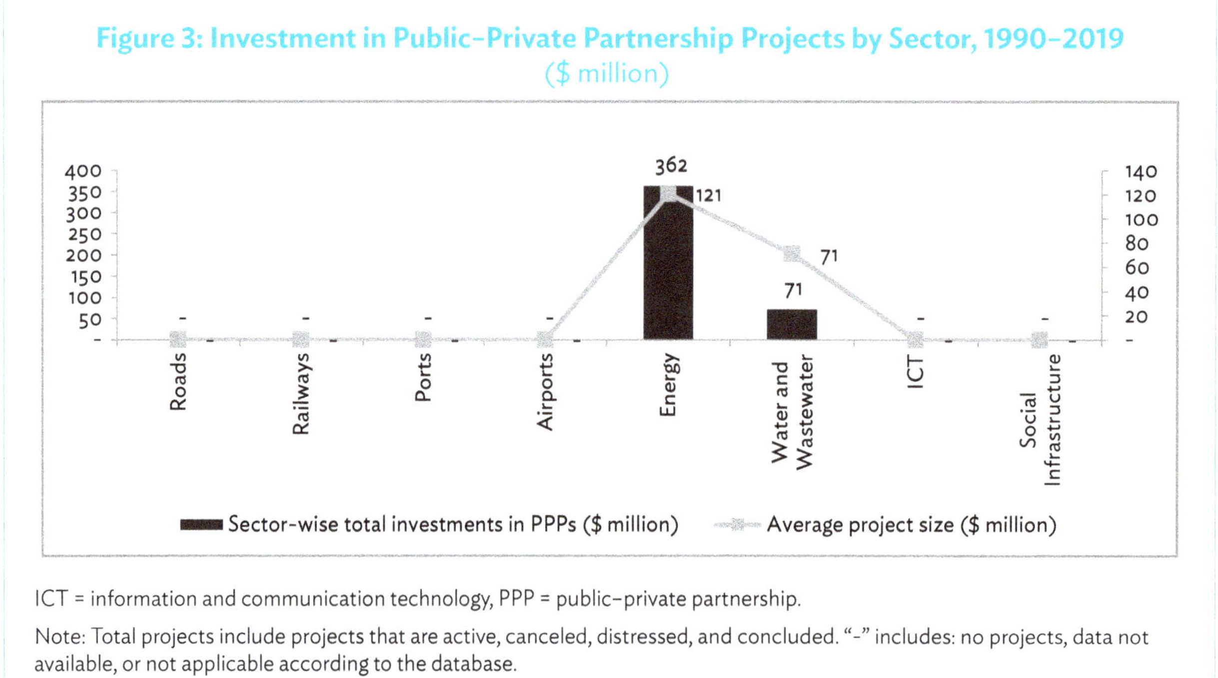

ICT = information and communication technology, PPP = public–private partnership.

Note: Total projects include projects that are active, canceled, distressed, and concluded. "-" includes: no projects, data not available, or not applicable according to the database.

Source: World Bank. Infrastructure Finance, PPPs and Guarantees. Country Snapshots. Papua New Guinea. https://ppi.worldbank.org/en/snapshots/country/papua-new-guinea (accessed 30 June 2020).

Table 1 presents the top private sector investors who have invested in PPPs in Papua New Guinea.

Table 1: Top Private Sector Investors for Public–Private Partnership Projects in Papua New Guinea

Private Sponsor	Country of Origin	Total Investment ($ million)	Total Investment (K million)	Number of PPP Projects
Brem Maju Berhad	Malaysia	71	245.67	1
George Malaysia Berhad	Malaysia	71	245.67	1

PPP = public–private partnership.

Source: World Bank. Infrastructure Finance, PPPs and Guarantees. Country Snapshots. Papua New Guinea. https://ppi.worldbank.org/en/snapshots/country/papua-new-guinea (accessed 30 June 2020).

Figure 4 shows the various modes through which PPP projects were procured from 1990 to 2019.

Figure 4: Various Modes of Procuring Public–Private Partnership Projects, 1990–2019

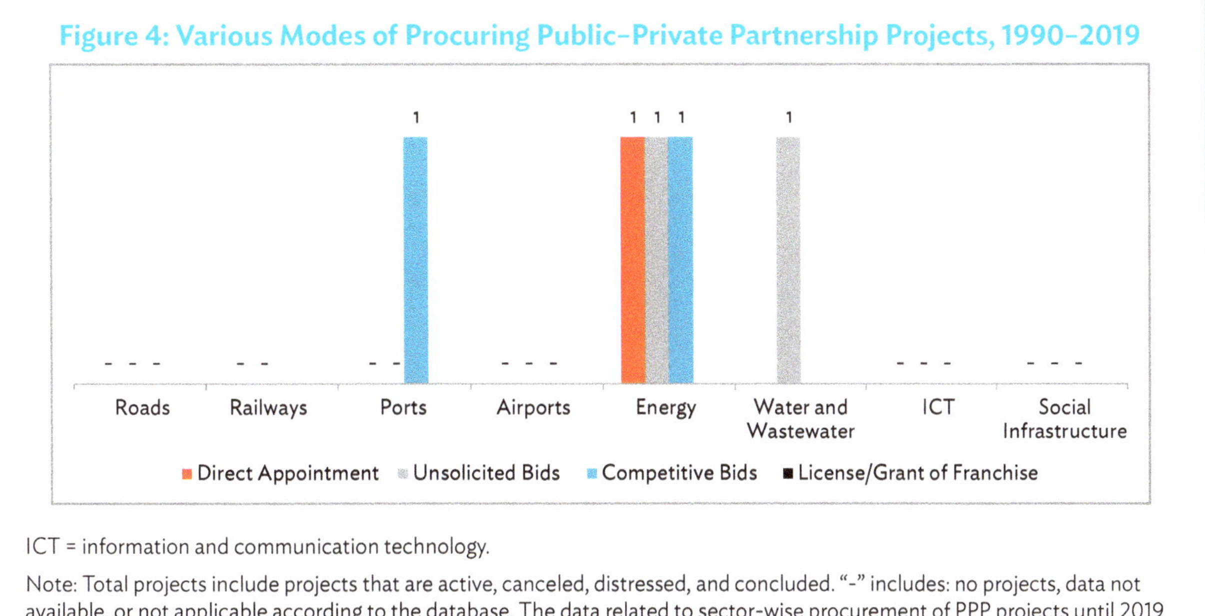

ICT = information and communication technology.

Note: Total projects include projects that are active, canceled, distressed, and concluded. "-" includes: no projects, data not available, or not applicable according to the database. The data related to sector-wise procurement of PPP projects until 2019 is not available.

Source: World Bank. Infrastructure Finance, PPPs and Guarantees. Country Snapshots. Papua New Guinea. https://ppi.worldbank.org/en/snapshots/country/papua-new-guinea (accessed 30 June 2020).

Figure 5 shows the PPP projects under preparation and procurement as of 2019.

Figure 5: Public–Private Partnership Projects under Preparation and Procurement, 2019

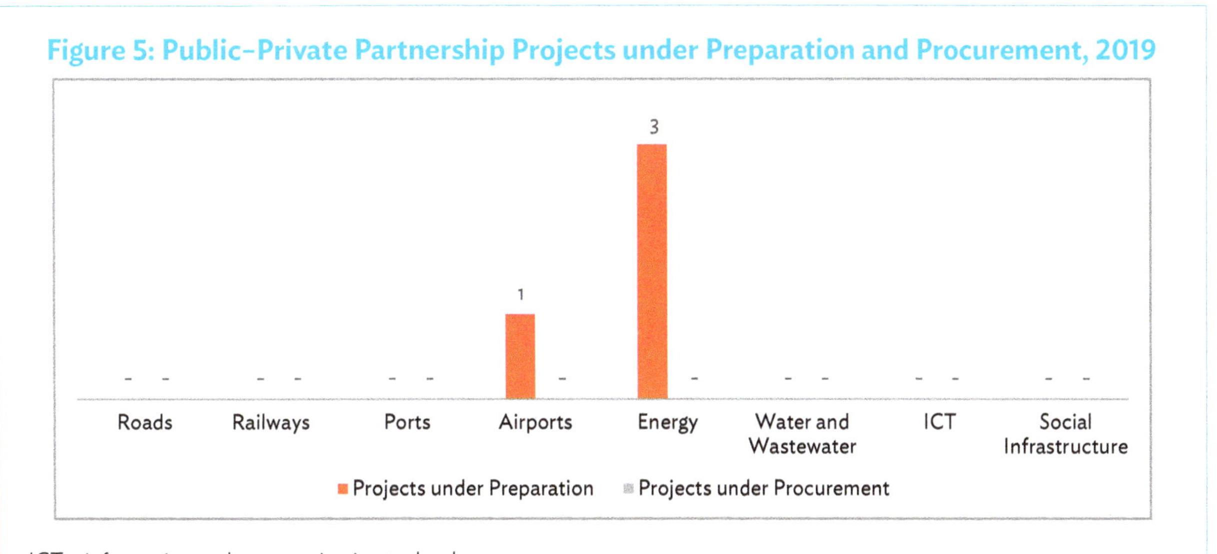

ICT = information and communication technology.

Note: "-" includes: no projects, data not available, or not applicable. Sector-wise data related to PPP projects under preparation and procurement until 2019 is not available.

Source: World Bank. Infrastructure Finance, PPPs and Guarantees. Country Snapshots. Papua New Guinea. https://ppi.worldbank.org/en/snapshots/country/papua-new-guinea (accessed 30 June 2020).

Figure 6 shows the PPP projects receiving government support in the period 1990–2019.

Figure 6: Public–Private Partnership Projects with Government Support, 1990–2019

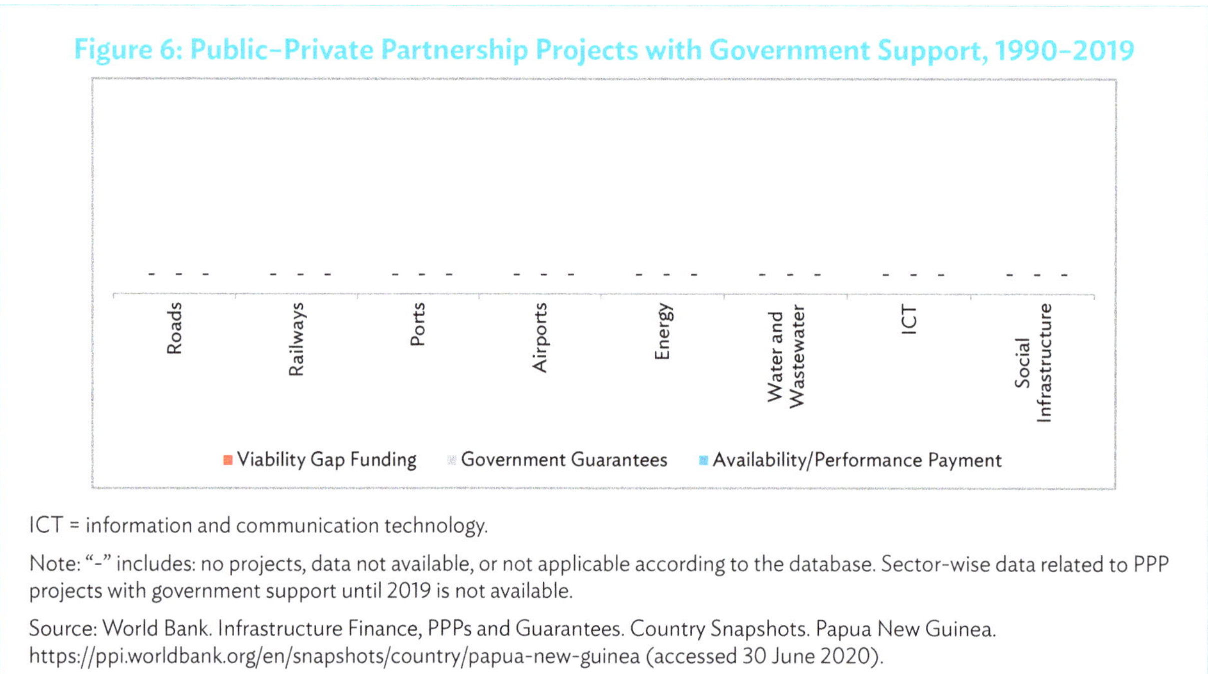

ICT = information and communication technology.

Note: "-" includes: no projects, data not available, or not applicable according to the database. Sector-wise data related to PPP projects with government support until 2019 is not available.

Source: World Bank. Infrastructure Finance, PPPs and Guarantees. Country Snapshots. Papua New Guinea. https://ppi.worldbank.org/en/snapshots/country/papua-new-guinea (accessed 30 June 2020).

Based on available data, from 1990 to 2019, there are two PPP projects based on user charges. The information on PPP projects based on government pay (off-take) in Papua New Guinea across various infrastructure sectors (i.e., roads, railways, ports, airports, energy, water and wastewater, ICT, social infrastructure) is not available. Figure 7 shows the payment mechanism of the PPP projects in the period 1990–2019.

Figure 7: Payment Mechanism for Public–Private Partnership Projects, 1990–2019

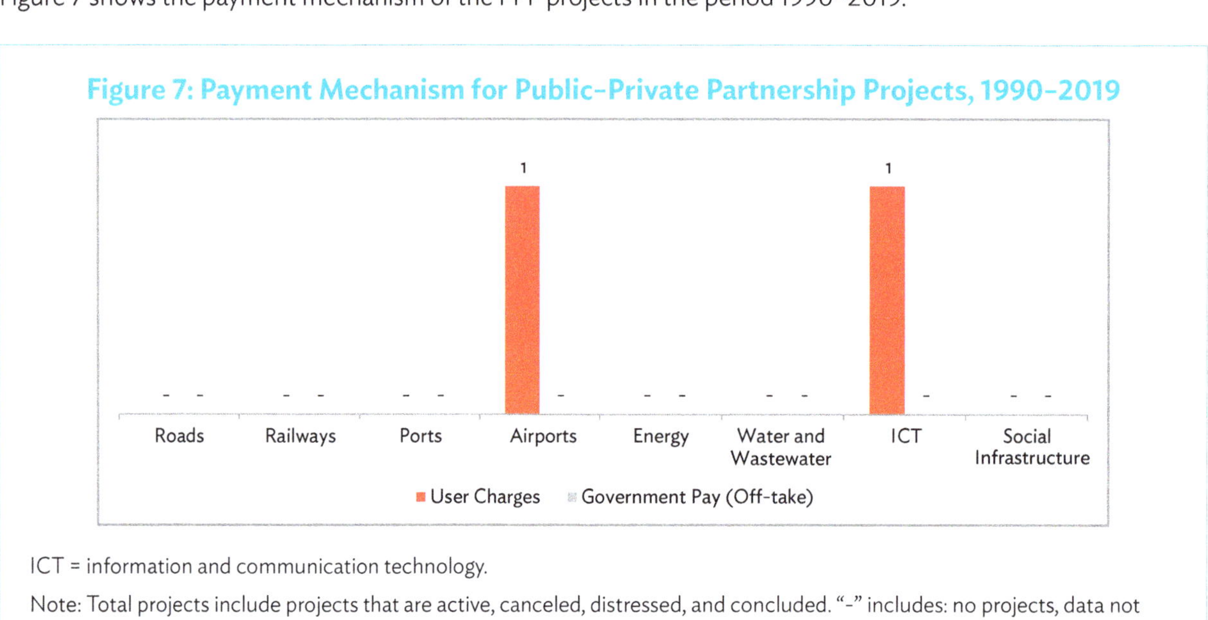

ICT = information and communication technology.

Note: Total projects include projects that are active, canceled, distressed, and concluded. "-" includes: no projects, data not available, or not applicable according to the database.

Source: World Bank. Infrastructure Finance, PPPs and Guarantees. Country Snapshots. Papua New Guinea. https://ppi.worldbank.org/en/snapshots/country/papua-new-guinea (accessed 30 June 2020).

Based on available data, from 1990 to 2019, five PPP projects in Papua New Guinea have witnessed participation from foreign sponsors. Figure 8 presents the distribution of these projects across various infrastructure sectors (i.e., roads, railways, ports, airports, energy, water and wastewater, ICT, social infrastructure). Figure 8 shows foreign sponsor participation in PPP projects from 1990 to 2019.

Figure 8: Foreign Sponsor Participation in Public–Private Partnership Projects, 1990–2019

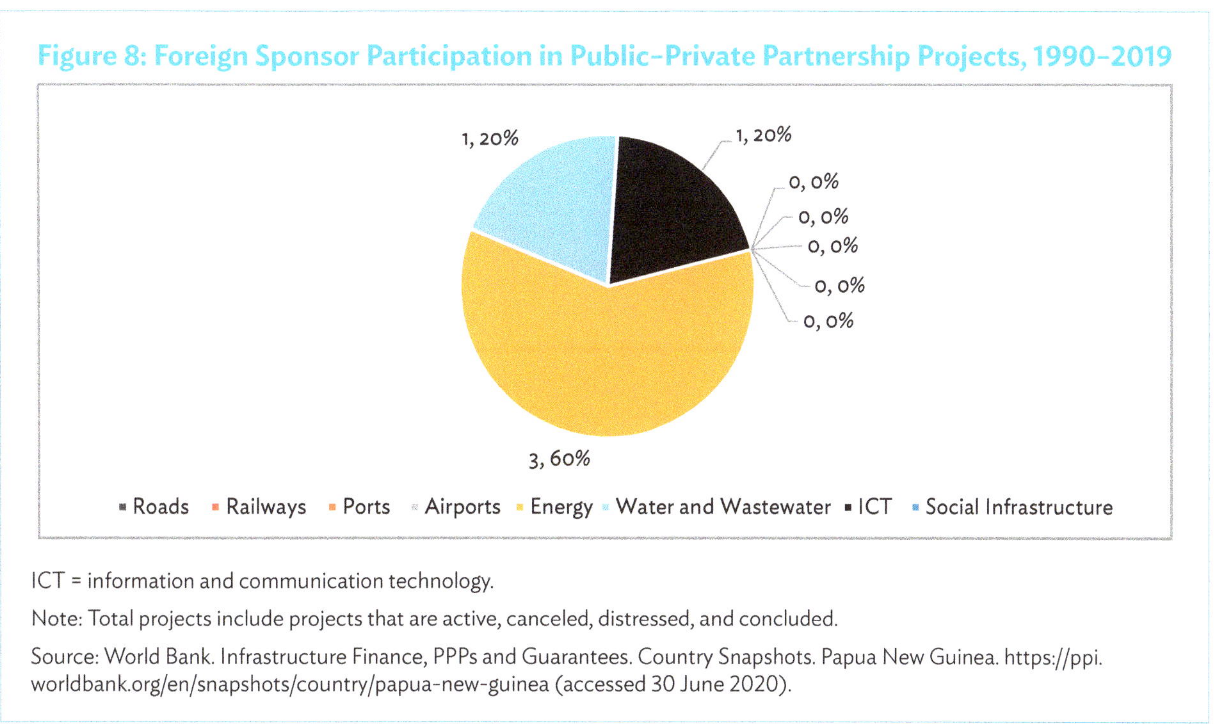

ICT = information and communication technology.

Note: Total projects include projects that are active, canceled, distressed, and concluded.

Source: World Bank. Infrastructure Finance, PPPs and Guarantees. Country Snapshots. Papua New Guinea. https://ppi.worldbank.org/en/snapshots/country/papua-new-guinea (accessed 30 June 2020).

Some of the major challenges associated with PPPs in Papua New Guinea are as follows:

- The PPP enabling framework in Papua New Guinea needs to be further developed and streamlined. The PPP Act needs to be amended and further strengthened to include provisions for PPP types, timelines for and approvals to be sought through the PPP process, government support to PPPs, dispute resolution mechanism, PPP contract termination provisions, lender's security rights and mechanisms, and other relevant provisions.
- The PPP Act needs to be supported by detailed regulations, standard operating procedures, and manuals to provide the relevant tools, frameworks, and guidance for identification, preparation, procurement, and management of PPP projects.
- Presently, there is no operational institution tasked with managing the PPP project development process. Therefore, the PPP Centre needs to be operationalized to fulfil its various functions as stipulated under the PPP Act. Also, the PPP Act has assigned substantial responsibility related to project preparation and procurement to the PPP Centre. The project preparation and procurement responsibilities of the Relevant Public Body need to be comprehensively defined and the functions of the PPP Centre need to be further streamlined.
- Presently, there is no database for PPP projects that have been procured and commercially and financially closed. Similarly, there is no pipeline of PPP projects at various stages of preparation, structuring, or procurement. Hence, a national database for PPP projects and a PPP project pipeline should be prepared and updated annually or semi-annually.

- The institutional capacity to develop, procure, and implement PPPs for the various Relevant Public Bodies in Papua New Guinea is limited. Also, the ability of the Government of Papua New Guinea to fund new infrastructure is limited, resulting into heavy reliance on assistance from the international development banks. As a result, very few PPPs have been developed in the country to date. Thus, there is a need for building institutional capacity to identify, prepare, structure, procure, and manage PPPs that are at par with international standards.
- The funding sources for project preparation and development, which could be tapped by the Relevant Public Bodies, are not clearly defined; and such funding is availed on an ad hoc basis. Hence, there is a need to clearly define the funding sources available for the Relevant Public Bodies and the eligibility criteria for availing such funding.
- The PPP Act does not provide for any government support to optimize the financial viability of the PPP projects. The government may consider introducing relevant government financial support mechanisms to improve the financial viability of PPP projects based on an assessment of international best practices on government support to PPPs.
- There is also a need to develop enabling institutions to support PPPs such as credit rating agencies for rating PPPs, development finance institutions to provide long-term financing to PPPs, and capital market and derivative market institutions and instruments to help PPPs raise funds from retail and international investors.
- Other challenges include the lack of provision for dispute resolution mechanisms, such as an independent tribunal for settling PPP disputes. Community opposition to PPPs is another key challenge. This reflects a lack of consultation with affected communities, as well as issues on potential exploitation of communities when local governments partner with private companies that dominate key sectors of the local economy in rural and isolated regions. These need to be adequately addressed through appropriate mechanisms and processes (footnote 2).

II. National Public–Private Partnership Landscape

The National Public–Private Partnership Policy (the PPP Policy) was endorsed by the Government of Papua New Guinea in 2008. This National PPP Policy forms the basis for the Public–Private Partnership Act 2014 (the PPP Act). The act was passed by the parliament in September 2014. However, the PPP Act was gazetted only in January 2018. The government has not implemented the PPP Act yet, as there are amendments to further strengthen it, and these amendments are yet to be circulated for comments and inputs from the public (footnote 2).

The PPP Act establishes the PPP Centre, which would implement the PPP Act and monitor its enforcement. It also establishes the PPP Steering Group, which includes the heads of the Department of Treasury and the Department of National Planning and Monitoring, and the PPP Forum (footnote 2).

Gas, mining, and petroleum projects, and all associated development agreements or projects undertaken as part of the government's tax credit scheme are excluded from the PPP Act. Infrastructure procurement projects involving a Relevant Public Body (footnote 1), wherein the value exceeds K50 million, would automatically qualify for a PPP arrangement under the PPP Act (footnote 3).

PPP agreements must also be in compliance with the ICCC regulations, the terms of the individual concession agreements related to the project, and with any umbrella regulations set by the ICCC related to the industry (footnote 1).

The first two PPP projects had reached financial closure long before the introduction of any of Papua New Guinea's PPP Policy and the recent commencement of Papua New Guinea's PPP Act. These projects are the Port Moresby Diesel-Fired Plant in 1996 and the PNG Water Limited potable water treatment plant in 1997. These projects involve a total investment of $136 million. In 2011, the Government of Papua New Guinea awarded a build–own–operate contract and a value-added services license for 15 years to Bemobile Limited, a PNG limited-liability company, to strengthen Papua New Guinea's backbone infrastructure for telecommunications and to reduce the country's reliance on the legacy infrastructure of Telikom PNG (the state-owned telecom service provider). The objective was to upgrade and expand its existing network in Papua New Guinea to increase national geographic and population coverage. The project was supported and partly financed by the Asian Development Bank (ADB). Other sponsors include Telikom PNG and General Enterprise Management Services (GEMS), a private equity fund based in Hong Kong, China.

In late 2017, the PPP Contract for Port Moresby and Lae was executed with the Philippines-based International Container Terminal Services, Inc. (ICTSI). The project is proposed to be implemented on a build–own–operate–transfer model.[8] ADB and the Papua New Guinea National Airports Corporation (NAC) have signed

---

[8] *Port Strategy News*. Close Collaboration Underpins PNG Port Reforms. https://www.portstrategy.com/news101/world/asia/close-collaboration-underpins-png-port-reforms.

a transaction advisory services agreement to develop a new international passenger terminal at Port Moresby (Jacksons) International Airport on 2 February 2017, on a design–build–finance–operate–maintain (DBFOM) basis.[9] In addition to this, the PPP Agreement for the $2 billion RAMU-2 hydroelectric power plant was signed in 2015 with the People's Republic of China's Shenzhen Energy Group. The construction of the RAMU-2 project was expected to commence by the end of 2019 by Kumul Consolidated Holdings (KCH).[10]

According to the 2018 budget, the government intends to develop a roadmap to help identify and implement a pipeline of PPP projects aligned with the country's Medium-Term Development Plan 3 for 2018–2022 (footnote 2).

National Public–Private Partnership Enabling Framework

1. Public–Private Partnership Legal and Regulatory Framework

Parameter	
Does the country have -	
• national PPP law and PPP regulations?	✓
• public financial management laws and regulations?	✓
• sector-specific laws and regulations?	✓
• procurement laws and regulations?	✓
• environmental laws and regulations?	✓
• laws and regulations for social compliance?	UA
• laws and regulations governing land acquisition and ownership?	✓
• taxation laws and regulations?	✓
• employment laws and regulations?	✓
• licensing requirements?	✓
What are the other components of the PPP legal and regulatory framework?	Other key supporting components (elaborated below) include • PPP Policy

✓ = Yes, ✗ = No, UA= Unavailable.

Source: Government of Papua New Guinea, Department of Treasury. 2014. *Public–Private Partnership Act 2014*. Port Moresby. https://www.treasury.gov.pg/html/legislation/files/acts/2014/Public.Private.Partnership.(PPP).Act.2014.pdf.

Evolution of the Public–Private Partnership Legal and Regulatory Framework in Papua New Guinea

Until 2008, PPPs in Papua New Guinea were implemented in an unorganized manner, without a formal PPP enabling framework governing PPP project identification, preparation, procurement, implementation, and management. In 2008, the Government of Papua New Guinea endorsed the National Public–Private Partnership Policy (the PPP Policy) to provide the policy framework and basis for PPPs (footnote 1). Based on this National PPP Policy, a PPP Act was drafted in 2010 to provide the legal basis for PPPs in Papua New Guinea. Following a

[9] *Asian Development Bank News*. 2017. ADB Helps PNG Expand Port Moresby International Airport Using PPP. 2 February. https://www.adb.org/news/adb-helps-png-expand-port-moresby-international-airport-using-ppp.

[10] *Post-Courier*. 2019. US2B Ramu 2 Hydro Power Project Stalled. 1 August. https://postcourier.com.pg/us2b-ramu-2-hydro-power-project-stalled/; Esila P. 2019. K3.31 billion Hydro Project to Start. *The National*. 8 August. https://www.thenational.com.pg/k3-31bil-hydro-project-to-start/.

few amendments to streamline the PPP Act, the modified PPP Act was passed by the Parliament in September 2014. The PPP Act was then gazetted in January 2018. Table 2 shows the modifications made from the PPP Act 2010 to PPP Act 2014.

Table 2: Amendments on the Public–Private Partnership Act

Aspects	Previous Regulation (PPP Act 2010)	Current Regulation (PPP Act 2014)
Public–Private Partnership (PPP) Arrangement	Does not cover the exclusions of the PPP arrangement	Covers the exclusions of the PPP arrangement in Schedule 3[a]
Government Line Agencies sponsoring PPPs	State Authorities including: • The Independent State of Papua New Guinea • A government department • A provincial government • A local-level government • An agency, branch, division, administrative unit, instrumentality, commission, board, authority, corporation (whether formed by statute or otherwise) of the National, a Provincial or Local-level Government, a state enterprise, public enterprise, a public body, a company or other body corporate including a corporation sole, or an unincorporated body, owned or controlled either directly or indirectly by the State, or a partnership under the management or control of the State or an entity that is carrying out functions and activities for and on behalf of the State, regardless of legal form or method of establishment, but which is not a private sector majority owned or controlled entity where control means the power to direct or cause the direction of the general management and policies of an entity.	Relevant Public Bodies including: • The Independent State of Papua New Guinea • Provincial or local-level governments • State-owned entities
Body responsible for registering project with PPP Centre	State authority	Relevant public body
Code of Practice	Must be consistent with public service management enactments	Must be consistent with Public Service (Management) Act 1995 and the General Orders made under the act.
Functional Assessment	No clause about functional assessment	PPP Centre must engage a firm to carry out a functional assessment every 5 years

PPP = public–private partnership.

[a] The PPP Act excludes mining, gas, and petroleum projects, and all associated development agreements or projects undertaken as part of the government's tax credit scheme. Infrastructure procurement projects involving a Relevant Public Body, wherein the value of which exceeds the referral threshold, would not automatically qualify as a public–private partnership arrangement under the PPP Act. The referral threshold would be set in the PPP Act regulations. However, there is a general indication that the referral threshold value of a project will be K50 million.

Source: Government of Papua New Guinea, Department of Treasury. 2014. *Public–Private Partnership Act 2014*. Port Moresby. https://www.treasury.gov.pg/html/legislation/files/acts/2014/Public.Private.Partnership.(PPP).Act.2014.pdf; ixueshu. PPP Act 2010. http://wk.ixueshu.com/file/27bbf54642ea6319.html.

The PPP Act provides for the procurement and delivery of infrastructure facilities and services through PPP arrangements, and gives power to certain public bodies to enter into such arrangements. However, the government has not implemented the PPP Act yet, as there are amendments to further strengthen the PPP Act, which are yet to be circulated for comments and inputs from the public. Upon adoption, the PPP Act would serve the following functions:

- Provide the state authorities with the necessary statutory powers to enter into PPP arrangements. These powers would supplement the existing powers of state authorities under relevant existing legislation. The PPP procurement process would cover all public infrastructure projects with a value of over K50 million (footnote 6).
- Provide for state authorities to form companies and to enter into joint ventures for the purpose of a PPP, including giving state authorities the legal capacity necessary to contract direct agreements with the private financiers of PPPs (footnote 6).
- Provide for the transfer of function of state authority, subject to it retaining the general control, to the private sector under the PPP.
- Provide for establishing the PPP Centre, the PPP Steering Group, and the PPP Forum, and their respective responsibilities and powers.
- Provide for reporting, accountability, and transparency in implementing the PPP program and managing the PPP Centre (footnote 6).
- Identify the role of the National Executive Council (NEC) as the sole decision-making body in approving the procurement for PPPs.

Though the PPP Act details the procedures for assessment and development of PPP projects, the PPP Act does not contain any significant provisions on the procurement options available, nor details on the specific procurement process of a PPP (footnote 6).

Provisions of the PPP Act indicate that the PPP Centre would be established to issue guidelines and regulations on PPP processes. However, the PPP Centre has not yet been established to date. While PPPs are not prohibited, currently there is no formal structure for the regulation of PPPs in Papua New Guinea. Procurement for government projects occurs on an ad hoc basis through normal government processes, and largely depends on the policies and priorities of the government of the day (footnote 6).

The PPP Act applies to the Independent State of PNG (State), provincial or local-level governments, and state-owned entities. Though the PPP Act applies for the grant of a lease, concession or license as part of a PPP arrangement, it does not apply to the grant of a right, license or lease, or that is subject to any other legislation. A PPP agreement may include terms and conditions in relation to the performance by the private partner and provision for charging user fees or collecting payment by a Relevant Public Body, or a combination of such payments.

The PPP Act defines "infrastructure" as any asset, facility, or service for the benefit of members of the public, including those specified in Schedule 2 of the PPP Act.[11]

[11] Asian Development Bank. 2019. *Public–Private Partnership Monitor, Second Edition*. Manila. https://www.adb.org/sites/default/files/publication/509426/ppp-monitor-second-edition.pdf.

Schedule 3 of the PPP Act specifies the arrangements that are classified as PPP for the purposes of the PPP Act. A PPP arrangement means an arrangement with a person other than a Relevant Public Body for the performance of functions related to (footnote 11):

- design and construction of infrastructure and the operation of services and provision of finance related to it,
- construction of infrastructure and the provision of finance related to it,
- design and construction of infrastructure and the provision of finance related to it, or
- provision of services relating to infrastructure for at least 5 years and the provision of finance related to the services.

Schedule 3 of the PPP Act explicitly excludes the following arrangements (footnote 11):

- those that are less than a referral threshold to be specified by a regulation in the future,
- mining projects under the Mining Act 1992 (and associated development agreements),
- gas projects and petroleum projects under the Oil and Gas Act 1998 (and associated development agreements), and
- where the infrastructure project is predominantly comprised of expenditure deemed as "income tax" under the Income Tax Act 1959 (footnote 11).

However, the responsible minister, following the recommendation of the PPP Steering Group, may amend Schedule 3 by adding or excluding any arrangement or class of arrangements, by notice in the National Gazette. Any arrangement or agreement entered into prior to the effective date of the PPP Act will remain in force as if the agreement or arrangement were made under the PPP Act. Where there are any inconsistencies between that arrangement or agreement and the PPP Act, the terms of the arrangement or agreement prevail (footnote 11).

Public–Private Partnership Regulatory Framework in Papua New Guinea

The PPP Act was passed by the National Parliament in September 2014 and was certified by the Acting Clerk and the Speaker of the National Parliament in October 2014. The PPP Act was brought into action on 31 January 2018 following its publication in the National Gazette. Moreover, there are laws governing certain aspects of the PPP procurement (Table 3).

Table 3: Laws on Public–Private Partnership Procurement

Law	Description
PPP Act 2014	• The PPP Act provides for the procurement and delivery of infrastructure facilities and services through PPP arrangements, and gives power to certain public bodies to enter into such arrangements
PPP Policy	• The PPP Policy forms the basis for the development of the components of the PPP Framework, including PPP Law, institutional arrangements, legal/regulatory framework, and implementing guidelines.

PPP = public–private partnership.

Source: Asian Development Bank. 2019. *Public–Private Partnership Monitor, Second Edition.* Manila. https://www.adb.org/sites/default/files/publication/509426/ppp-monitor-second-edition.pdf.

2. Types of Public–Private Partnerships

The PPP Act does not provide for specific types of PPP contracts. However, based on the revenue model, the PPP Act allows for PPPs based on user charges, off-take payments by a Relevant Public Body, or a combination of user charges and off-take payments.

Based on the experience from PPP projects implemented in the past, the PPP types used include

- **Build-Operate-Transfer (BOT),** where the private party builds and operates the project assets with some encouragement/support from the Relevant Public Body. The project assets are transferred back to the Relevant Public Body at the end of the PPP contract period (e.g., Port Moresby Diesel-Fired Plant, 1996);[12]
- **Rehabilitate-Operate-Transfer (ROT),** in which the private party is permitted to refurbish, operate, and maintain the existing facility. These activities will be performed for a specific period of time after which the project assets are transferred back to the Relevant Public Body (e.g., PNG Water Limited potable water treatment plant, 1997);[13] and
- **Design-Build-Finance-Operate-Transfer (DBFOT),** where the private party is responsible for designing, financing, constructing, operating, and maintaining the project assets. At the end of the concession period, the project assets are transferred back to the Relevant Public Body (e.g., Port Moresby [Jacksons] International Airport [PMIA] PPP project).[14]

3. Eligible Sectors for Public–Private Partnerships

As per *Schedule 2–Infrastructure* of the PPP Act, there are 19 economic and social infrastructure sectors across which projects can be procured through the PPP route (Table 4). A PPP project may also be proposed for a combination of two or more infrastructure sectors.

Table 4: Projects Eligible for Public–Private Partnership Mode of Procurement

Sectors	Subsectors
1. Transportation infrastructure	• Airports – Airport runways, air traffic control, terminals, and other airside and landside facilities • Rail • Bridges • Tunnels • Ports and harbor facilities on water or land
2. Road infrastructure	• Roads, highways, and road facilities
3. Water resources and irrigation infrastructure	• Dams • Irrigation
4. Water supply infrastructure	• Potable water supply, distribution, and delivery
5. Infrastructure for centralized water waste management systems	• Desalination • Wastewater treatment and disposal • Drainage and sewerage

continued on next page

12 World Bank PPI Database.

13 The Constructor. PPP Construction Projects—Types and Benefits. https://theconstructor.org/construction/public-private-partnership-ppp-construction-projects-types-benefits/1319/#12_Rehabilitate_Operate_and_Transfer_ROT.

14 National Airports Corporation. Airports. https://www.nac.com.pg/airports/pmia-ppp/.

continued from previous page

Sectors	Subsectors
6. Infrastructure for local water waste management system	• Unavailable
7. Infrastructure for waste management system	• Solid waste management including waste collection and disposal
8. Telecommunication and informatics infrastructure	• Fixed or mobile local telephony • Domestic long distance telephony • Internet and broadband and facilities related to satellites • Broadcasting facilities
9. Energy and electricity infrastructure including renewable energy	• Generation • Transmission • Distribution • Supply • Ancillary facilities including dam for hydro power • Gas transmission • Public gas distribution • Gas and gas works
10. Energy conservation infrastructure	• Street lighting
11. Urban facilities infrastructure	• Land reclamation • Environmental management • Remediation and clean-up • Urban development • Government and public buildings including office accommodation and courts
12. Zone infrastructure	• Industrial zone
13. Tourism infrastructure, such as tourism information center (TIC)	• Tourism development projects • Trade fair complexes • Convention, exhibition, and cultural centers
14. Education facilities, research and development infrastructure	• Schools and colleges • Residential facilities • Training • Research and development
15. Sports, arts, and culture facility infrastructure	• Sports recreation facilities
16. Health infrastructure	• Hospitals
17. Penitentiary infrastructure	• Prisons • Remand centers
18. Public housing infrastructure	• Affordable housing
19. Traditional market	• Unavailable

Source: Government of Papua New Guinea, Department of Treasury. 2014. *Public–Private Partnership Act 2014*. Port Moresby. https://www.treasury.gov.pg/html/legislation/files/acts/2014/Public.Private.Partnership.(PPP).Act.2014.pdf.

The PPP Act specifies the following infrastructure subsectors as eligible for PPPs:

- assets, facilities, and services for the provision of power or electricity (generation, transmission, distribution, and supply);
- transport (airports, rails, roads, bridges, tunnels, ports, and dams);
- telecommunications;

- water;
- real property;
- health (hospitals);
- education;
- correctional management (prisons);
- gas transmission and distribution; and
- any other project/sector that may be notified by the responsible minister in the National Gazette.

The PPP Act specifically excludes (i) arrangements of a size or value lower than any referral threshold which may be set in a regulation made under the PPP Act, (ii) gas and petroleum projects under the Oil and Gas Act 1998 (and associated development agreements), (iii) mining projects under the Mining Act 1992 (and associated development agreements), and (iv) any infrastructure project in which the expenditure is predominantly comprised of expenditure deemed to be income tax under section 219C of the Income Tax Act 1959 (footnote 11).

The responsible minister may also include or exclude an arrangement or class of arrangements from being a PPP arrangement under the PPP Act by National Gazette notice (footnote 11).

4. Public–Private Partnership Institutional Framework

Parameter	
Does the country have a national PPP unit?	×
What are the functions of the national PPP unit?	
• Supporting the design and operationalization of the national PPP enabling framework?	NA
• Helping develop a national PPP pipeline?	NA
• Supporting the arrangement of funding for project preparation (budgetary allocations, technical assistance funding from multilateral development agencies, operating a dedicated project preparation/ project development fund)?	NA
• Guidance for project preparation to and coordination with the government agencies responsible for sponsoring the projects?	NA
• Making recommendations to the PPP committee and/ or other approving authorities to provide approvals associated with various stages of PPP process?	NA

✓ = Yes, × = No, UA= Unavailable, NA = Not Applicable.

The PPP Act provides for the establishment of the PPP Centre, a statutory agency to be established to implement the PPP Act and monitor its enforcement. The PPP Centre arrangements are guided by the National PPP Policy and the PPP Act. The PPP Act also provides for the establishment of the PPP Steering Group, which would include the heads of the Department of Treasury and the Department of National Planning and Monitoring, and the PPP Forum.

However, none of these entities are operational yet (footnote 2). Presently, there is no operational centralized government PPP authority. PPP matters are currently being partially managed by the PPP Policy and Strategy Unit of Treasury (footnote 11).

Table 5 outlines the key entities and institutions and their respective roles in promoting PPPs in Papua New Guinea (footnote 11):

Table 5: Key Agencies and Their Roles in Promoting Public–Private Partnerships

Key Agencies	Function/Role in Promoting PPPs
PPP Centre	• Part III of the PPP Act establishes the PPP Centre. It is an unincorporated statutory body with a range of powers and functions to assist the state and other Relevant Public Bodies on all aspects of PPP arrangements. Its functions include – encouraging Relevant Public Bodies to consider PPP arrangements in procuring infrastructure; – advising and assisting Relevant Public Bodies on all aspects of PPP arrangements; – acting as secretariat to the PPP Steering Group and PPP Forum; – reviewing and evaluating proposals for projects and advising the PPP Steering Group; – coordinating the implementation of PPP policy, program, and projects by the national, – provincial, and local-level governments; and – performing any other function concerning PPP arrangements. • The PPP Centre has broad powers that can be exercised on behalf of the state in connection with the performance of its functions, including accessing premises (subject to providing notice), giving directions (subject to approval of the responsible minister), engaging consultants and advisors, charging fees, and managing and administering funds. • The operation of the PPP Centre must be in accordance with a code of practice prepared by the chief executive officer and approved by the responsible minister. • With prior consultation with the responsible minister, the PPP Steering Group, appropriate Relevant Public Bodies, and other appropriate persons recommended by the PPP Forum, the PPP Centre may issue or revoke procedures, guidelines, and instructions as it deems necessary (PPP Centre Rules). Any issue or revocation of PPP Centre Rules must be published in the National Gazette. • The PPP Centre is subject to control and supervision of the responsible minister who is accountable to the National Parliament for the PPP Centre. The PPP Centre must report to the PPP Steering Group on policy, program, and projects, and carry out the decisions of the PPP Steering Group and the National Executive Council (NEC) on these matters.
PPP Steering Group	• Part V of the PPP Act establishes the PPP Steering Group to procure and develop infrastructures through PPPs. Its functions include – coordinating and monitoring the PPP Policy and program of the NEC, – ensuring that the PPP Policy and program are implemented appropriately, – recommending to and advising the NEC on measures that may be taken to advance PPP policy and program generally, – making recommendations to the NEC on an individual PPP project or a group of projects, – ensuring public communications and interaction with the private sector on PPP is successful in building understanding and confidence among the general public, and – ensuring highest standards of probity are maintained in the procurement of PPP arrangements.

continued on next page

continued from previous page

Key Agencies	Function/Role in Promoting PPPs
PPP Forum	• Part VI of the PPP Act provides that the Chief Executive Officer must convene and hold a forum called the PPP Forum to discuss specific issues, such as PPP legislation, policy, and procedures for any proposals for change, but not any specific PPP arrangement. • The purpose of the PPP forum is to allow all stakeholders of society who have an interest in PPP arrangements and implementation of PPP projects to discuss and exchange views on specific issues. • The Chief Executive Officer must invite the significant private sector interest groups in Papua New Guinea that represent consumers and users of infrastructure facilities and services, as well as members of the PPP Steering Group and senior representatives of state authorities involved in infrastructure development and PPP policy. • The Chief Executive Officer must convene the PPP Forum at least once per calendar year.
National Executive Council	• Approving the execution of an agreement for a PPP arrangement
Responsible Minister	• Amending the schedule in accordance with the recommendation of the Steering Committee • Giving directions concerning the management of the company established for the purpose of PPP arrangement and other general directions and guidelines to the PPP Centre • Serving as the chairperson of the PPP Centre appointments committee • Tabling each six monthly report and the annual report of the PPP Centre at the national parliament
Relevant Public Body or Government Contracting Agency	• Entering into a PPP arrangement • Arranging for or making payment to a partner • Entering into agreements with operators, service providers, and contractors, among others, for the purpose of a PPP arrangement • Forming and registering a company for the purpose of a PPP arrangement • Seeking the PPP Centre's approval or confirmation of a PPP arrangement in compliance with the PPP Act • Conducting initial assessment for procurement of a project • Submitting the initial assessment to the PPP Centre within 30 days of conducting the assessment

NEC = National Executive Council, PPP = public–private partnership.

Sources: Government of Papua New Guinea, Department of Treasury. 2014. *Public–Private Partnership Act 2014*. Port Moresby. https://www.treasury.gov.pg/html/legislation/files/acts/2014/Public.Private.Partnership.(PPP).Act.2014.pdf; Asian Development Bank. 2019. *Public–Private Partnership Monitor, Second Edition*. Manila. https://www.adb.org/sites/default/files/publication/509426/ppp-monitor-second-edition.pdf.

Entities Responsible for Public–Private Partnership Project Identification, Approval, and Oversight

Parameter	
Who is responsible for identifying, preparing, and procuring the PPP projects?	Line Agency or State-owned entities with the help of the PPP Center
Is there a PPP committee for providing approvals at various stages of PPP projects?	✓
Who are the other approving authorities than the PPP committee for PPP projects?	National Executive Council
Does the country have an independent think tank for various PPP planning, budgeting, and policy decisions?	UA
Is there a legislature for the PPP program oversight?	UA

✓ = Yes, × = No, UA= Unavailable, NA = Not Applicable.

Source: Government of Papua New Guinea, Department of Treasury. 2014. *National PPP Policy 2014*. Port Moresby. https://www.treasury.gov.pg/html/misc/Special%20Projects/PPP/PNG%20National%20PPP%20Policy%202014.pdf.

Entities Responsible for Public–Private Partnership Project Monitoring

Parameter	
Is there an entity for monitoring of PPP projects post commercial close?	✓
Is there an entity for monitoring and management of fiscal risks and liabilities from PPP projects for Ministry of Finance (MOF)?	✓

✓ = Yes, × = No, UA= Unavailable, NA = Not Applicable.

PPP = public–private partnership.

Source: Government of Papua New Guinea, Department of Treasury. 2014. *National PPP Policy 2014*. Port Moresby. https://www.treasury.gov.pg/html/legislation/files/acts/2014/Public.Private.Partnership.(PPP).Act.2014.pdf.

Line agency surveys the status of projects, including assets, and reviews and concludes the PPP. The PPP Centre helps assess options after contract termination (footnote 1).

5. Public–Private Partnership Process Details

Parameter	
Does the PPP legal and regulatory framework provide for a ppp implementation process covering the entire PPP lifecycle?	✓
Does the feasibility assessment stage cover – • Technical feasibility? • Socioeconomic feasibility? • Environmental sustainability? • Financial feasibility? • Fiscal affordability assessment? • Legal assessment? • Risk assessment and ppp project structuring? • Value for Money (VFM) assessment? • Market sounding with stakeholders?	 × ✓ ✓ × × × ✓ ✓ ✓
Is the PPP procurement plan required?	UA
Is there a need to set up a separate PPP procurement committee?	UA
Is competitive bidding the only method for selection of PPP private developer?	×
Is the prequalification stage necessary? Or does the PPP legal and regulatory framework allow flexibility to skip the prequalification stage?	UA
Does the PPP legal and regulatory process provide the option to the preferred bidder for contract negotiations?	UA
Does the PPP legal and regulatory framework allow unsuccessful bidders to challenge the award/ submit complaints?	UA
What is the maximum time allowed for submitting a complaint/ challenging the award by unsuccessful bidders from the announcement of the preferred bidder?	UA
Does the PPP legal and regulatory framework provide for transparency?	UA
Which of the following are required to be published?	
• Findings from the feasibility assessment?	UA
• Procurement notice?	UA
• Outcome of stakeholder consultations from market sounding?	UA

continued on next page

continued from previous page

Parameter	
• Clarifications to prequalification queries?	UA
• Prequalification results?	UA
• Clarifications to pre-bid queries?	UA
• Results for the bid stage and selection of preferred bidder?	UA
• Final concession agreement to be entered between the government agency and the preferred bidder? and other PPP project agreements executed between government agency and preferred bidder?	UA
• Confidentiality?	UA

✓ = Yes, × = No, UA = Unavailable, NA = Not Applicable.

PPP = public–private partnership.

While the National PPP Policy contemplates that studies regarding the PPP process details would be required as part of an Outline Business Case, this is not yet a legal requirement.

As per the National PPP Policy and the PPP Act, the PPP project process consists of four stages:

- development stage,
- procurement stage,
- implementation (construction and operation) stage, and
- termination stage.

The PPP Act envisages the PPP Centre to play a central role throughout the PPP process, especially in the development and procurement stages (Figure 9). The PPP Centre would help ensure that sufficient standards of project preparation and analysis are used as a basis of determining whether the project should be offered in the PPP mode, the suitable PPP model, and that the best value for money is derived from the awarded private entity.

Figure 9: Public–Private Partnership Development and Procurement Process

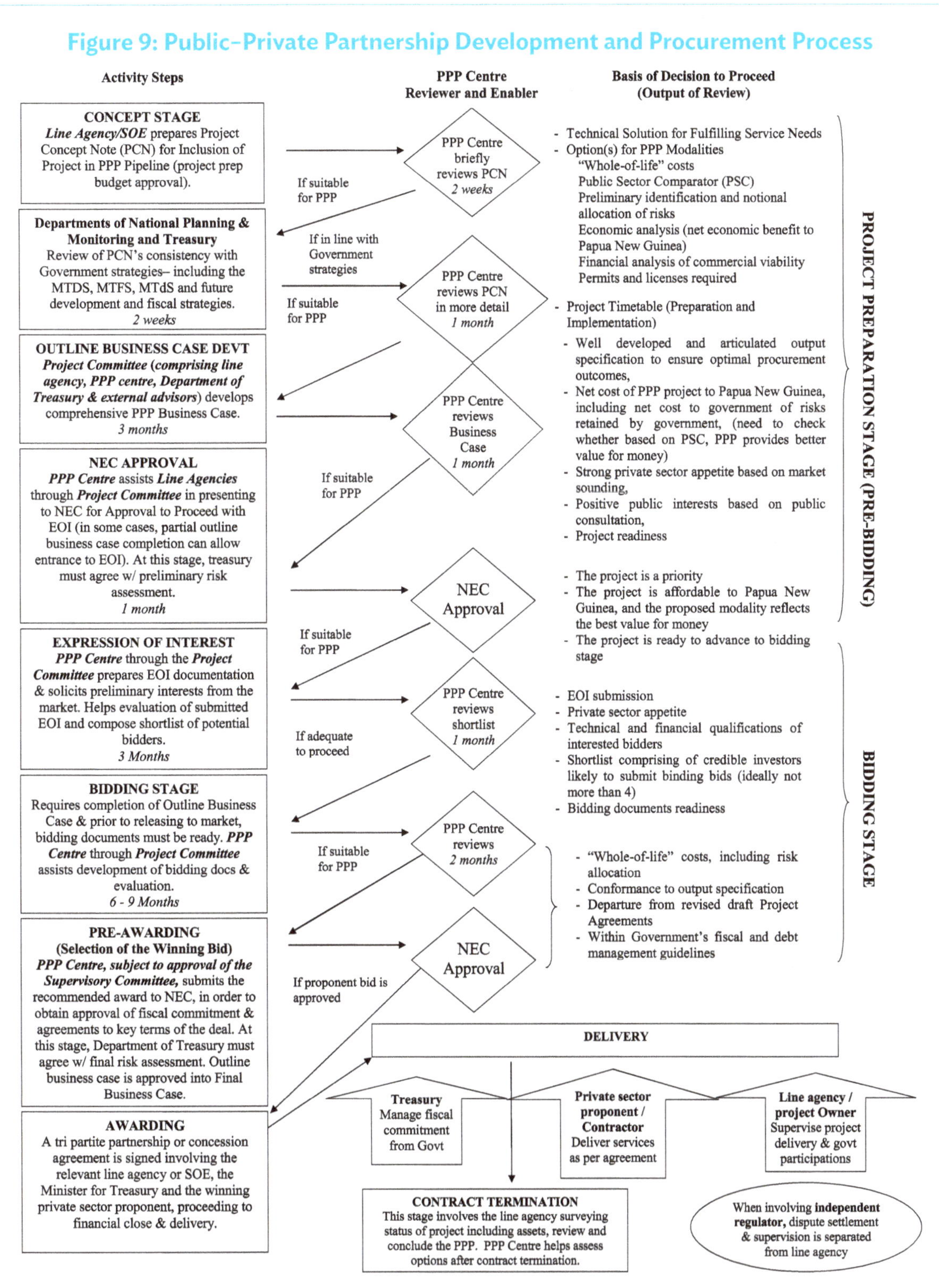

EOI = expression of interest, MTDS = medium-term development strategy, MTdS = medium-term debt strategy, MTFS = medium- term fiscal strategy, NEC = National Executive Council, PCN = project concept note, PPP = public–private partnership, PSC = Public Service Commission, SOE = state-owned enterprise.

Source: Government of Papua New Guinea, Department of Treasury. 2014. *National PPP Policy 2014*. Port Moresby. https://www.treasury.gov.pg/html/misc/Special%20Projects/PPP/PNG%20National%20PPP%20Policy%202014.pdf.

Figure 10 and Table 6 describe the various steps involved in each stage of the PPP process.

Figure 10: Stages of the Public–Private Partnership Process

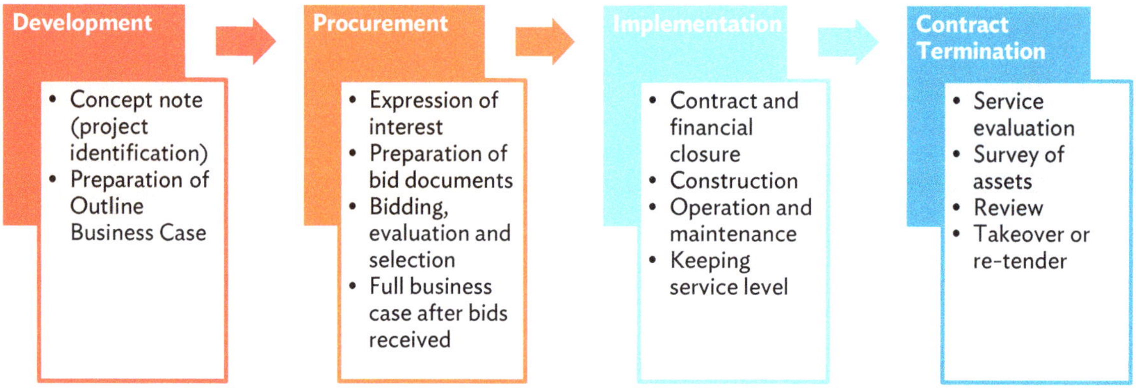

Source: Government of Papua New Guinea, Department of Treasury. 2014. *National PPP Policy 2014*. Port Moresby. https://www.treasury.gov.pg/html/misc/Special%20Projects/PPP/PNG%20National%20PPP%20Policy%202014.pdf.

Table 6: Features of the Public–Private Partnership Process

DEVELOPMENT STAGE	
Submission of project concept note from line agency or state-owned enterprise (SOE) to the PPP Centre	• The line agency or SOE identifies the public infrastructure or service needs that can be fulfilled through a PPP project and prepares a project concept note. Projects submitted to the PPP Centre must be approved by the NEC through inclusion in the National PPP Infrastructure Pipeline, an allocation in the national budget, or an NEC Decision. • The line agency or SOE submits the project concept note to the PPP Centre. The PPP Centre forwards the project concept note to the Departments of Treasury and National Planning and Monitoring, for initial appraisal against the Medium-Term Fiscal Strategy (MTFS), Medium-Term Development Strategy (MTDS), Medium-Term Debt Strategy (MTdS), and future development strategies and fiscal guidelines. • The PPP Centre assists the line agency or SOE by reviewing the project concept note. Since development of the Outline Business Case may involve significant costs, only projects that accord with the government's development priorities, such as public goods and those that have strong potential as a PPP project, would proceed beyond this stage. A project appraisal manual would be prepared to provide guidance on this issue. • The analytical framework, which should accompany the project concept note and which would form the basis for the review by the PPP Centre, includes details on: – whether the project accords with current and future national development and fiscal strategies and/or identified within the "National PPP Infrastructure Pipeline."[a] This would be done primarily by the Department of National Planning and Monitoring and the Department of Treasury, in consultation with relevant stakeholders; – technical solution for fulfilling service needs; – options for PPP modalities versus other modalities such as purely private provision; – "whole-of-lifecycle" costs; – a public sector comparator or other equivalent benchmarking analysis to ensure that the project has value for money; – preliminary identification and notional allocation of risks; – economic analysis (net economic benefit to the country); – social cost benefit analysis;

continued on next page

continued from previous page

DEVELOPMENT STAGE	
	– preliminary project financial appraisal; – the required land for the project; – the required permits and licenses; and – project timetable (preparation and implementation). • Based on the above information, the PPP Centre advises the line agency whether or not the project qualifies as a priority project (priority is also determined in reference to other potential PPP projects which the PPP Centre may have under consideration. The line agency's strategic plan plays a strong role in this determination) and whether or not the project is affordable and of optimal value to the country. If the project is deemed to be a priority, the PPP Centre then includes the project in the pipeline and the project can then proceed to the Outline Business Case development stage.
Development of the Outline PPP Business Case	• The PPP Centre plays a more active role in this process and assists the line agency in accessing resources to support the Outline Business Case, including as appropriate, support in engaging specialist external advisors. A project committee comprising representatives from the PPP Centre, line agency/SOE, and the Department of Treasury and supported by external specialists are formed to manage the development of the Outline Business Case. • The Outline Business Case phase develops the PPP project proposal to a level where it is ready to enter the bidding stage, and is presentable for NEC to make a decision on approving fiscal commitments and the release of the project to the market. • The Outline Business Case builds upon the initial work done by the line agencies, and the latter play an important role in providing input to the Outline Business Case development. • An Outline Business Case prepared for NEC approval includes the following analyses: – a well-developed and articulated output specification; – a public sector comparator analysis, which is an assessment of the net cost of the PPP project to the country, including the net cost to the government of retained risks. The analysis aims to determine whether a PPP represents better value for money than public sector implementation. A risk management manual will be developed to guide this process during the Outline Business Case preparation and the Final Business Case development at the later stage of procurement; – strong private sector appetite based on market sounding; – positive public interest based on public consultation; and – project readiness, including assessment of land acquisition, environmental approval, and other statutory approval issues. • The PPP Centre uses its expertise to ensure that submissions of the Outline Business Case to the NEC are well-prepared and qualified for consideration as a PPP project. The PPP Centre ensures that the information used and the analyses are reliable. • If the project is affordable, and both the Department of Treasury and the Department of National Planning and Monitoring concur that the project should proceed to the next stage, then the PPP Centre presents the Outline Business Case to the NEC.
NEC Approval	• The PPP Centre, the line agency or SOE, and the parties involved in the project committee jointly submits the PPP Outline Business Case to the NEC for approval. The NEC then confirms whether the project is: – a priority public infrastructure or service that conforms to the country's development priorities and that the project meets the fiscal and debt management guidelines, upon advice from the Department of Treasury and the Department of National Planning and Monitoring; – affordable to Papua New Guinea, and the proposed modality reflects the best value for money; and – ready to advance to the bidding stage.

continued on next page

continued from previous page

PROCUREMENT STAGE	
Advertising for expressions of interest (EOI) and prequalification	• At this stage, the government is not yet obliged to proceed with the project, and the cost to the private proponent to participate at this stage is not yet high. The absence of obligation to proceed allows the PPP Centre to test the market's propensity for the project. This is often the reason that projects, which have only partially completed the Outline Business Case, subject to NEC's approval, proceed to EOI stage in parallel with finalizing the PPP Outline Business Case. • Expressions of interest solicited by the government reveal the level of market interest for the potential PPP project, and at this stage the private proponent is not required to prepare detailed submissions. • In soliciting expressions of interest, the government develops an EOI document which provides clear guidance to potential private proponents on the information required for submission and how the government would evaluate this information. • The project committee develops the documentation, and the PPP Centre guides this process. The documentation includes brief service requirements to be met by the PPP project, including a proposed timeline, the information required in the EOI, and the evaluation criteria. • The project committee, which may be assisted by advisors appointed by the PPP Centre, evaluates the prequalification documents submitted by the bidders. The PPP Centre ensures that a technically skilled team is involved during the evaluation stage. In shortlisting investors, the project committee ensures that it selects an optimal number of potential bidders (a shortlist of more than four is likely to lead to a loss of interest among bidders, as the probability of award is reduced and the bidder may consider that it is not worth the resources required to prepare a bid). The quality of the shortlist is critical because it may be indicative of a successful tender. • If the results of the prequalification round indicate a low level of interest, the PPP Centre can recommend that the project does not proceed to the bidding stage.
Bidding stage, bid opening and evaluation, and awarding	• At this stage, the Outline Business Case should already be fully developed and completed, with NEC approval. The project structure agreed by the NEC as presented in the Outline Business Case forms the basis for preparing the bidding documents. Once the shortlist has been reviewed and the PPP Centre recommendation obtained to proceed to the bidding stage, the project committee begins the process of soliciting binding bids from the shortlisted private proponents. • The PPP Centre and the project committee actively participates together with the line agency in developing the bidding documents. Once prepared, the bidding documents should provide comprehensive project information to allow the shortlisted private proponents to fully understand the service requirements, develop a complete project proposal, and commit to enter into a binding contract to implement and operate the project. • If the proposals received from shortlisted bidders are non-compliant, the PPP Centre can recommend to NEC that the project be withdrawn. Alternatively, the bidders may be requested to resubmit their bids. If the bids received from compliant proposals suggest costs to the government that are in excess of the costs assumed at the initial appraisal stage, the project is reassessed to ensure that the principal of value for money is achieved and that it is affordable in the context of the government's fiscal and debt strategies. • All bidding documents should contain an information memorandum, or its equivalent in the Request for Proposal (RFP), as well as full drafts of all project agreements. Aside from the evaluation criteria to be used in determining the first ranked bidder, the documents should allow the private proponent to understand the project background, output specifications, proposed risk allocation, any constraints or a requirement arising from the legal or regulatory environment, and the expected support that the government is willing to assume.

continued on next page

continued from previous page

PROCUREMENT STAGE	
	• The draft project agreement is intended to be broadly non-negotiable, and this forms the basis for the private proponent to submit a binding bid, committing them to enter a contract to implement and operate the project. The project committee may opt to allow shortlisted proponents to propose amendments to the draft project agreements during bid conferences, and any proposed amendments accepted by the government must not be substantially divergent from the currently approved Outline Business Case, otherwise NEC approval will have to be obtained anew. Once the suggested amendments are incorporated into a revised agreement, the document is distributed to all shortlisted private proponents. The government can comfortably commit to accept the responsive binding bids because the bidding documents have clearly set out the project fundamentals in line with the NEC-approved Outline Business Case. • If the private proponent still needs to request some change to the project agreement, the proponents should submit, with its binding bid, a revised set of project agreements with detailed explanation on the requested changes. These additional changes are incorporated in the evaluation of the binding bid. • The criteria for evaluation of submitted bids broadly cover: – "whole-of-lifecycle" costs, including value for money and risk allocation; – conformance to output specification; and – departure from the revised draft project agreements, if permitted by the Request for Proposal (RFP) documents. • The PPP Centre reviews the evaluation report and the recommended or preferred private proponent. Should there be no bid deemed responsive to the bidding documents, the PPP Centre can recommend that the project does not continue to the award stage. • At this stage, the supervisory committee considers the PPP Centre's recommended bid. In their decision, the supervisory committee takes into consideration the best interests of the country and the adherence to the principles of the PPP Policy, namely, value for money in the deal, competitive tension in the selection of the winning proponent, and a transparent procurement process. • Following the supervisory committee's approval, a full Business Case is prepared and submitted for final approval by the NEC. Consideration by the NEC should be based on the analysis of how the preferred proponent will achieve value for money through the delivery of the PPP project. At this stage, the estimated net cost of the PPP can be confirmed with the submitted bid. • The Minister for Treasury forwards the supervisory committee's recommendation for the winning bidder to the NEC. • Subject to consistency with the government's existing policies on investment projects, approval by the NEC forms the basis for the fiscal authority to commit to the project. The PPP Centre can, through the project committee, finalize project agreements with the awarded proponent. • The concession or partnership agreement is then signed on a tri-partite basis involving the line agency, the Minister for Treasury, and the successful private sector proponent. • In keeping with the anticipated role of the Head of State in the PPP Law and in accordance with the Public Finances (Management) Act, the signed agreement is sponsored by the Minister for Treasury and submitted for consent and ratification to the Head of State.
CONSTRUCTION AND OPERATION STAGE	
	• Upon signing of the concession or partnership agreement, the private proponent is provided with a reasonable period in which to proceed to financial closure. The government and contractor should then proceed to satisfy the conditions precedent as soon as possible. • When independent regulators are involved, the government focuses on its role as project owner, and the regulator acts as a referee to monitor service delivery and as an objective party to take decisions ensuring that the best interests of all parties are safeguarded. • The project committee then completes its work and the contract management team within the relevant line agency, assisted by the PPP Centre, begins its work in ensuring that the private proponent delivers the project on schedule and according to specifications. Given that the PPP Centre understands the project contract, it is expected to provide assistance to the contract management team. Advisors' services can be sought to assist the contract management team.

continued on next page

continued from previous page

CONTRACT TERMINATION	
	• Contract termination may occur during the partnership period due to triggers as stipulated in the agreement or by the end of the partnership period. The line agency, and the independent regulatory body if any, is responsible for this process. This involves surveying project status, including assets and future needs for the project. In reviewing the options for continuing the project, the PPP Centre should provide advice and expertise in selecting the most economically favorable option, prior to concluding the PPP with the existing private counterpart.

EOI = expression of interest, NEC = National Executive Council, PPP = public–private partnership, RFP = request for proposal, SOE = state-owned enterprise.

[a] It is envisaged that the Department of National Planning and Monitoring will develop a "National PPP Infrastructure Pipeline" in consultation with the key line agencies including the Departments of Works, Transport, Health, Education, the National Roads Authority, and the IPBC in tandem with the development of PPP laws and institutional arrangements. In the 2018 national budget presentation, it was mentioned that activities envisaged in 2018 include developing a roadmap that will assist the government to identify and implement a pipeline of projects under PPP arrangements.

Source: Government of Papua New Guinea, Department of Treasury. 2014. *National PPP Policy 2014*. Port Moresby. https://www.treasury.gov.pg/html/misc/Special%20Projects/PPP/PNG%20National%20PPP%20Policy%202014.pdf.

The features of the PPP process, as provided in Table 6, are only described in high-level terms, with little detail offered over timelines or regarding actual procedures. There have been no PPP projects implemented using this procedure yet, and the PPP Centre is not yet in operation.

6. Public–Private Partnership Standard Operating Procedures, Toolkits, Templates, and Model Bidding Documents

Parameter	
Does the country have PPP Guidelines/PPP Guidance Manual?	×
Does the PPP Guidelines/PPP Guidance Manual adequately cover the process, entities involved, roles and responsibilities of various entities, approvals required at various stages, and the timelines for the various stages of the PPP project lifecycle?	×
What are the templates and checklists available in the PPP Guidelines/PPP Guidance Manual?	
• Project needs assessment and options analysis checklist?	×
• Project due diligence checklist?	×
• Technical assessment checklist?	×
• Environmental assessment checklist?	×
• Ppp procurement plan template?	×
Does the country have standardized/model bidding documents for PPPs?	
• Model request for qualification (RFQ) document?	×
• Model request for proposal (RFP) document?	×
• Model ppp/concession agreement?	×
• State support agreement?	×
• VGF agreement?	×
• Guarantee agreement?	×
• Power purchase agreement?	×
• Capacity take-or-pay contract?	×
• Fuel supply agreement?	×
• Transmission and use of system agreement?	×
• Performance-based operations and maintenance contract?	×
• Engineering, procurement, and construction contract?	×

continued on next page

continued from previous page

Parameter	
Does the country have standardized PPP agreement terms?	×
Does the Country have standardized/model toolkits to facilitate identification, preparation, procurement, and management of PPP projects?	
• PPP family indicator?	×
• PPP mode validity indicator?	×
• PPP suitability filter?	×
• PPP screening tool?	×
• Financial viability indicator model?	×
• Economic viability indicator model?	×
• VFM indicator tool?	×
• Readiness filter?	×
Is there a framework for monitoring fiscal risks from PPPs including the following?	
• Process for assessing fiscal commitments?	×
• Process for approving fiscal commitments?	×
• Process for monitoring fiscal commitments?	×
• Process for reporting fiscal commitments?	×
• Process for budgeting fiscal commitments?	×
Are there fiscal prudence norms/thresholds to limit fiscal exposure to PPPs?	×
Is there a process for assessing and budgeting contingent liabilities from PPPs?	×

✓ = Yes, × = No, UA = Unavailable NA = Not Applicable.

PPP = public–private partnership, VFM = value for money, VGF = viability gap funding.

Source: Government of Papua New Guinea, Department of Treasury. 2014. *Public Private Partnership Act 2014*. Port Moresby. https://www.treasury.gov.pg/html/legislation/files/acts/2014/Public.Private.Partnership.(PPP).Act.2014.pdf; Asian Development Bank. 2019. *Public–Private Partnership Monitor, Second Edition*. Manila. https://www.adb.org/sites/default/files/publication/509426/ppp-monitor-second-edition.pdf.

Key Clauses Related to Public–Private Partnership Agreement

There is no information available on the key clauses of the PPP Agreement such as Performance Security, Transfer of Ownership, and other relevant clauses.

Other Critical Contractual Provisions and Public–Private Partnership Enabling Considerations

Parameter	
Does the law specifically enable lenders the following rights:	
• Security over the project assets?	×
• Security over the land on which they are built (land use right)?	×
• Security over the shares of a PPP project company?	×
• Can there be a direct agreement between the government and lenders?[A]	×
• Do lenders get priority in the case of insolvency?	×
• Can lenders be given step-in rights? (Footnote a)	×

[a] There is no explicit regulation, but there are provisions to give comfort to lenders under the Foreign Private Investment Act, 1980.

✓ = Yes, × = No, UA = Unavailable NA = Not Applicable.

PPP = public–private partnership.

Source: Asian Development Bank. 2019. *Public–Private Partnership Monitor, Second Edition*. Manila. https://www.adb.org/sites/default/files/publication/509426/ppp-monitor-second-edition.pdf.

The PPP Act does not specify the lender's security rights (other than to permit a Relevant Public Body to enter into a direct agreement with a person who has arranged or provided funding for the partner to carry out the PPP arrangement); likewise the PPP Act does not specify termination or compensation rights. However, these limitations could be addressed in the Regulations, or in the PPP Centre Rules or by the PPP Tenders Board, in the future (footnote 11).

Parameter	
Does the law specifically enable compensation payment to the private partner in case of early termination due to:	
• Public sector default or termination for reasons of public interest?	×
• Private sector default?	×
• Force majeure?	×
Does the law enable the concept of economic/financial equilibrium?	×
Does the law enable compensation payment to the private partner due to:	
• Material adverse government action?	×
• Force majeure?	×
• Change in law?	×

✓ = Yes, × = No, NA = Not Applicable, UA = Unavailable.

Source: Asian Development Bank. 2019. *Public–Private Partnership Monitor, Second Edition*. Manila. https://www.adb.org/sites/default/files/publication/509426/ppp-monitor-second-edition.pdf.

7. Unsolicited Public–Private Partnership Proposals

Parameter	
Does the PPP legal and regulatory framework allow submission and acceptance of unsolicited proposals?	✓
What are the advantages provided to the project proponent for an unsolicited bid?	
• Competitive advantage at bid evaluation?	×
• Swiss challenge?	×
• Compensation of the project development costs?	×
• Government support for land acquisition and resettlement cost?	×
• Government support in the form of VGF and guarantees?	×

✓ = Yes, × = No, NA = Not Applicable, UA = Unavailable.

PPP = public–private partnership, VGF = viability gap funding.

Source: Asian Development Bank. 2019. *Public–Private Partnership Monitor, Second Edition*. Manila. https://www.adb.org/sites/default/files/publication/509426/ppp-monitor-second-edition.pdf; Government of Papua New Guinea, Department of Treasury. 2014. *Public–Private Partnership Act 2014*. Port Moresby. https://www.treasury.gov.pg/html/legislation/files/acts/2014/Public.Private.Partnership.(PPP).Act.2014.pdf.

In Papua New Guinea, the two PPPs that reached financial closure in the 1990s were unsolicited proposals. These projects were closed in 1996 and 1997, prior to the introduction of the PPP Act and the PPP Policy. The PPP Act does not specify the preferential treatment that may be afforded to unsolicited bidders for having spent their own resources to develop a feasibility study or business case for such projects (footnote 11).

The PPP Policy envisages that it will consider unsolicited proposals from the private sector for infrastructure projects that are not in the project list of any line agencies and/or SOEs (i.e., the unsolicited project has attributes that justify its inclusion in this category, and has not already been considered by the government, line agencies, and/or the SOEs) (footnote 1).

The process for consideration of an unsolicited bid is expected to be defined in due course. However, in principle, the proponents of an unsolicited project will be given an opportunity to develop a business case at their own costs on an understanding that the technical sections of their business case will be used for a competitive bidding process should the project be deemed a priority. The PPP Law, to be developed in due course, will specify in detail the preferential treatment that may be afforded to unsolicited bidders for having spent their own resources to develop a feasibility study or business case for such projects (footnote 1).

8. Foreign Investor Participation Restrictions

Parameter	
Is there any restriction for foreign investors on:	
• Land use/ownership rights as opposed to similar rights of local investors	✓
• Currency conversion	×
PPP Projects with foreign sponsor participation (number)	5

✓ = Yes, × = No, NA = Not Applicable, UA = Unavailable.

PPP = public–private partnership.

The Investment Promotion Act facilitates, regulates, and monitors foreign investments in Papua New Guinea:[15]

- Section 37 of this Act guarantees that the property of a foreign investor would not be nationalized or expropriated except in accordance with law, for a public purpose defined by law and in payment of compensation as defined by law.[16]
- There are no sector-specific restrictions, limitations, or requirements applied to foreign goods.
- Foreigners are not allowed to own land in Papua New Guinea. Most foreign businesses use long-term leases for land instead of direct purchases. Any dealing involving land being granted or transferred to a foreign person or a corporate entity requires ministerial approval (footnote 16).
- Papua New Guinea recently changed its citizenship laws to allow dual citizenship, which had previously been a limiting factor for Papua New Guineans returning from overseas having naturalized elsewhere. Another change allows long-term residents to naturalize as Papua New Guinea citizens with full legal rights and responsibilities (footnote 16).
- Foreign exchange controls have been largely deregulated in Papua New Guinea. Foreign exchange transactions no longer require prior approval provided they are reported to the Bank of Papua New Guinea (BPNG). Controls remain in place in relation to foreign currency bank accounts held by residents. The BPNG also maintains the ability to impose reporting and other administrative obligations, supervises tax clearance processes, regulates foreign currency accounts, and generally gives directions in relation to foreign exchange. The BPNG may give specific directions about exchange control matters, or reinstate exchange controls partially or wholly (footnote 16).

[15] Government of Papua New Guinea. 1992. *Investment Promotion Act 1992*. Port Moresby. *https://www.italaw.com/sites/default/files/laws/italaw6297.pdf*.

[16] United States Department of State. 2019. *2019 Investment Climate Statements: Papua New Guinea*. Washington, DC. *https://www.state.gov/reports/2019-investment-climate-statements/papua-new-guinea/*.

- An employer must obtain an entry permit (visa) under the Migration Act (Chapter 16) and a work permit under the Employment of Non-Citizens Act 2007 for any non-citizens employed in Papua New Guinea. These visas and work permits are particular to the employee, his/her roles, and the employer. Employers must also maintain a register of all work permits (footnote 16).
- The PPP Act does not specify any restrictions on foreign ownership in PPP arrangements, although this could be addressed in the Regulations, or in the PPP Centre Rules or by the PPP Tenders Board, in the future (footnote 16).

9. Dispute Resolution

PPP regulations (both old and new) prescribe PPP contracts to determine the dispute resolution mechanism. However, there are no standard dispute-resolution procedures for PPPs as there are no model concession documents available. Most contractual disputes for "less-than-termination" events are resolved through negotiation. If unresolved, domestic or international arbitration is called for, commonly with the Singapore International Arbitration Centre (footnote 11).

Parameter	
Does the country have a Dispute Resolution Tribunal (DRT)?	UA
Does the country have an institutional arbitration mechanism?	✓
Can a foreign law be chosen to govern PPP contracts?	✓
What dispute resolution mechanisms are available for PPP agreements?	
• Court litigation?	✓
• Local arbitration?	✓
• International arbitration?	✓
Has the country signed New York Convention On The Recognition And Enforcement Of Foreign Arbitral Awards?	✓

✓ = Yes, × = No, NA = Not Applicable, UA = Unavailable.

Sources: Pacific Islands Treaty Series PACLII. Arbitration Act 1951. http://www.paclii.org/pg/legis/consol_act/aa1951137/; Allens. Insights & News. PNG Proposes a New Regime for Arbitration. https://www.allens.com.au/insights-news/insights/2020/02/png-proposes-a-new-regime-for-arbitration/; Allens. Insights & News. PNG Accedes to the New York Convention: What Will Change. https://www.allens.com.au/insights-news/insights/2019/08/png-accedes-to-the-new-york-convention-what-will-change/.

A foreign choice of law is generally upheld and recognized as valid in Papua New Guinea. The National Court of Papua New Guinea is a court of unlimited jurisdiction and frequently determines commercial disputes. Domestic arbitration can be conducted under Arbitration Act 1951, although it is not frequently used for commercial disputes. The Arbitration Act makes no distinction between domestic and international arbitration. It does not outline the arbitration process, and does not refer to disputes between states or between investor and the state. Papua New Guinea is not a party to the New York Convention on the Recognition and Enforcement of Foreign Arbitral Awards. A Papua New Guinea court order is needed to enforce any foreign arbitral award in Papua New Guinea. Investor–state dispute settlement mechanisms may also be available if a free trade agreement or investment treaty, which contains an investor–state dispute settlement mechanism, exists among the relevant jurisdictions (footnote 11).

The PPP Act does not specify any particular dispute resolution processes for PPP arrangements, although this could be addressed in the Regulations, or in the PPP Centre Rules or by the PPP Tenders Board, in the future (footnote 11).

10. Environmental and Social Issues

Parameter	
Is there a local regulation establishing a process for environmental impact assessment?	✓
Is there a legal mechanism for the private partner to limit environmental liability for what is outside of its control or caused by third parties?	✓
Is there a local regulation establishing a process for social impact assessment?	✓
Is there involuntary land clearance for public–private partnership projects?	✓

✓ = Yes, × = No, NA = Not Applicable, UA = Unavailable.

The Environment Act 2000 provides the regulatory framework for environmental impact assessment through an environmental approval and permit system.[17] As per the Environment Act 2000, the following activities require permit:

- construction of works, land clearance, demolition, excavation, or other works in relation to land or water;
- installation, operation, or maintenance of plant or equipment;
- activities for the purpose of extracting or harvesting natural resources; and
- release of contaminants to air, land, or water, in connection with any of these activities.

The Environment Act was amended in May 2010, restricting landowners' rights in respect of projects ruled to be of national interest.

11. Land Rights

Parameter	
Which of the following is permitted to the private partner:	
• Transfer land lease/use/ownership rights to third party?	✓
• Use leased/owned land as collateral?	UA
• Mortgage leased/owned land?	✓
Is there a legal mechanism for granting wayleave rights, for example, laying water pipes or fiber cables over land occupied by persons other than the government or the private partner?	✓
Is there a land registry/cadastre with public information on land plots?	×
Which of the following information on land plots is available to the private partner:	
• Appraisal of land value?	×
• Landowners?	×
• Land boundaries?	×
• Utility connections?	×
• Immovable property on land?	×
• Plots classification?	×

✓ = Yes, × = No, NA = Not Applicable, UA = Unavailable.

Sources: Asian Development Bank. 2019. *Public–Private Partnership Monitor, Second Edition*. Manila. https://www.adb.org/sites/default/files/publication/509426/ppp-monitor-second-edition.pdf; Jones Lang Lasalle. 2014. *PNG Property Investment Guide*. Port Moresby. http://www.joneslanglasallesites.com/investmentguide/uploads/attachments/2014AP_PropertyInvestmentGuide-PapuaNewGuinea_88np1ap4.pdf.

[17] Pacific Islands Treaty Series PACLII. Environment Act 2000. http://www.paclii.org/pg/legis/consol_act/ea2000159/.

Approximately 97% of Papua New Guinea's land is held under customary ownership for which there is generally no recorded title, which may only be acquired by the state from traditional owners. If a foreign person requires access to customary land, it would need to be acquired from the traditional owners by the state and leased from the state (footnote 11).

All other land in Papua New Guinea is alienated land held by the state (i.e., land that at some time in the past has been acquired by the state). Alienated land is subject to Land Act 1996.[18] Alienated land can be held as freehold or leasehold from the state. Non-citizens are not permitted to own freehold land in Papua New Guinea.

Most dealings in land are by way of leasehold from the state via state leases. State leases may be registered under the Land Registration Act (Chapter 191).[19] State leases generally give the leaseholder indefeasibility of title (subject to certain exceptions) and a certificate of title is issued after registration. Encumbrances such as mortgages may be registered on the title and take priority over unregistered dealings. Any dealing involving land being granted or transferred to a foreign person or a corporate entity requires ministerial approval (footnote 11).

A lease–leaseback scheme is designed in Papua New Guinea for the owners of customary land to develop their land for special agricultural or other business projects. Under the Land Act, customary landowners (either in their own name or through a special purpose corporation or incorporated land group, which acts as an agent for the customary landowners) may dispose of their land to the state, which then grants a special agricultural or business lease back to one or more incorporated land groups in their capacity as agent for the customary landowners (footnote 11).

Under the PPP Act, a Relevant Public Body may grant, transfer, convey, or assign an interest in real or personal property or a leasehold interest owned or held by that Relevant Public Body to a company to enable it to carry out its financing functions under the PPP arrangement, subject to certain ministerial approvals. It may also take such steps as may otherwise be available to it to assist a partner to obtain rights related to land (and to enjoy those rights) (footnote 11).

For compliance with the Constitution and the Land Act, the PPP Act deems the purpose and reason for which the PPP Act permits any compulsory acquisition of land (or rights in land) under PPP arrangements as reasonably justified in a democratic society that has a proper regard for the rights and dignity of humankind (footnote 11).

Government Support for Public–Private Partnership Projects

Parameter	
Project Funding Support	
Is there a dedicated government financial support mechanism for PPP projects?	x
What are the instruments of government financial support available under this government financial support mechanism?	
• Capital grant	x
• Operations grant	x

continued on next page

[18] Government of Papua New Guinea. 1996. *Land Act 1996*. Port Moresby. http://extwprlegs1.fao.org/docs/pdf/png20843.pdf (The Land Act provides that all land in Papua New Guinea, which is not customary land, are the property of the state subject to any estates, rights, titles, or interests in force under any law).

[19] Government of Papua New Guinea. 1981. *Land Registration Act 1981*. Port Moresby. http://extwprlegs1.fao.org/docs/pdf/png24837.pdf.

continued from previous page

Parameter	
• Annuity/availability payments	×
• Guarantees to cover – Currency inconvertibility and transfer risk – Foreign exchange risk – War and civil disturbance risk – Breach of contract risk – Regulatory risk – Expropriation risk – Government payment obligation risk – Credit risk – Minimum demand/revenue risk – Risk of making annuity/availability payments in a timely manner	 × × × × × × × × × ×
What are the caps/ceilings for the government financial support under each of the abovementioned government financial support instruments?	UA
Is there a minimum PPP project size (investment) for a PPP project to be eligible for receiving government financial support?	UA
Are there minimum equity investment requirements which the private developer should meet for availing any of the above government support mechanism?	UA
Are there minimum financial commitment requirements for the private developer equity before the government support could be drawn?	UA
Is the government financial support required, usually the bid parameter for PPP projects?	UA
Are unsolicited PPP proposals eligible to receive government financial support?	UA
Are there standard operating procedures for providing government financial support to PPP projects? • Appraisal and approval process • Budgeting process • Disbursement process • Monitoring process • Accounting, auditing, and reporting process	UA
Who are the signatories to the government financial support agreement?	UA
Who is responsible for monitoring the performance of PPP projects availing government financial support? • Independent engineer? • Government agency? • Ministry of finance?	UA
What are the other forms of government support available for PPP projects?	
• Land acquisition funding support?	UA
• Funding support for resettlement and rehabilitation of affected parties?	UA
• Tax holidays/exemptions?	UA
• Real estate development rights?	UA
• Advertising and marketing rights?	UA
• Interest rate/cost of debt subventions?	UA

continued on next page

continued from previous page

Parameter	
• Other subsidies and subventions?	UA
Can the other forms of government support be availed over and above the government financial support through various instruments listed above?	UA

✓ = Yes, × = No, NA = Not Applicable, UA = Unavailable.

PPP = public–private partnership.

[a] Regulations are silent on this, but some energy independent power producer (IPP) projects received payment guarantees, therefore it is understood that this type of guarantee can be provided on a case-by-case basis.

[b] Regulations are silent on this; however, all energy generation projects have been implemented on availability payment basis under a Power Purchase Agreement.

Source: Government of Papua New Guinea, Department of Treasury. 2014. *Public–Private Partnership Act 2014*. Port Moresby. https://www.treasury.gov.pg/html/legislation/files/acts/2014/Public.Private.Partnership.(PPP).Act.2014.pdf; Government of Papua New Guinea, Department of Treasury. 2014. *National PPP Policy 2014*. Port Moresby. https://www.treasury.gov.pg/html/legislation/files/acts/2014/Public.Private.Partnership.(PPP).Act.2014.pdf; Asian Development Bank. 2019. *Public–Private Partnership Monitor, Second Edition*. Manila. https://www.adb.org/sites/default/files/publication/509426/ppp-monitor-second-edition.pdf.

There is no specific law enabling government support for PPP projects in Papua New Guinea. However, it is possible to provide some guarantees within an individual contract. Also, depending on the revenue model, PPPs in some sectors, such as the energy sector, may be based on annuity/availability payments. The PPP Policy stipulates that the Treasury would manage any fiscal commitment from the government (footnote 11).

The PPP Act does not specify government support arrangements—other than that the state does not and will not provide a guarantee or indemnity unless it has been approved by the National Executive Council—although this could be addressed in the regulations, or in the PPP Centre Rules or by the PPP Tenders Board, in the future (footnote 11).

The PPP Act also provides that a Relevant Public Body may enter into a direct agreement with a person who has arranged or provided funding for the partner to carry out the PPP arrangement (footnote 11).

Parameter	
Project Development Funding	
What are the various sources of funds for PPP project preparation?	
• Budgetary allocations?	UA
• Dedicated project preparation/project development fund?	UA
• Technical assistance from multilateral/bilateral/and donor agencies?	UA
• Recovery of project preparation funding from the preferred bidder?	UA
At what stage of the PPP project, can the project preparation/development funding be availed by the government agency?	
• Pre-feasibility stage?	UA
• Detailed feasibility stage?	UA
• Transaction stage?	UA
Is there a list of project preparation/project development activities towards which the project development funding can be utilized?	UA

continued on next page

continued from previous page

Parameter	
Can the project development funding be utilized to appoint transaction advisors for PPP projects?	UA
Is there a specific process to be followed by government agencies to appoint transaction advisors?	UA
What are the payment mechanisms for making payments to transaction advisors?	
• Time-sheet based?	UA
• Milestone based?	UA
Are there standard agreements and documents to avail project development funding?	UA
Who are the signatories to the project development funding agreements?	UA

✓ = Yes, × = No, NA = Not Applicable, UA = Unavailable.

There is no information available on the project development funding available for PPP projects in Papua New Guinea.

Maturity of the Public–Private Partnership Market

Parameter	
PPP Project Statistics?	
– Is there a national PPP database for the country?	×
Is the distribution of PPP projects across infrastructure sectors available?	✓
Is the distribution of PPP projects across various stages of the PPP lifecycle available?	UA

✓ = Yes, × = No, NA = Not Applicable, UA = Unavailable.

PPP = public–private partnership.

Parameter	
Does the country publish a national PPP project pipeline?	×
At what frequency is the national PPP project pipeline published?	NA
Is the national PPP project pipeline based on the national infrastructure plan for the country?	NA

✓ = Yes, × = No, NA = Not Applicable, UA = Unavailable.

PPP = public–private partnership.

It is envisaged that the Department of National Planning and Monitoring will develop a "National PPP Infrastructure Pipeline" in consultation with key line agencies including the Departments of Works, Transport, Health, and Education; the National Roads Authority; and the Independent Public Business Corporation (IPBC), in tandem with the development of PPP laws and institutional arrangements (footnote 1).

The first two PPP projects had reached financial closure long before the introduction of any of Papua New Guinea's PPP Policy and the recent commencement of the PPP Act. These include the Port Moresby Diesel-Fired Plant in 1996 and the PNG Water Limited potable water treatment plant in 1997. These projects involved a total investment of $136 million. In 2011, the Independent Consumer and Competition Commission (ICCC) of Papua New Guinea awarded a build-own-operate contract and a value-added services license for 15 years to Bemobile Limited, a PNG limited-liability company, to strengthen Papua New Guinea's backbone infrastructure for telecommunications and to reduce the country's reliance on the legacy infrastructure of Telikom PNG (the state-owned telecom service provider). The objective was to upgrade and expand its existing network in Papua New Guinea to increase national geographic and population coverage. The project was supported and partly financed by ADB. Other sponsors include Telikom PNG and GEMS, a private equity fund based in Hong Kong, China. In late 2017, the PPP Contract for Port Moresby and Lae was executed with the Philippines-based International Container Terminal Services, Inc. (ICTSI). The project is proposed to be implemented on a build-own-operate-transfer model (footnote 8). ADB and the Papua New Guinea National Airports Corporation (NAC) have signed a transaction advisory services agreement to develop a new international passenger terminal at Port Moresby (Jacksons) International Airport on 2 February 2017 on a design-build-finance-operate-maintain (DBFOM) basis (footnote 9). In addition to this, the PPP Agreement for the $2 billion RAMU-2 hydroelectric power plant was signed in 2015 with China's Shenzhen Energy Group. The construction of the RAMU-2 project by Kumul Consolidated Holdings (KCH) was expected to commence by the end of 2019 (footnote 10).

Australia and Papua New Guinea's prime ministers have agreed to jointly fund energy network and generation projects worth A$250 million ($175 million as of June 2020) in Papua New Guinea.[20] Also, PPPs would be considered for the electrification of Papua New Guinea, for which Australia, New Zealand, Japan, and the US have pledged to support. In a joint statement at the annual Asia-Pacific Economic Cooperation meeting in Papua New Guinea, the five countries confirmed they would help build an electricity network as well as new internet connections across the country to meet its goal of connecting 70% of the population to electricity by 2030 (footnote 20).

According to the 2018 budget, the government intends to develop a roadmap to help identify and implement a pipeline of PPP projects aligned with the country's Medium-Term Development Plan 3 for 2018–2022 (footnote 2).

Parameter	
Sources of PPP Financing	
Who are the typical entities financing PPP projects in the country?	
• Private developers	UA
• Construction contractors	UA
• Institutional/financial/private equity investors	UA
• Pension funds	UA
• Insurance companies	UA
• Banks	UA
• NBFCs/financial institutions	UA
• Donor agencies	UA
• Government agencies and state-owned enterprises	UA
What is the distribution of financing among these entities financing PPP projects?	UA
Does the country have the history/track record of issuing bonds by infrastructure projects?	UA

continued on next page

[20] *Inframation News*. Australia and Papua New Guinea Plan—A$250 Million Energy Project Spending. https://www.inframationnews.com/news/3748526/australia-and-papua-plan-aud-250m-energy-project-spending.thtml.

continued from previous page

Parameter	
How many infrastructure projects/private developers for infrastructure projects have raised funding through bond issuances?	UA
What is the value of funding raised through capital markets by PPPs?	UA
Does the country have a matured derivatives market to hedge certain risks associated with PPPs?	UA
Does the country have a national development bank?	✓
Does the country have credit rating agencies to rate infrastructure projects?	UA
Typically, what are the credit ratings achieved/received by infrastructure projects?	UA
Is there a threshold credit rating for infrastructure PPPs below which institutional investors, pension funds, and insurance companies would not invest in infrastructure PPPs?	UA
What is the typical funding model for infrastructure PPPs—corporate finance or project finance?	UA
Are there regulatory limits/restrictions for the maximum exposure that can be taken by banks to infrastructure projects?	UA

✓ = Yes, × = No, NA = Not Applicable, UA = Unavailable.

NBFC = non-banking financial company, PPP = public–private partnership.

The National Development Bank of Papua New Guinea is a development finance institution wholly owned by Kumul Consolidated Holdings (KCH). The National Development Bank provides long-term loans to all the sectors including infrastructure sector PPPs.[21]

Parameter	Non/Limited Recourse Loan	Non/Limited Recourse Local Currency Loan	Project Financing, Local Public Sector Banks	Interest Rate Swaps	Currency Swaps	Project Financing through Project Bond Issuance
Maximum tenor, in years	UA	5–10 years	UA	NA	NA	NA
Upfront arrangement fee, (bps)	UA	100–150 bps	UA	NA	NA	NA
Floor rate	UA	KFR	UA	NA	NA	NA
Margin rate (bps)	UA	400–600 bps	UA	NA	NA	NA
Percentage of foreign debt out of total debt for project financing	UA	UA	UA			
Percentage of project bonds out of total debt for project financing	NA	NA	UA			
Typical debt–equity ratio	UA	60:40	60:40			
Timeline to financial close (month)		6–12 months				

continued on next page

21 Kumul. What we do. https://www.kch.com.pg/what-we-do/our-portfolio/national-development-bank/.

continued from previous page

Parameter	Non/Limited Recourse Loan	Non/Limited Recourse Local Currency Loan	Project Financing, Local Public Sector Banks	Interest Rate Swaps	Currency Swaps	Project Financing through Project Bond Issuance
Minimum DSCR covenant levels (x)		1.2x – 1.5x				
Nominal interest rates		UA				
Real interest rates		UA				
Security package		UA				

✓ = Yes, × = No, UA =Unavailable, NA = Not Applicable.

bps = basis points, D = debt, DSCR = debt-service coverage ratio, E = equity, KFR = Kina Facility Rate published by the Bank of Papua New Guinea.

Source: Asian Development Bank. 2019. *Public–Private Partnership Monitor, Second Edition*. Manila. https://www.adb.org/sites/default/files/publication/509426/ppp-monitor-second-edition.pdf.

There is little information in the public domain regarding the financing of PPPs in Papua New Guinea. There are limited sources of finance domestically. International development agencies contribute significantly to the funding of infrastructure projects (Table 7).

Table 7: Sources of Loans in Papua New Guinea

Source	Institution	Loan Amount ($ billion)
Export credit agencies	• Export–Import Bank of the United States • Export–Import Bank of China • SACE • Export Finance and Insurance Corporation • Japan Bank for International Cooperation • Nippon Export and Investment Insurance	8.30
Commercial banks	• Sumitomo Mitsui Banking Corporation • Mizuho Corporate Bank Limited • Mitsubishi UFJ Financial Group	1.95
Corporate entity	• ExxonMobil	3.75
Total		**14.00**

SACE = Servizi Assicurativi del Commercio Estero, UFJ = United Financial of Japan.

Source: Asian Development Bank. 2019. *Public–Private Partnership Monitor, Second Edition*. Manila. https://www.adb.org/sites/default/files/publication/509426/ppp-monitor-second-edition.pdf.

III. Sector-Specific Public–Private Partnership Landscape

ROADS

Parameter	Value	Unit
Length of the Total Road Network	19,600	km
Quality of Road Infrastructure	UA	1(low) – 7(high)

✓ = Yes, × = No, NA = Not Applicable, UA = Unavailable, km = kilometer.

Sources: Trading Economics. Papua New Guinea—Road Total Network. https://tradingeconomics.com/papua-new-guinea/roads-total-network-km-wb-data.html; The Global Economy. Compare Countries. https://www.theglobaleconomy.com/compare-countries/.

1. Contracting Agencies in the Road Sector

The Department of Works and Implementation, the National Roads Authority, and the Road Traffic Authority are the executing agencies for all road transport projects and programs. The Department of Transport as the lead transport sector agency provides overall policy support, and monitoring and evaluation of all projects.[22]

2. Road Sector Laws and Regulations

Originally, the Land Transport Division of the Department of Transport and the National Road Safety Council were responsible for regulating road transport infrastructure and services in the country. Since the establishment of the Road Traffic Authority through Road Traffic Act 2014, the functions of the Land Transport Division of the Department of Transport and the National Road Safety Council have been transferred to the Road Traffic Authority. The Road Traffic Authority is responsible for managing and administering land transport regulations, safety, and efficient use of land transport throughout Papua New Guinea. For road transport, the Parliament of Papua New Guinea has enacted the following laws and regulations:[23]

Road Traffic Act 2014

The purpose of this Act is to provide for the:

- safety of land transport;
- administration and regulation of land transport, and the use of public streets; and
- creation of the Road Traffic Authority to administer the regulation, safety, and use of land transport.

22 Papua New Guinea Department of Transport. Road Projects. http://www.transport.gov.pg/projects/road-projects.

23 Papua New Guinea Department of Transport. Land Transport. http://www.transport.gov.pg/land-transport; Papua New Guinea Road Transport Authority. Acts of Parliament. http://www.rta.gov.pg/legislation/acts-of-parliament/.

Road Traffic (Amendment) Act 2017

The purpose of this Act is to:

- amend and insert definitions,
- provide for an additional member of the Board to be nominated by the Minister,
- provide for traffic enforcement officers to seize vehicles in certain circumstances, and
- amend the wording of some other provisions.

Table 8 presents a snapshot of the functions of various agencies associated with the road transport sector in Papua New Guinea.[24]

Table 8: Agencies and their Functions in the Road Transport Sector of Papua New Guinea

Agency	Function
Department of Transport and Infrastructure (DoTI)	• Conducts sector planning and prepares sector budget • Coordinates with the 12 transport sector agencies and develops an integrated transport sector plan
Department of Works and Implementation (DoWI)	• Conducts programming and contract management for national road and bridge construction and maintenance • Specifies technical standards for road and bridge engineering and training, and advises the government on engineering costs, technical design, and construction matters • Maintains provincial works units in most provinces • Maintains the road asset management system and the bridge asset management system, which inform maintenance plans and budget deliberations
National Roads Authority (NRA)	• Administers the regulation, safety, and use of land transport • Conducts routine maintenance of the national road network • Ensures continual and reliable supply of funds for maintaining the national road network
National Road Safety Council (NRSC)	• Promotes road safety and collects road traffic accident data
National Land Transport Board (NLTB)	• Regulates land transport services
Motor Vehicle Insurance Ltd. (MVIL)	• Conducts vehicle, driver, and transport licensing; vehicle type approval and roadworthiness standards; and motor vehicle testing and dealer licensing

Source: Government of Australia, Department of Foreign Affairs and Trade. 2018. *Road Management in Papua New Guinea: An Evaluation of a Decade of Australian Support 2007–2017*. Canberra. http://www.oecd.org/derec/australia/australia-ode-evaluation-road-management-in-papua-new-guinea.pdf.

2.1 Foreign Investment Restrictions in the Road Sector

Parameter	2017	2018	2019
Maximum allowed foreign ownership of equity in greenfield projects	100%	100%	100%

[24] Government of Australia, Department of Foreign Affairs and Trade. 2018. *Road Management in Papua New Guinea: An Evaluation of a Decade of Australian Support 2007–2017*. Canberra. http://www.oecd.org/derec/australia/australia-ode-evaluation-road-management-in-papua-new-guinea.pdf.

Foreign investments in Papua New Guinea are governed by the Investment Promotion Act, 1992. Although joint ventures with local partners are highly encouraged in Papua New Guinea, many businesses are foreign owned, and a 100% foreign-owned enterprise within the roads sector is allowed. The Department of Transport has its own procedures for approving foreign investment in the roads sector. However, there are no sector-specific restrictions, limitations, or requirements applied to foreign investment (footnote 16).

2.2 Standard Contracts in the Road Sector

Type of Contract	Availability
PPP/concession agreement	×
Performance-based operation and maintenance contract	×
Engineering procurement and construction contract	×

✓ = Yes, × = No, NA = Not Applicable, UA = Unavailable.

3. Road Sector Master Plan

The national road network carries nearly 89% of the total national passenger and freight traffic in Papua New Guinea. Over the medium term, the Government of Papua New Guinea aims to make substantial investments in rehabilitation, maintenance, reconstruction, and upgrading of roads to further strengthen the national road network. It also aims to construct economically vital missing link roads, and undertake design, reconstruction, and upgrading of bridges.[25]

While there is no specific Road Sector Master Plan, the Papua New Guinea Development Strategic Plan (PNGDSP) 2010–2030 and the National Transport Strategy consider maintenance of the national priority roads as the transport sector's greatest priority. The PNGDSP 2010–2030 aims to increase the country's share of national roads in "good" condition from 28.7% in 2010 to 100% by 2030, in addition to tripling the network's length to 25,000 kilometers. Under this strategy, priority highways include the Highlands, New Britain, and Buluminski highways, as well as the Koroba–Mendi and Pogera–Togoba roads. The PNGDSP is also targeting the construction of missing link roads, including a coastal line connecting Aitape and Vanimo, a highway linking Madang to East Sepik from Bogia to Angoram, and a highway connecting Gulf Province to Southern Highlands Province, between the Kerema and Kopi roads (footnote 25).

Aligned with the PNGDSP 2010–2030 and the National Transport Strategy, some of the critical ongoing road sector programs and projects in Papua New Guinea are as follows:

- Highlands Highway Rehabilitation Program,
- Other National Highways Rehabilitation Program (NHRP),
- Rural Economic Road and Bridge Program (RERBP),
- Coastal District Road and Rehabilitation and Maintenance Program,
- Provincial Road Rehabilitation and Maintenance Program,
- Missing Link Road (Baiyer–Madang Highway),
- Missing Link Road (Gulf–Southern Highlands Province),

[25] Oxford Business Group. Overview. https://oxfordbusinessgroup.com/overview/beaten-track-investing-infrastructure-key-unlocking-potential.

- Missing Link Road (Central–Milne Bay),
- Capacity Development of Transport Sector Agencies,
- National Bridge Program (NBP),
- Momase Highway,
- District Town Roads,
- Provincial Town Roads,
- Road Maintenance and User-Pay Program,
- Lae–Nadzab Road,
- Manus Provincial Highway, and
- Morobe–Gulf Highway.[26]

There is no clarity on which of these programs/projects are proposed to be implemented through the PPP route.

No.	Project	Implementing Agency	Estimated Project Cost ($ million)	Estimated Project Cost (K million)	Status
1.	UA	UA	UA	UA	UA

✓ = Yes, × = No, NA = Not Applicable, UA = Unavailable.

3.1 Projects under Preparation and Procurement in the Road Sector

Figure 11 shows the number of PPP projects which are under preparation and procurement in Papua New Guinea's road sector.

Figure 11: Public–Private Partnership Road Projects under Preparation and Procurement

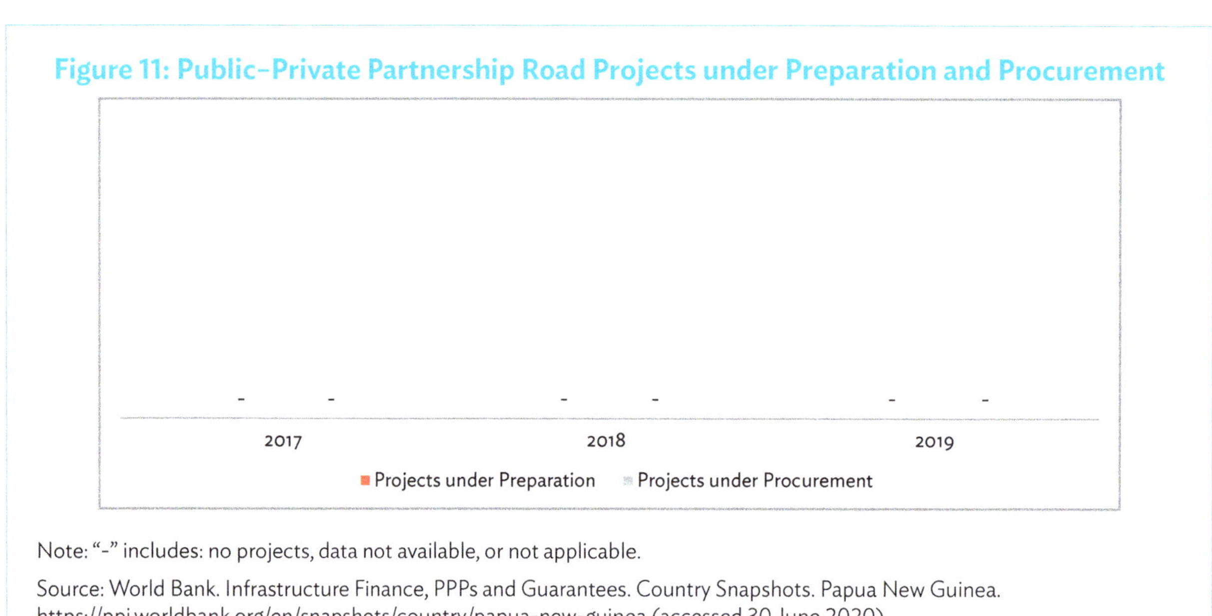

Note: "-" includes: no projects, data not available, or not applicable.

Source: World Bank. Infrastructure Finance, PPPs and Guarantees. Country Snapshots. Papua New Guinea. https://ppi.worldbank.org/en/snapshots/country/papua-new-guinea (accessed 30 June 2020).

[26] Government of Papua New Guinea, Department of Transport. Road Projects. *http://www.transport.gov.pg/projects/road-projects;* Asian Development Bank. 2016–2020. *Sector Assessment (Summary): Transport.* Manila. https://www.adb.org/sites/default/files/linked-documents/cps-png-2016-2020-ssa-01.pdf.

4. Features of Past Public–Private Partnership Projects

Figure 12 presents the number of PPP projects procured through various modes including direct appointment, unsolicited bids, and competitive bids in Papua New Guinea's road sector.

Figure 12: Modes of Procurement for Public–Private Partnership Road Projects

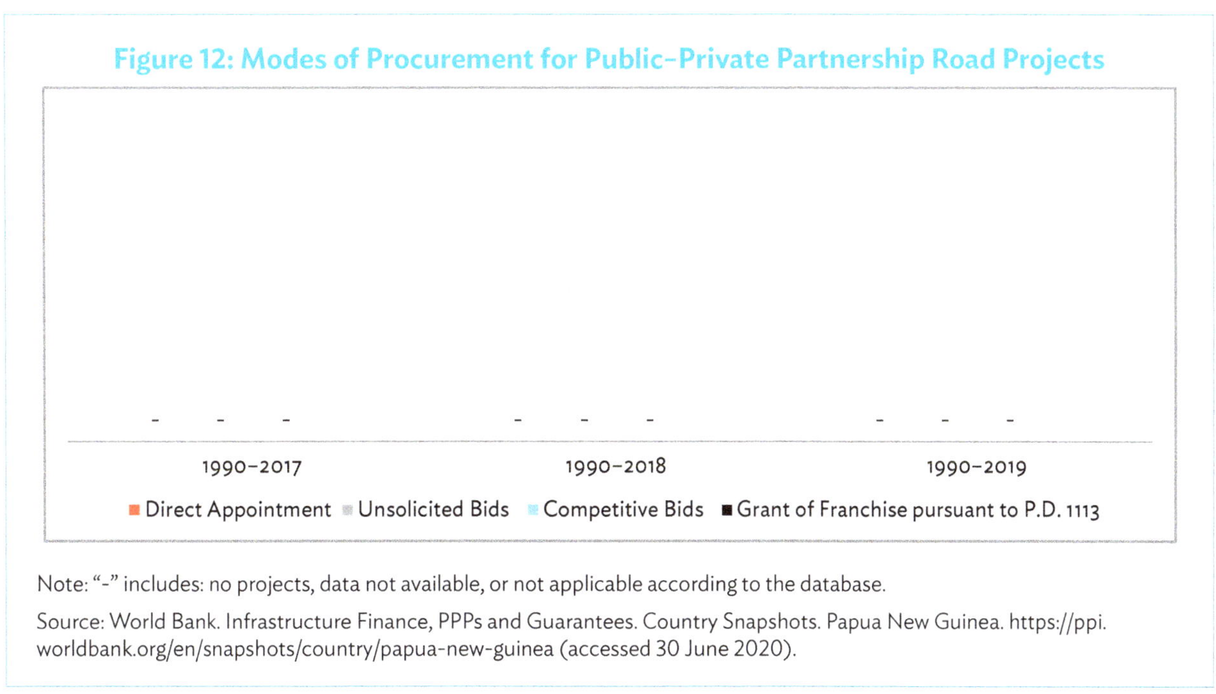

Note: "-" includes: no projects, data not available, or not applicable according to the database.

Source: World Bank. Infrastructure Finance, PPPs and Guarantees. Country Snapshots. Papua New Guinea. https://ppi.worldbank.org/en/snapshots/country/papua-new-guinea (accessed 30 June 2020).

Figure 13 shows the number of PPP projects which have reached financial closure and the total value of those projects in Papua New Guinea's road sector.

Figure 13: Public–Private Partnership Road Projects Reaching Financial Closure

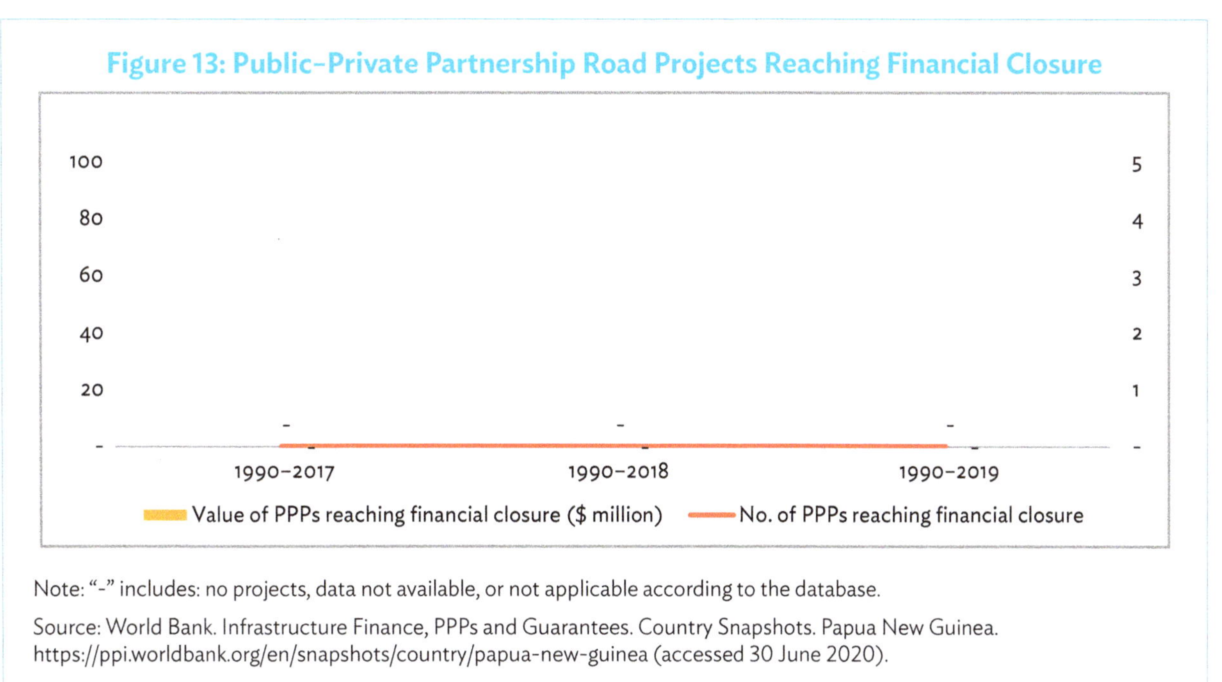

Note: "-" includes: no projects, data not available, or not applicable according to the database.

Source: World Bank. Infrastructure Finance, PPPs and Guarantees. Country Snapshots. Papua New Guinea. https://ppi.worldbank.org/en/snapshots/country/papua-new-guinea (accessed 30 June 2020).

Figure 14 presents the number of PPP projects that have foreign sponsor participation in Papua New Guinea's road sector.

Figure 14: Public–Private Partnership Road Projects with Foreign Sponsor Participation

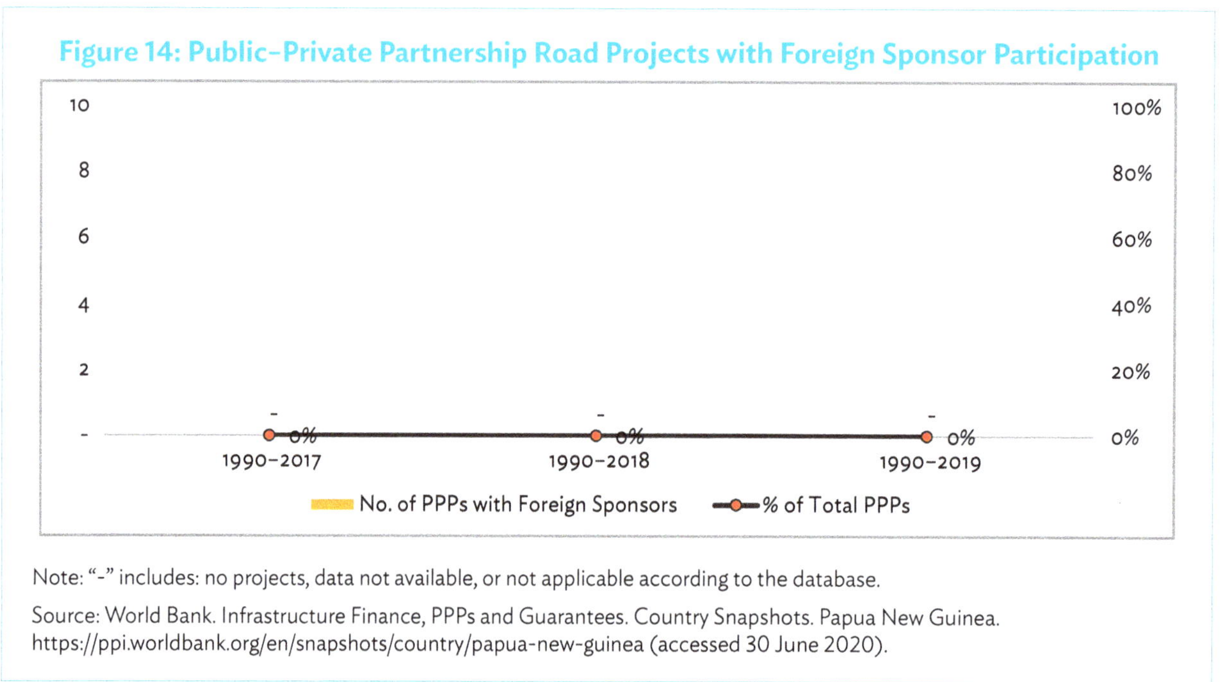

Note: "-" includes: no projects, data not available, or not applicable according to the database.

Source: World Bank. Infrastructure Finance, PPPs and Guarantees. Country Snapshots. Papua New Guinea. https://ppi.worldbank.org/en/snapshots/country/papua-new-guinea (accessed 30 June 2020).

Figure 15 shows the number of PPP projects that have received government support including viability gap funding (VGF) mechanism, government guarantees, and availability/performance payment in Papua New Guinea's road sector.

Figure 15: Government Support to Public–Private Partnership Road Projects

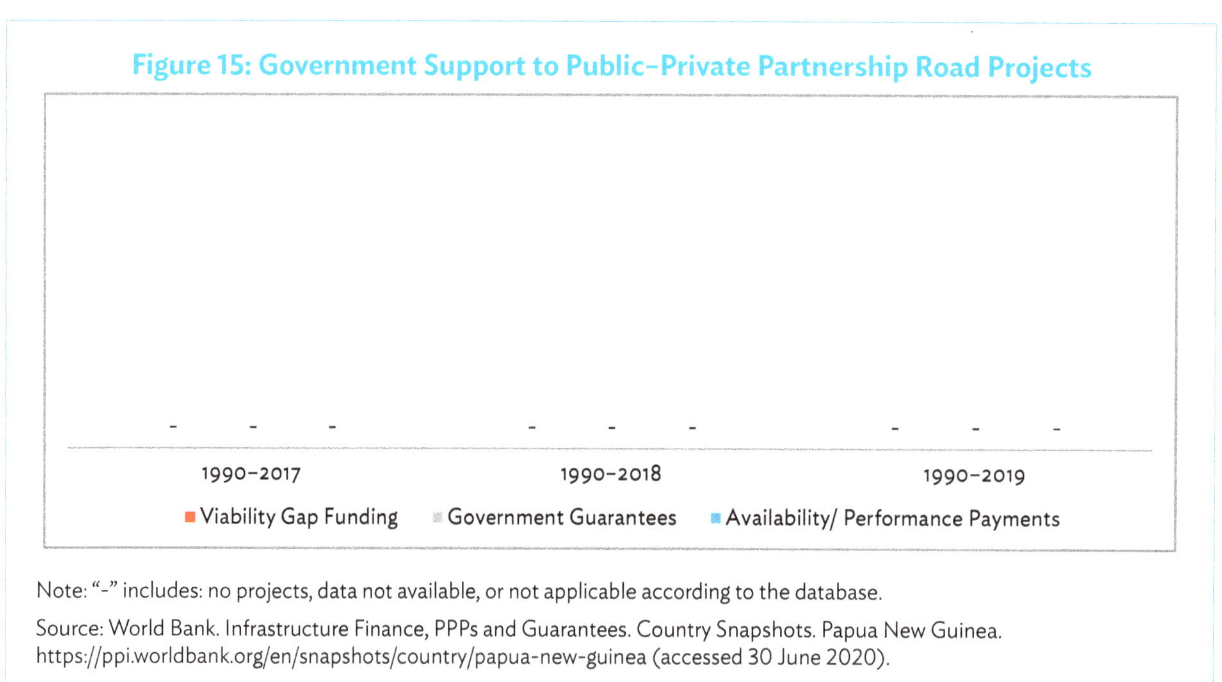

Note: "-" includes: no projects, data not available, or not applicable according to the database.

Source: World Bank. Infrastructure Finance, PPPs and Guarantees. Country Snapshots. Papua New Guinea. https://ppi.worldbank.org/en/snapshots/country/papua-new-guinea (accessed 30 June 2020).

Figure 16 presents the number of PPP projects which have received payment in the form of user charges and government pay (off-take) in Papua New Guinea's road sector.

Figure 16: Payment Mechanisms for Public–Private Partnership Road Projects

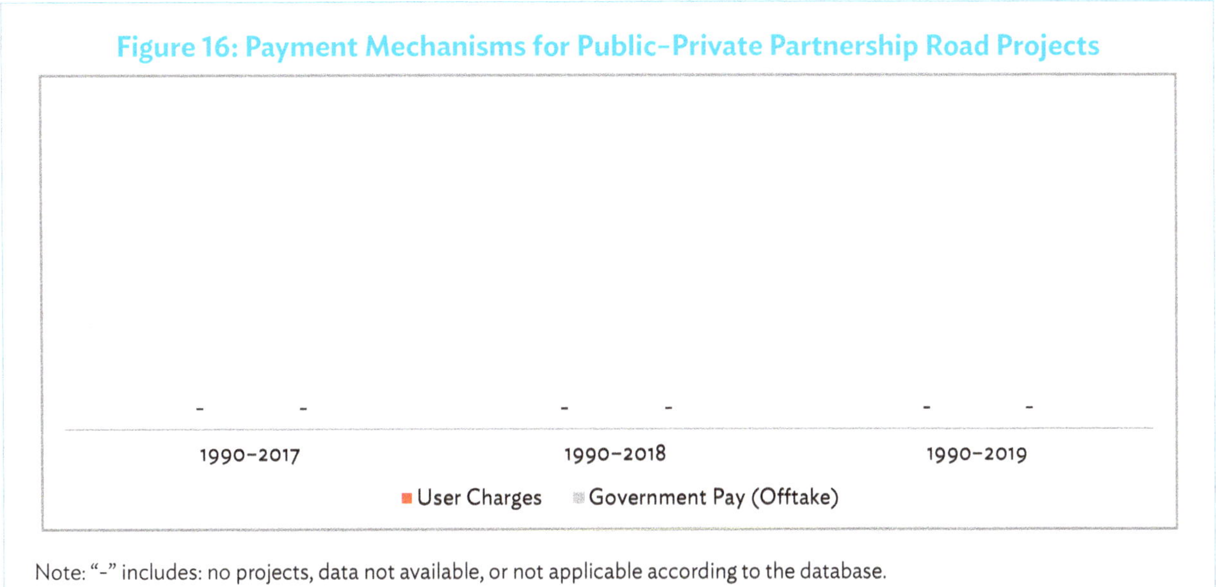

Note: "-" includes: no projects, data not available, or not applicable according to the database.

Source: World Bank. Infrastructure Finance, PPPs and Guarantees. Country Snapshots. Papua New Guinea. https://ppi.worldbank.org/en/snapshots/country/papua-new-guinea (accessed 30 June 2020).

4.1 Tariffs in the Road Sector

Since there have been no implemented PPP projects in the road sector thus far, information on tariffs applicable to such projects is not available. However, according to the Road Traffic Act 2014, it is the function of the Road Traffic Authority to set fees and charges for road transport services. Further, to partly finance the substantial capital investment required in the roads sector, the road user charges would be extended to include a charge on both petrol and diesel, an annual charge on registered vehicles, and a charge for heavy vehicle axle loads.[27]

4.2 Typical Risk Allocation for Public–Private Partnership Projects in the Road Sector

Since there have been no implemented PPP projects in the road sector thus far, information on typical risk allocation for such projects is not available.

As per the generic risk allocation prescribed by the National PPP Policy and the PPP Act, the private sector is expected to assume the completion and delivery risks while the public sector is expected to assume approval and regulatory risks. The detailed risk allocation is determined on a case-by-case basis through negotiation between the government and the private sector service providers (footnote 1).

[27] Papua New Guinea Road Traffic Authority. 2014. *Road Traffic Act 2014*. Port Moresby. http://rta.gov.pg/pdfs/RoadTrafficAct2014.pdf ; Government of Australia, Department of Foreign Affairs and Trade. 2018. *Road Management in Papua New Guinea: An Evaluation of a Decade of Australian Support 2007–2017*. Canberra. http://www.oecd.org/derec/australia/australia-ode-evaluation-road-management-in-papua-new-guinea.pdf.

4.3 Financing Details in the Road Sector

Parameter	1990-2017	1990-2018	1990-2019
PPP projects with foreign lending participation	UA	UA	UA
PPP projects that received export credit agency/international financing institution support	UA	UA	UA
Typical debt–equity ratio	UA	UA	UA
Time for financial close		UA	
Typical concession period		UA	
Typical financial internal rate of return		UA	

✓ = Yes, × = No, NA = Not Applicable, UA = Unavailable.

5. Challenges in the Road Sector

Some of the challenges faced in the roads sector of Papua New Guinea are as follows:

- Underfunding and capacity constraints have led to poor road management and maintenance.
- Despite the road sector's positive economic return, sufficient funding to road maintenance has not been allocated by successive governments in Papua New Guinea due to political incentives.[28]
- Construction of new roads is prioritized over maintenance of existing roads and funding is allocated without consideration of economic or financial impact (footnote 28).
- The lack of political support and engagement and the opposition to the Road Fund among parts of the civil service have resulted to the limited impact of the Road Fund and the National Roads Authority (NRA) on road management and road conditions in Papua New Guinea (footnote 28).

RAILWAYS

Parameter	Value	Unit
Length of total railway network	UA	total route (km)
Total number of passengers carried	UA	million passenger-km
Total volume of freight carried	UA	million ton-km
Quality of railways infrastructure	UA	1 (low) – 7 (high)

✓ = Yes, × = No, NA = Not Applicable, UA = Unavailable.

Sources: The Economist Intelligence Unit. Papua New Guinea. https://infrascope.eiu.com/; The Global Economy. Railway Passengers—Country Rankings. https://www.theglobaleconomy.com/rankings/railway_passengers/; The Global Economy. Railway Transport of Goods—Country Rankings. https://www.theglobaleconomy.com/rankings/Railway_transport_of_goods/; The Global Economy. Railroad Infrastructure Quality—Country Rankings. https://www.theglobaleconomy.com/rankings/railroad_quality/.

[28] Wiley. The Political Economy of Road Management Reform: Papua New Guinea's National Road Fund. https://onlinelibrary.wiley.com/doi/full/10.1002/app5.142.

Papua New Guinea has no major railways, but some mine sites have disused tracks. In September 2007, a mining company proposed to build a new railway to link the coast to a copper-molybdenum mine at Yandera in Madang province. Although the country may be regarded as without railways, there have been a surprising number of light tramways and railways over the past century.[29]

There are no further details available about this sector.

PORTS

Parameter	Value	Unit
Total number of ports	19.00	No.
Total freight capacity of all the ports	UA	MTPA
Total container traffic at ports	341,300	TEUs
Quality of port infrastructure	UA	1(low) - 7(high)
Quality of trade and transport-related infrastructure index	2.3	1=low to 5=high

✓ = Yes, × = No, NA = Not Applicable, UA = Unavailable.

MTPA = million tons per annum, TEUs = twenty-foot equivalent unit.

Sources: World Port Source. Ports. http://www.worldportsource.com/countries.php; The Global Economy. Port Traffic—Country Rankings. https://www.theglobaleconomy.com/rankings/Port_traffic/; The Economist Intelligence Unit. Papua New Guinea. https://infrascope.eiu.com/.

1. Contracting Agencies in the Port Sector

While the Relevant Public Body is the state, the appropriate minister—following the approval of the National Executive Council (NEC)—has the power to execute an agreement for a PPP arrangement on behalf of the state.[30]

2. Port Sector Laws and Regulations

The various sector-specific regulations governing the maritime sector (ports and shipping) in Papua New Guinea are as follows:

- Harbours Act, 2002;
- Merchant Shipping Act (Chapter 242), 1975;
- Merchant Shipping (Coasting Trade) Regulation, 1978; and the
- Merchant Shipping (Maritime Security) Regulation, 2013.[31]

[29] Wiley. The Political Economy of Road Management Reform: Papua New Guinea's National Road Fund. https://onlinelibrary.wiley.com/doi/full/10.1002/app5.142; PNG BUAI. Transport - Railways - German New Guinea (1884 - 1914). http://www.pngbuai.com/300socialsciences/transport/railgerman1a.html.

[30] Government of Papua New Guinea, Department of Transport. Maritime Sector Institutions. http://www.transport.gov.pg/maritime-transport/maritime-sector-institutions; Asian Development Bank. 2019. *Public–Private Partnership Monitor, Second Edition.* Manila. https://www.adb.org/sites/default/files/publication/509426/ppp-monitor-second-edition.pdf.

[31] Government of Papua New Guinea, Department of Transport. Maritime Sector Institutions. *http://www.transport.gov.pg/maritime-transport/maritime-sector-institutions*; Government of Papua New Guinea, Department of Transport. Ports Landings. http://www.transport.gov.pg/maritime-transport/ports-landings; Government of Papua New Guinea, Department of Transport. Maritime Sector Legislations. http://www.transport.gov.pg/maritime-transport/maritime-sector-legislations.

Maritime shipping in Papua New Guinea is regulated by the Department of Transport, in conjunction with the National Maritime Safety Authority under the National Maritime Safety Authority Act of 2003. The National Maritime Safety Authority is responsible for maritime safety, registration of domestic vessels, and marine pollution control.[32]

Following a delegation from the Department of Transport, the state-owned PNGPCL regulates, manages, and controls 16 declared ports in Papua New Guinea under the Harbors Act. The declared ports are regulated under the Independent Consumer and Competition Commission (ICCC) Act of 2002, where ICCC has a regulatory contract with PNGPCL related to tariffs for essential port and stevedoring services. Charges are reviewed and approved annually.[33]

The Department of Transport regulates the private ports operated by companies for specific industries, such as mining. Table 9 presents the key institutions involved in regulating the ports sector.

Table 9: Key Agencies Regulating the Ports Sector in Papua New Guinea

Agency	Function
National Maritime Safety Authority	• Issue and enforce pollution control standards following international agreements. • Ensure that the vessels meet the safety standards required by Papua New Guinea's (PNG) legislation, regulations, and commitments under the International Maritime Organization's conventions.
PNG Ports Corporation Limited	• Control and regulate all waters and the use of all waters within a declared port. • Act as a pilotage authority for the purposes of Part VIII of the Merchant Shipping Act (Chapter 242) where appointed as such under that act. • Erect and place in position buoys, markers, beacons, and leads, and other things that are necessary or desirable to facilitate navigation in or into a declared port. • Dredge and maintain channels and berthing places. • Build retaining walls for the purpose of reclaiming, and claim and obtain title to land that is the bed of the declared port.
Kumul Consolidated Holdings (KCH)	• KCH is a holding company with ownership in state-owned enterprises, including PNG Power Limited. It provides management oversight of the companies. It may also take operational actions in companies that require support. KCH participates in monthly review meetings in the energy sector and supports the PNG Power Limited.
Independent Consumer and Competition Commissions	• Any functions that a regulatory contract—issued under the Independent Consumer and Competition Commission Act, 2002, which relates to the essential port services industry—contemplates will be performed by the commission for the purposes of that regulatory contract. • Perform licensing functions conferred by the Harbours Act – Economic monitoring, control, inspection, and regulation of the essential port services industry. – Consulting, where appropriate, in commercial, industrial, and consumer organizations about any matter relating to the supply of essential port services.

KCH = Kumul Consolidated Holdings, PNG = Papua New Guinea.

Source: National Maritime Safety Authority. 2013. *Separation of PNG Ports Corporation's Regulated and Unregulated Businesses.* Port Moresby. http://www.pngports.com.pg/docs/Public-notices/Issues-Paper_Seperation-of-Regulated-and-Unregulated-Buinesses.pdf.

[32] Government of Papua New Guinea, Department of Transport. Ports Landings. http://www.transport.gov.pg/maritime-transport/ports-landings.

[33] Government of Papua New Guinea, Department of Transport. Maritime Sector Institutions. *http://www.transport.gov.pg/maritime-transport/maritime-sector-institutions.*

2.1 Foreign Investment Restrictions in the Port Sector

Parameter	2017	2018	2019
Maximum allowed foreign ownership of equity in greenfield projects	100%	100%	100%

Sources: United States Department of State. 2019 Investment Climate Statements. https://www.state.gov/reports/2019-investment-climate-statements/papua-new-guinea/; Asian Development Bank. 2019. *Public–Private Partnership Monitor, Second Edition*. Manila. https://www.adb.org/sites/default/files/publication/509426/ppp-monitor-second-edition.pdf.

Although joint ventures with local partners are highly encouraged in Papua New Guinea, many businesses are foreign owned and a 100% foreign-owned enterprise within the port sector is allowed. The Department of Transport has its own procedures for approving foreign investment in the port sector (footnote 11). There are no sector-specific restrictions, limitations, or requirements applied to foreign investment.

2.2 Standard Contracts in the Port Sector

Type of Contract	Availability
PPP/concession agreement	×
Performance-based operation and maintenance contract	×
Engineering procurement and construction contract	×

✓ = Yes, × = No, UA = Unavailable, NA = Not Applicable.

Source: World Bank. 2017. *Benchmarking PPP Procurement 2017 in Papua New Guinea*. Washington, DC. https://www.procurementinet.org/wp-content/uploads/2017/02/Papua-New-Guinea.pdf.

3. Port Sector Master Plan

There are 22 declared ports, of which 16 are operated by PNG Ports Corporation, either directly or through agents (Aitape and Samarai). There are four ports under PNG Ports that are not currently operational—Kerema, Kinim (Karkar Island, Madang Province), Siassi (Morobe Province), and Kupiano (Central province). The ports of Lihir (New Ireland) and Misima (Milne Bay) are also declared as ports under the Harbours Act but are developed and operated by the mining industry. There are also leased and privately owned port facilities within the declared ports (footnote 32).

While there is no specific Port Sector Master Plan, the PNG Development Strategic Plan (PNGDSP) 2010–2030 and the National Transport Strategy consider developing an easily accessible sea transport system to stimulate economic activities in the rural maritime regions and improve the efficiency of international shipping in the next 5 years as an important priority. With an estimated 59% of the country's population dependent on sea transport, the PNGDSP also targets tripling the number of routes served and vessels serviced by 2030, as well as upgrades across the country's ports network. This would also reduce international turnaround times at ports in Lae and Port Moresby from an average of three days into one day (footnote 11).

Aligned with the PNGDSP 2010–2030 and the National Transport Strategy, some of the critical port sector programs and projects in Papua New Guinea which the government would invest into are as follows:[34]

[34] Government of Papua New Guinea, Department of Transport. Maritime Projects. http://www.transport.gov.pg/projects/maritime-projects; Asian Development Bank. 2016–2020. *Sector Assessment (Summary): Transport*. Manila. https://www.adb.org/sites/default/files/linked-documents/cps-png-2016-2020-ssa-01.pdf.

- National wharves development,
- National ports development,
- Jetty development and maintenance programs, and
- National Shipping Service (footnote 34).

Based on the above, some of the maritime projects and programs in the pipeline in Papua New Guinea are as follows:[35]

- **Wewak Wharf Development** – Construction of a new wharf facility to enable increased movement of cargo and passenger, thus creating trade and socioeconomic development.
- **Manus Wharf Development** – Construction of a new wharf facility to complement the new N'Drauke township development on the West Coast of Manus Island.
- **Vanimo Wharf Development** – Construction of a new wharf facility to enable increased movement of cargo and passenger, thus creating trade and socioeconomic development.
- **Kikori Wharf Development** – Construction of a new wharf facility to exploit the huge potential for economic development in the Gulf Province given the oil and gas explorations and fisheries development.
- **Inland Jetty Program** – Construction of jetties within inland waterways to provide easy access for transportation and tourism intervention
- **NGI Transport Connectivity Project** – Provision of sustainable, efficient, and reliable transport connectivity network in the NGI region, and connectivity to the rest of the maritime spots of PNG to allow for service accessibility, eventually resulting into economic growth
- **National Shipping Service** – Replacement of the old and obsolete Navigational Bridge Stimulator with new, state-of-the-art Navigational Bridge Stimulator and other related infrastructure developments.

Based on the above maritime projects and programs, significant opportunities for PPP projects are expected in the maritime sector. However, the details regarding a PPP project pipeline are not available presently.

No.	Project	Implementing Agency	Estimated Project Cost ($ million)	Estimated Project Cost (K million)	Status
1.	UA	UA	UA	UA	UA

✓ = Yes, × = No, NA = Not Applicable, UA = Unavailable.

3.1 Projects under Preparation and Procurement in the Port Sector

Figure 17 presents the number of PPP projects which are under preparation and procurement in Papua New Guinea's port sector.

[35] Papua New Guinea Department of Transport. Maritime Projects. http://www.transport.gov.pg/projects/maritime-projects.

Figure 17: Public–Private Partnership Port Projects under Preparation and Procurement

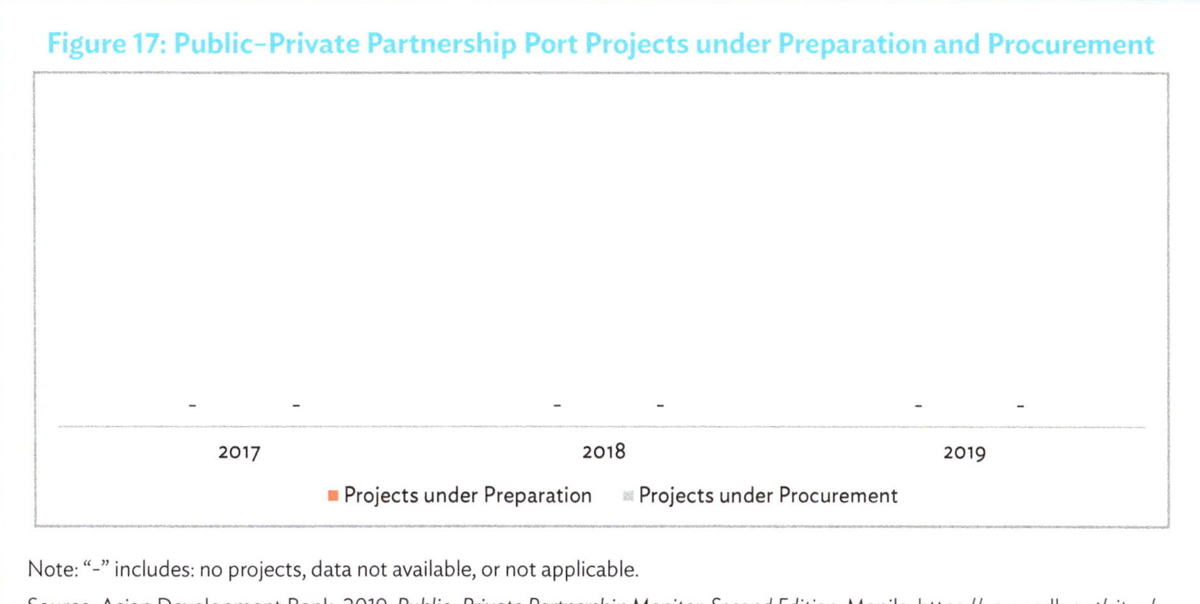

Note: "-" includes: no projects, data not available, or not applicable.

Source: Asian Development Bank. 2019. *Public–Private Partnership Monitor, Second Edition.* Manila. https://www.adb.org/sites/default/files/publication/509426/ppp-monitor-second-edition.pdf.

4. Features of Past Public–Private Partnership Projects in the Port Sector

Figure 18 shows the number of PPP projects procured through various modes including direct appointment, unsolicited bids, and competitive bids in Papua New Guinea's port sector.

Figure 18: Modes of Procurement for Public–Private Partnership Port Projects

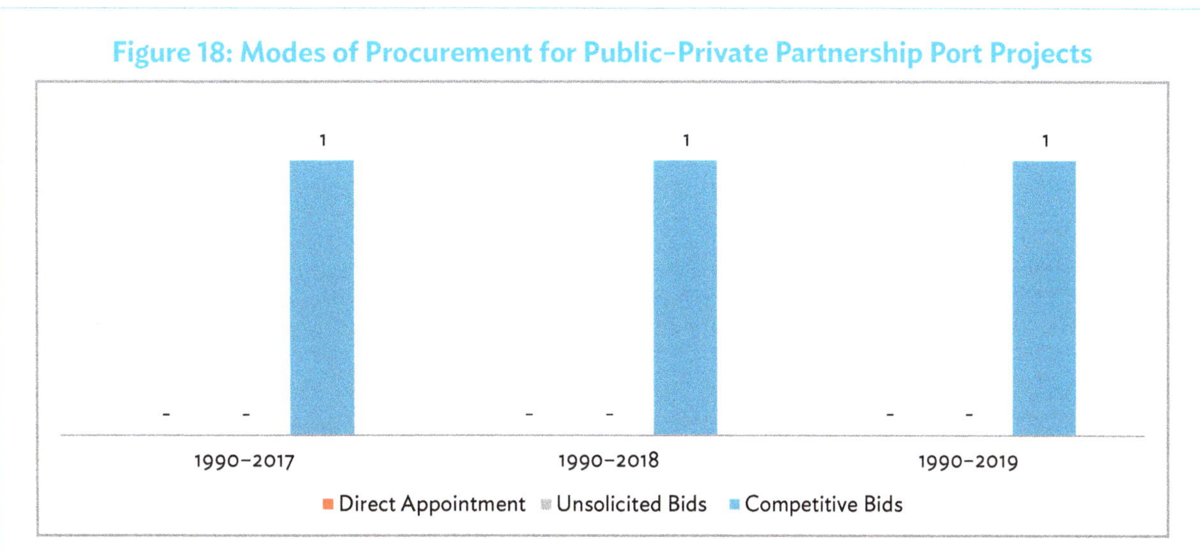

Note: Only active and concluded projects are considered in the above graph. "-" includes: no projects, data not available, or not applicable according to the database.

Source: Asian Development Bank. 2019. *Public–Private Partnership Monitor, Second Edition.* Manila. https://www.adb.org/sites/default/files/publication/509426/ppp-monitor-second-edition.pdf.

Figure 19 presents the number of PPP projects which have reached financial closure and the total value of those projects in Papua New Guinea's port sector.

Figure 19: Public–Private Partnership Port Projects Reaching Financial Closure

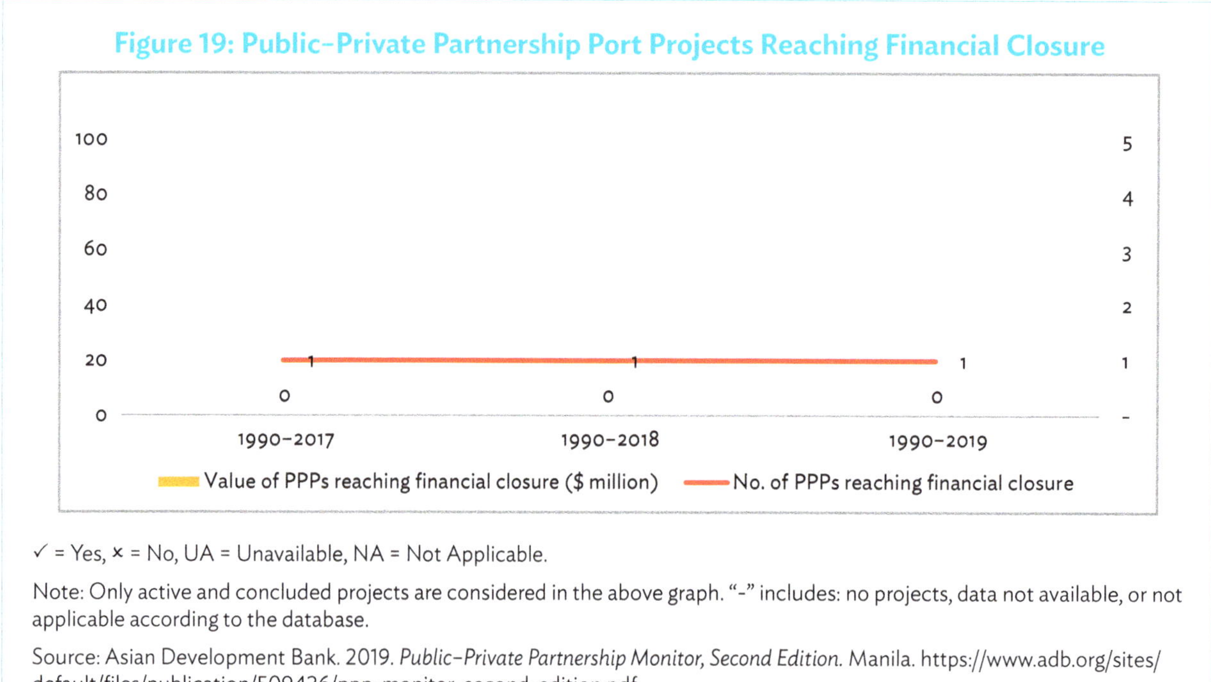

✓ = Yes, × = No, UA = Unavailable, NA = Not Applicable.

Note: Only active and concluded projects are considered in the above graph. "-" includes: no projects, data not available, or not applicable according to the database.

Source: Asian Development Bank. 2019. *Public–Private Partnership Monitor, Second Edition.* Manila. https://www.adb.org/sites/default/files/publication/509426/ppp-monitor-second-edition.pdf.

Figure 20 shows the number of PPP projects that have foreign sponsor participation in Papua New Guinea's port sector.

Figure 20: Public–Private Partnership Port Projects with Foreign Sponsor Participation

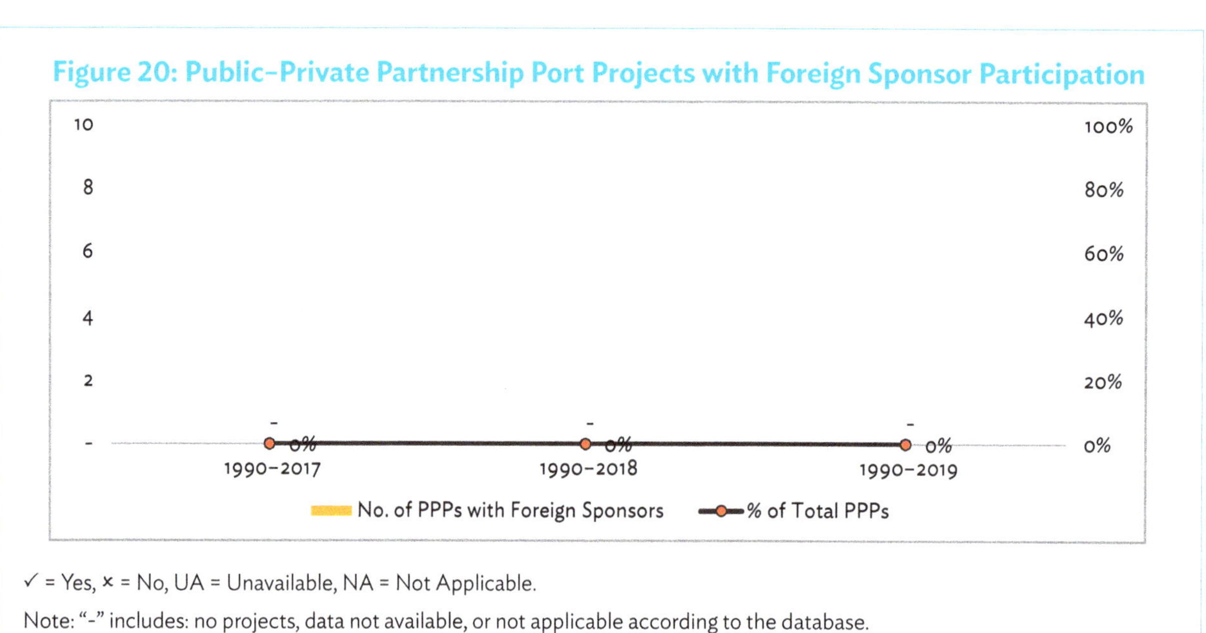

✓ = Yes, × = No, UA = Unavailable, NA = Not Applicable.

Note: "-" includes: no projects, data not available, or not applicable according to the database.

Source: World Bank. Infrastructure Finance, PPPs and Guarantees. Country Snapshots. Papua New Guinea. https://ppi.worldbank.org/en/snapshots/country/papua-new-guinea (accessed 30 June 2020).

Figure 21 presents the number of PPP projects that have received government support including viability gap funding (VGF) mechanism, government guarantees, and availability/performance payment in Papua New Guinea's port sector.

Figure 21: Government Support to Public–Private Partnership Port Projects

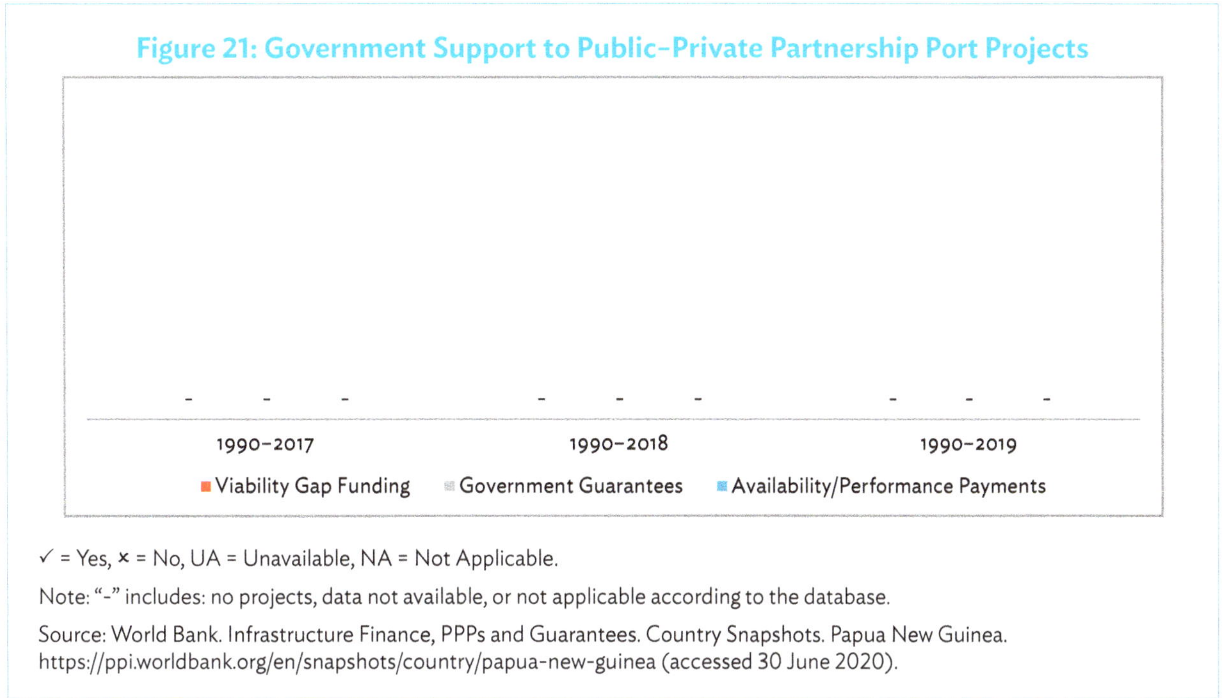

✓ = Yes, × = No, UA = Unavailable, NA = Not Applicable.

Note: "-" includes: no projects, data not available, or not applicable according to the database.

Source: World Bank. Infrastructure Finance, PPPs and Guarantees. Country Snapshots. Papua New Guinea. https://ppi.worldbank.org/en/snapshots/country/papua-new-guinea (accessed 30 June 2020).

Figure 22 provides the number of PPP projects that have received payment in the form of user charges and government pay (off-take) in Papua New Guinea's port sector.

Figure 22: Payment Mechanisms for Public–Private Partnership Port Projects

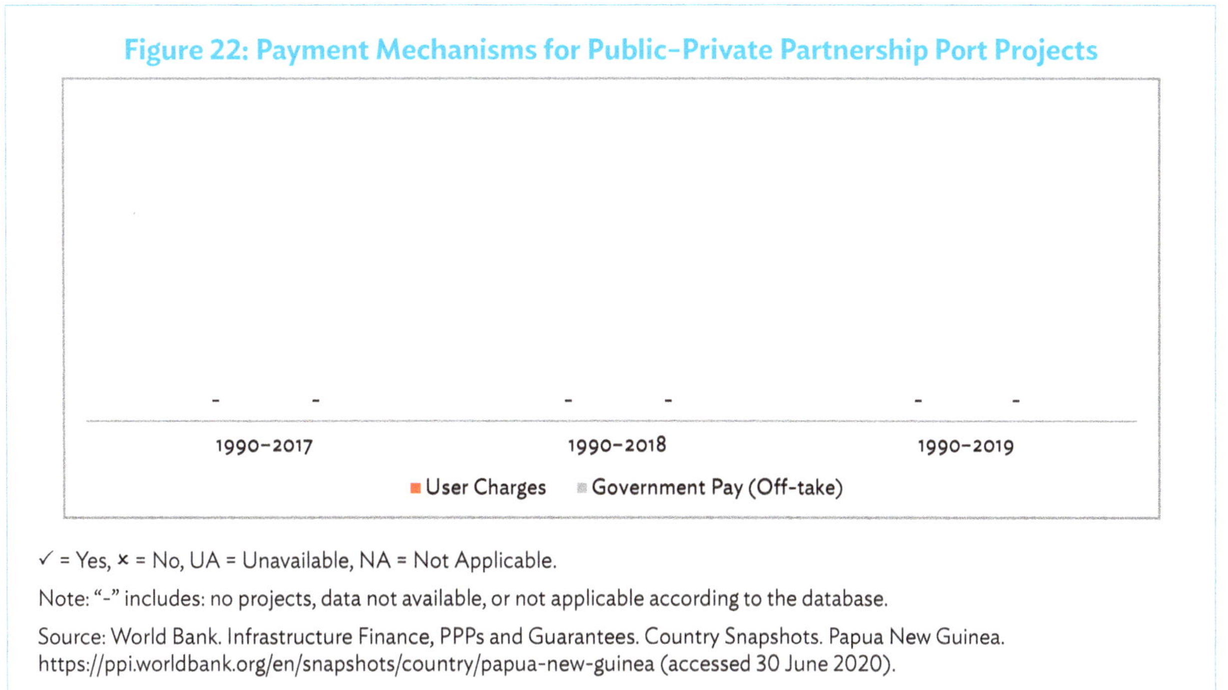

✓ = Yes, × = No, UA = Unavailable, NA = Not Applicable.

Note: "-" includes: no projects, data not available, or not applicable according to the database.

Source: World Bank. Infrastructure Finance, PPPs and Guarantees. Country Snapshots. Papua New Guinea. https://ppi.worldbank.org/en/snapshots/country/papua-new-guinea (accessed 30 June 2020).

4.1 Tariffs in the Port Sector

The private sector has the freedom to set tariffs and user charges under PPP in the port sector.

Terminal handling charges (THCs) are charges made by the terminal operators in respect of container movements and services performed at a terminal. For container terminals, THCs cover the movement of a container between the ship's hold and the exit–entry gate via the container terminal yard. The ICCC has approved the 2020 maximum tariffs for the regulated services representing two groups of declared ports.[36]

For the ports of Moresby, Lae, Kimbe, Vanimo, and Samarai, the maximum THCs for "Overseas Cargo—Inward" are $232 (K803 as of June 2020) per twenty-foot equivalent unit (TEU) and $465 per forty-foot equivalent unit (FEU). For the ports of Madang, Rabaul, Alotau, Oro Bay, Kavieng, Daru, Buka, Aitape, Lorengau, and Wewak, the maximum THCs are $298 per TEU and $596 per FEU.

It should be noted that the THCs are the maximum allowed charges and that PNGPCL may choose to apply a lower tariff if it is deemed appropriate by management and is consistent with the development goals of the port.

4.2 Typical Risk Allocation for Public–Private Partnership Projects in the Port Sector

The information on typical risk allocation for PPP projects in the port sector is not available.

As per the generic risk allocation prescribed by the National PPP Policy and the PPP Act, the private sector is expected to assume the completion and delivery risks while the public sector is expected to assume approval and regulatory risks. The detailed risk allocation is determined on a case-by-case basis through negotiation between the government and the private sector service providers.[37]

4.3 Financing Details in the Port Sector

Parameter	1990–2017	1990–2018	1990–2018
PPP projects with foreign lending participation	1	1	1
PPP projects that received export credit agency/international financing institution support	UA	UA	UA
Typical debt–equity ratio	UA		
Time for financial closure	UA		
Typical concession period	UA		
Typical financial internal rate of return	UA		

✓ = Yes, × = No, UA = Unavailable, NA = Not Applicable.

[36] Papua New Guinea Ports. 2020. *2020 Essential Port Services Tariff Schedule*. Port Moresby. http://www.pngports.com.pg/docs/tariff/2020/2020-Essential-Port-Services-Tariff-Schedule.pdf.

[37] Government of Papua New Guinea, Department of Treasury Papua New Guinea. 2014. *Public–Private Partnership Act 2014*. Port Moresby. *https://www.treasury.gov.pg/html/legislation/files/acts/2014/Public.Private.Partnership.(PPP).Act.2014.pdf.*

5. Challenges in the Port Sector

Some of the challenges faced in the ports sector of Papua New Guinea are as follows:

- Majority of Papua New Guinea's population residing along the coastline and waterways does not have access to roads. There are innumerable small wharves, jetties, and beach landings providing the basic infrastructure for maritime services, but the majority of these are in poor condition and carry very little traffic. This also results into many deaths due to the sinking of overloaded ferries.
- The state-owned PNG Ports Corporation (PNGPCL), which operates 16 ports, enjoys a monopoly from low cargo processing costs and a competitive national shipping market.
- PNG's international shipping is one of the most expensive in the Pacific region, wherein the competition that is meant to drive costs is inexistent. On the other hand, export distances are aligned with the regional average. The World Bank's survey reveals that the average border compliance costs for exports amount to $675 in Papua New Guinea, compared to East Asia and the Pacific average of $402. On the other hand, documentary export compliance takes an average of 96 hours, compared to 73 hours in Asia and the Pacific region. Border compliance costs for imports are at $810 on average, compared to the regional average of $436. Whereas documentary compliance for imports takes 120 hours and costs $425 in Papua New Guinea, the regional average is 71 hours and $128.
- The ports sector lacks a sound PPP project pipeline.
- The Cabotage Policy, which plays as a market protection regulation against foreign entry to coastal shipping, is gradually getting lifted.

AIRPORTS

Parameter	Value	Unit
Number of airports	561	number
Total passenger capacity	0.96	million passengers
Quality of air transport infrastructure	UA	1(low) – 7(high)
Total number of projects with cumulative lending, grant, and technical assistance commitments in transport sector	79	number
Total amount of cumulative lending, grant, and technical assistance commitments in transport sector	1,816	$ million

✓ = Yes, × = No, NA = Not Applicable, UA = Unavailable.

Sources: City Population. Airports. https://www.citypopulation.de/en/world/bymap/airports.html; World Bank. Air Transport, Passengers Carried. https://data.worldbank.org/indicator/is.air.psgr?locations=bd-kh-ge-kz-mm-pk-pg-lk-uz-vn-cn-in-id-ph-th; The Global Economy. Compare Countries. https://www.theglobaleconomy.com/compare-countries/; Asian Development Bank. Cumulative Lending, Grant, and Technical Assistance Commitments. https://data.adb.org/dataset/cumulative-lending-grant-and-technical-assistance-commitments.

1. Contracting Agencies in the Airport Sector

The National Airports Corporation (NAC), a state-owned enterprise (SOE), is mandated by the Government of Papua New Guinea to own, operate, manage, and maintain airports in the country. NAC presently operates the 22 national airports in the country, and is responsible for operating and managing other airports established by the Ministry of Transport and Infrastructure on its own or as a joint venture.[38]

NAC is mandated by the Government of Papua New Guinea to enter into a lease, management, or any other type of PPP agreement with a private developer for developing, operating, managing, and maintaining any airport in the country, on the terms and conditions approved by the Ministry of Transport and Infrastructure (footnote 38).

NAC, with the support of the Asian Development Bank as the PPP transaction advisors, is expanding the Port Moresby (Jacksons) International Airport (PMIA) through a PPP route, to develop a new international passenger terminal (footnote 38).

2. Airport Sector Laws and Regulations

The two institutions responsible for administering, regulating, and managing the civil aviation sector in Papua New Guinea are the Department of Transport and Infrastructure and the Civil Aviation Safety Authority.

The Department of Transport and Infrastructure, through its Air Transport Division, ensures that all government policies and relevant legislation on economic regulation of civil aviation are enforced and complied with for sustainable, cost-effective, efficient, safe, and secure air transportation service delivery.[39]

The Civil Aviation Safety Authority promotes aviation safety and security through effective safety regulation of the civil aviation industry, focusing on preventing aviation accidents and incidents within the civil aviation system in Papua New Guinea.[40]

The civil aviation subsector in Papua New Guinea is governed by the following legislations:

- Civil Aviation Act, 2000;
- Civil Aviation Regulation, 1975;
- PNG Civil Aviation Rules;
- Civil Aviation Policy; and
- International Civil Aviation Organization Annex 14.[41]

38 National Airports Corporation. Airports. https://www.nac.com.pg/airports/pmia-ppp/;
National Airports Corporation. About us. https://www.nac.com.pg/about-us/services/;
Asian Development Bank. News. https://www.adb.org/news/adb-helps-png-expand-port-moresby-international-airport-using-ppp;
Papua New Guinea Department of Transport. Civil Aviation Institutions. http://www.transport.gov.pg/air-transport/civil-aviation-institutions.

39 Government of Papua New Guinea, Department of Transport. Air Transport. http://www.transport.gov.pg/air-transport.

40 Government of Papua New Guinea, Civil Aviation Safety Authority. About Us. https://casapng.gov.pg/about-us/.

41 Government of Papua New Guinea, Department of Transport. Civil Aviation Legislation. http://www.transport.gov.pg/air-transport/civil-aviation-legislation.

Table 10 presents the key government agencies associated with the airport sector in Papua New Guinea.

Table 10: Key Agencies Regulating Papua New Guinea's Airports

Agency	Function
Department of Transport	The Department of Transport (DOT) provides ministerial advisory services and policy and planning input to the air transport sector. The Air Transport Division of DOT is responsible for (i) international and domestic air transport operations encompassing safety, security, market, policy, legislation, and regulation; (ii) negotiation and administration of international air service licensing agreements for overseas carriers to provide services into and through Papua New Guinea; and (iii) issuing air services licenses to carriers.
The Civil Aviation Safety Authority	The Civil Aviation Safety Authority (CASA) is the principal regulatory agency in the sector and is responsible for safety certification of air operators, aircraft, aircrew, air traffic controllers, and airports. It ensures that PNG complies with international air safety conventions under the International Civil Aviation Organization. The Aviation Facilities division of CASA manages and facilitates the regulatory oversight of Air Traffic Services and Air Navigation Services and Airports/Aerodromes operations, and monitors and assesses the performance of aviation security outcomes by the industry and associated agencies, which aim to deter, detect, and prevent attempted acts of unlawful interference in Papua New Guinea.
PNG Air Services Ltd.	The PNG Air Services Ltd. (PNGASL) is a state-owned enterprise (SOE) responsible for providing, maintaining, and developing air navigation and airways services infrastructure, comprising ground and satellite-based navigation systems and management of the upper, middle and lower airspace, including overflying. PNGASL also coordinates aviation search and rescue.
National Airports Corporation	The National Airports Corporation (NAC) is an SOE responsible for the provision, maintenance, and development of the 22 government-owned airports, including aviation security, airport fire crash and rescue services, and control of ground movements of aircraft and other airport vehicles and equipment.
The Accident Investigation Commission	The Accident Investigation Commission is responsible for the investigation of the circumstances of air accidents on a "no-fault" basis with a view of future prevention.

PNG = Papua New Guinea.

Sources: Government of Papua New Guinea, Department of Transport. Civil Aviation Legislation. http://www.transport.gov.pg/air-transport/civil-aviation-legislation; Government of Papua New Guinea, Department of Transport. Civil Aviation Institutions. http://www.transport.gov.pg/air-transport/civil-aviation-institutions; Civil Aviation Safety Authority of PNG. About Us. https://casapng.gov.pg/about-us/; Government of Papua New Guinea, Department of Transport. Air Transport. http://www.transport.gov.pg/air-transport; National Airports Corporation. Airports. https://www.nac.com.pg/airports/pmia-ppp/.

2.1 Foreign Investment Restrictions in the Airport Sector

Parameter	2017	2018	2019
Maximum allowed foreign ownership of equity in greenfield projects	100%	100%	100%

Although joint ventures with local partners are highly encouraged in PNG, many businesses are foreign owned and a 100% foreign-owned enterprise within the airport sector is allowed. The Department of Transport has its own procedures for approving foreign investment in the airport sector. There are no sector-specific restrictions, limitations, or requirements applied to foreign investment (footnote 16).

2.2 Standard Contracts in the Airport Sector

Type of Contract	Availability
PPP/concession agreement	×
Performance-based operation and maintenance contract	×
Engineering procurement and construction contract	×

✓ = Yes, × = No, UA = Unavailable, NA = Not Applicable.

3. Airport Sector Master Plan

Papua New Guinea's air service system has evolved and improved over time into a relatively well-developed network. The government focuses on connecting remote isolated regions that are hard to access by road and on providing a safe, secure, reliable, and cost-effective air transport system to promote economic growth.[42]

Aligned with these objectives, the key government programs to further streamline the civil aviation sector in Papua New Guinea are:

- national airport upgrading and development program,
- Nadzab airport re-development,
- air transport safety program,
- rural airstrip rehabilitation program, and
- airport development.

Civil Aviation Development Investment Program (CADIP)

The Civil Aviation Development Investment Program is closely aligned with GoPNG's Development Strategic Plan 2011–2030 and the National Transport Strategy. The program recognizes the need for the country's remote communities to have basic access to air transport and services as a national priority and to establish a sustainable civil aviation network to support PNG's economic growth (footnote 42).

The program focuses on the 21 national airports aiming for a safer, more efficient, and more accessible all-weather air transport services.[43] CADIP is being implemented in the following tranches:

- **CADIP Tranche 1** – Upgrading of airports to strengthen aviation safety and services, including (i) improving pavements and fencing in five airports, (ii) installing new security fences to comply with the International Civil Aviation Organization's safety and security standards, and (iii) improving institutional and sector reforms (footnote 43).
- **CADIP Tranche 2** – Strengthening of the operations of air transport agencies (NAC, PNGASL, and CASA PNG) that were established under Tranche 1, and improvement of air traffic management, navigation services, and airport infrastructure to comply with international and domestic regulations and standards (footnote 43).

[42] Government of Papua New Guinea, Department of Transport. Air Projects. http://www.transport.gov.pg/113-investment/air-projects.
[43] Papua New Guinea Department of Transport. Air Projects. http://www.transport.gov.pg/113-investment/air-projects.

- **CADIP Tranche 3** – Continued improvement and strengthening of airport infrastructure, level of compliance with safety and security standards, air transport agency operations, and other activities under Tranches 1 and 2 (footnote 43).

The executing agency for the Civil Aviation Development Investment Program is the National Airports Corporation (NAC) which has been implementing the program since 2010 (footnote 43).

CADIP provides committed funding for security works, upgrading of airport runways to F100 standard, and other priority works at the national airports. CADIP also provides committed funding for air communications, navigation, and air traffic management systems grading (footnote 43).

Under CADIP, the NAC, with ADB support, is preparing the PPP project for the Port Moresby (Jacksons) International Airport (PMIA), which involves developing a new passenger terminal and expanding the runway and other airside facilities on a design–build–finance–operate–maintain basis. The project is presently at the preparation stage.

No.	Project	Implementing Agency	Estimated Project Cost		Status
			($ million)	(K million)	
1.	UA	UA	UA	UA	UA

✓ = Yes, × = No, NA = Not Applicable, UA = Unavailable.

3.1 Projects under Preparation and Procurement in the Airport Sector

Figure 23 presents the number of PPP projects that are under preparation and procurement in Papua New Guinea's airport sector.

Figure 23: Public–Private Partnership Airport Projects under Preparation and Procurement

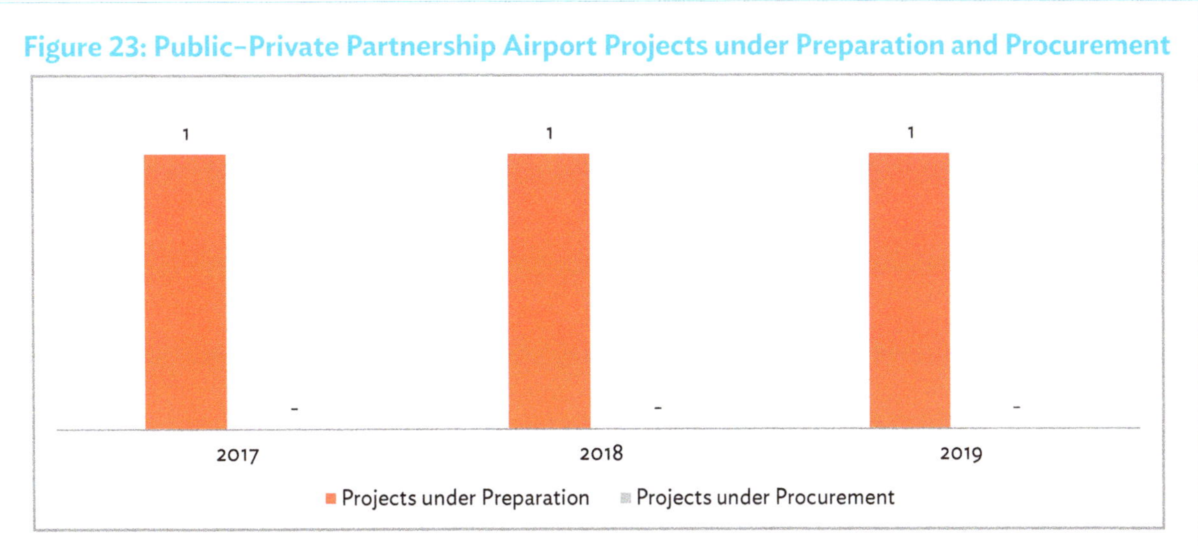

Note: "-" includes: no projects, data not available, or not applicable.

Source: World Bank. Infrastructure Finance, PPPs and Guarantees. Country Snapshots. Papua New Guinea. https://ppi.worldbank.org/en/snapshots/country/papua-new-guinea (accessed 30 June 2020).

4. Features of Past Public–Private Partnership Projects in the Airport Sector

Figure 24 shows the number of PPP projects procured through various modes including direct appointment, unsolicited bids, and competitive bids in Papua New Guinea's airport sector.

Figure 24: Modes of Procurement for Public–Private Partnership Airport Projects

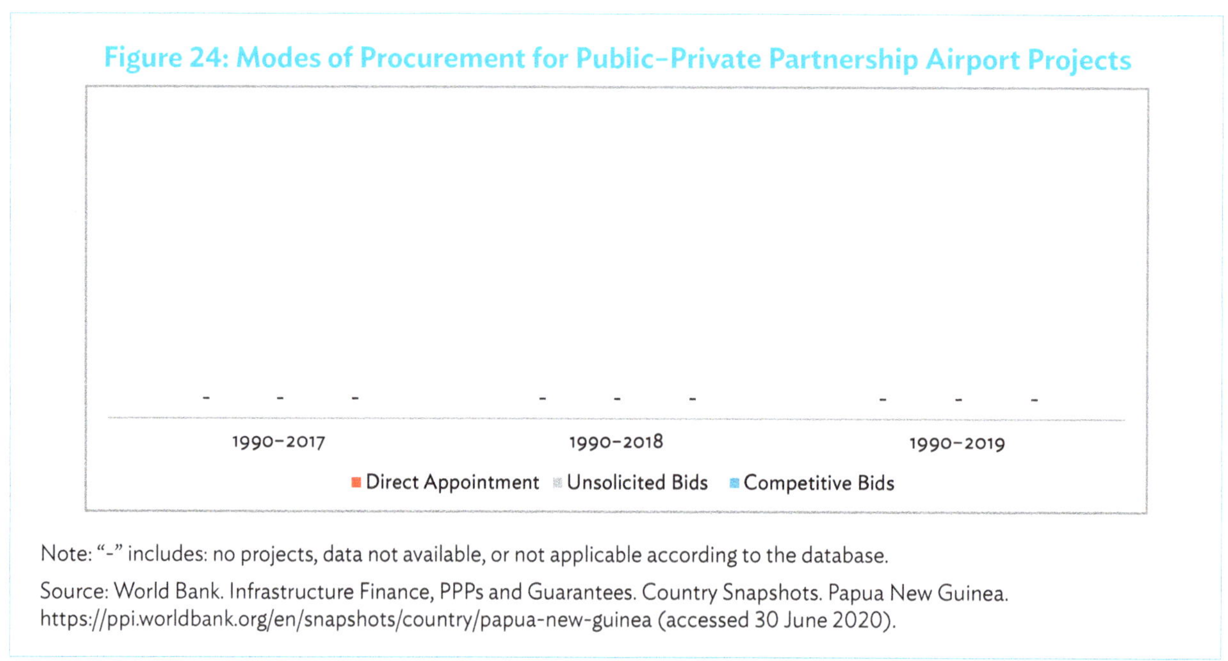

Note: "-" includes: no projects, data not available, or not applicable according to the database.

Source: World Bank. Infrastructure Finance, PPPs and Guarantees. Country Snapshots. Papua New Guinea. https://ppi.worldbank.org/en/snapshots/country/papua-new-guinea (accessed 30 June 2020).

Figure 25 presents the number of PPP projects that have reached financial closure and the total value of those projects in Papua New Guinea's airport sector.

Figure 25: Public–Private Partnership Airport Projects Reaching Financial Closure

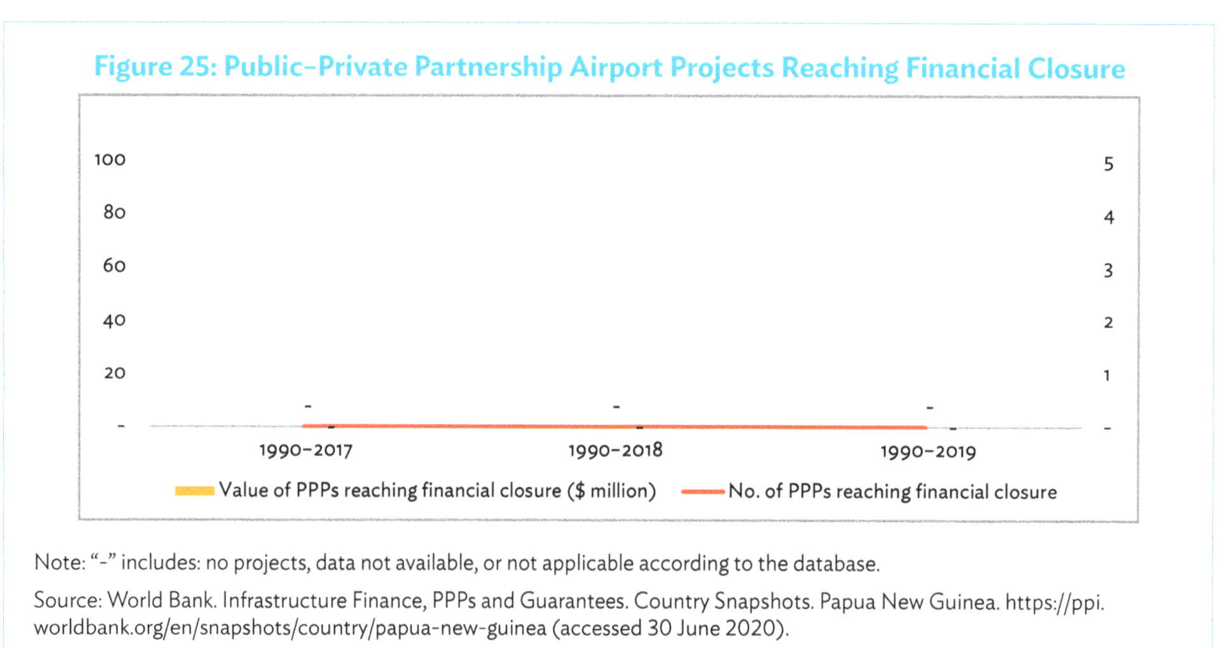

Note: "-" includes: no projects, data not available, or not applicable according to the database.

Source: World Bank. Infrastructure Finance, PPPs and Guarantees. Country Snapshots. Papua New Guinea. https://ppi.worldbank.org/en/snapshots/country/papua-new-guinea (accessed 30 June 2020).

Figure 26 shows the number of PPP projects that have foreign sponsor participation in Papua New Guinea's airport sector.

Figure 26: Public–Private Partnership Airport Projects with Foreign Sponsor Participation

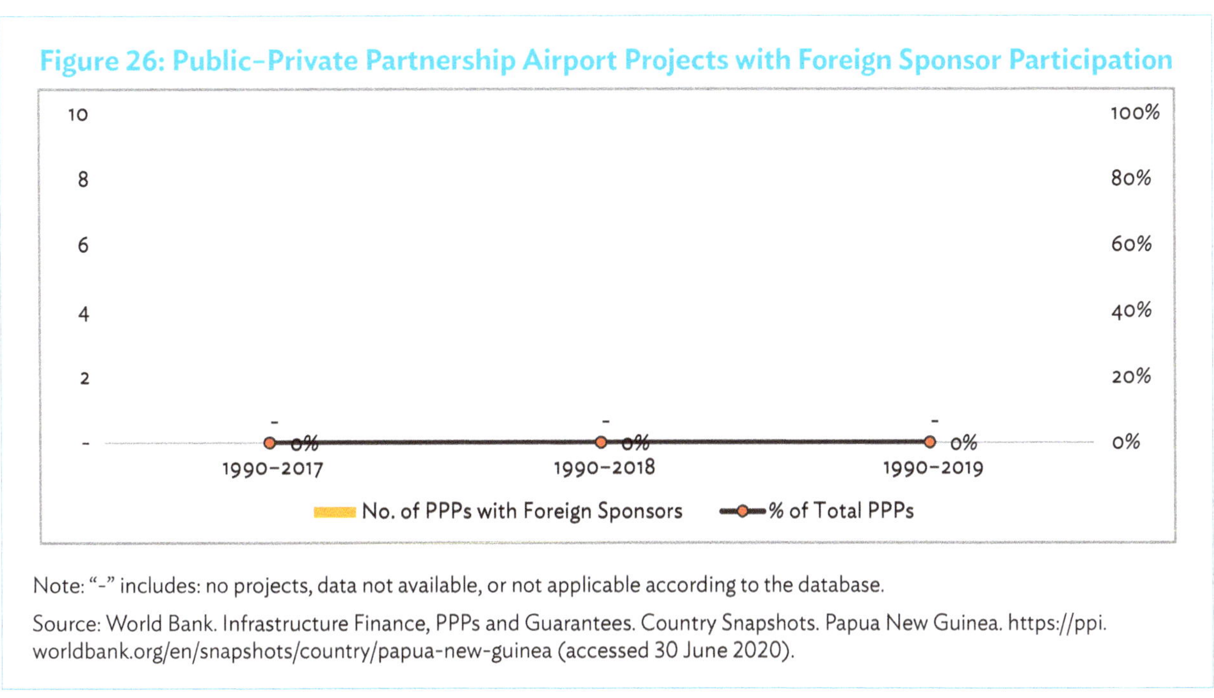

Note: "-" includes: no projects, data not available, or not applicable according to the database.

Source: World Bank. Infrastructure Finance, PPPs and Guarantees. Country Snapshots. Papua New Guinea. https://ppi.worldbank.org/en/snapshots/country/papua-new-guinea (accessed 30 June 2020).

Figure 27 shows the number of PPP projects that have received government support including viability gap funding (VGF) mechanism, government guarantees, and availability/performance payment in Papua New Guinea's airport sector.

Figure 27: Government Support to Public–Private Partnership Airport Projects

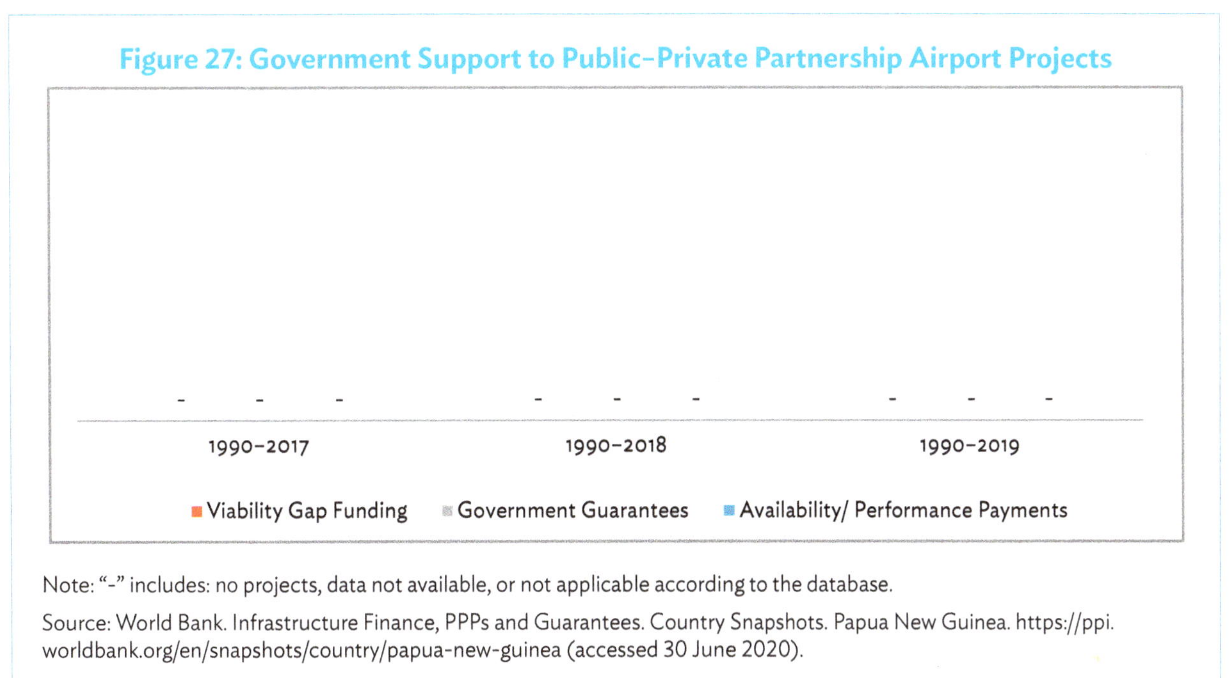

Note: "-" includes: no projects, data not available, or not applicable according to the database.

Source: World Bank. Infrastructure Finance, PPPs and Guarantees. Country Snapshots. Papua New Guinea. https://ppi.worldbank.org/en/snapshots/country/papua-new-guinea (accessed 30 June 2020).

Figure 28 presents the number of PPP projects that have received payment in the form of user charges and government pay (off-take) in Papua New Guinea's airport sector.

Figure 28: Payment Mechanisms for Public–Private Partnership Airport Projects

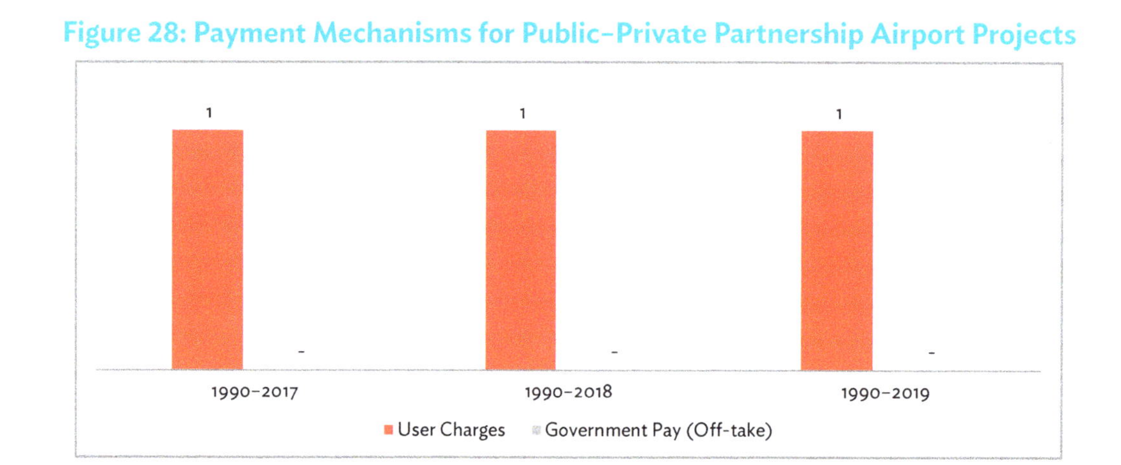

Note: Only active and concluded projects are considered in the above graph. "-" includes: no projects, data not available, or not applicable according to the database.

Source: World Bank. Infrastructure Finance, PPPs and Guarantees. Country Snapshots. Papua New Guinea. https://ppi.worldbank.org/en/snapshots/country/papua-new-guinea (accessed 30 June 2020).

4.1 Tariffs in the Airport Sector

There is no information available on the tariffs applicable for PPPs in the airport sector in Papua New Guinea.

4.2 Typical Risk Allocation for Public–Private Partnership Projects in the Airport Sector

Since there have been no PPP projects implemented in the airport sector thus far, the information on typical risk allocation for such projects is not available.

As per the generic risk allocation prescribed by the National PPP Policy and the PPP Act, the private sector is expected to assume the completion and delivery risks while the public sector is expected to assume approval and regulatory risks. The detailed risk allocation is determined on a case-by-case basis through negotiation between the government and the private sector service providers.

4.3 Financing Details in the Airport Sector

Parameter	1990–2017	1990–2018	1990–2018
PPP projects with foreign lending participation	0	0	0
PPP projects that received export credit agency/international financing institution support	0	0	0
Typical debt-equity ratio	UA		
Time for financial closure	UA		
Typical concession period	UA		
Typical financial internal rate of return	UA		

✓ = Yes, × = No, UA = Unavailable, NA = Not Applicable.

5. Challenges in the Airport Sector

- The airports operated by the NAC have been deteriorating, posing a threat to air safety. Air navigation systems are outdated and unreliable. Hence, the air transport system in Papua New Guinea requires substantial upgrades. Recent investments financed by ADB have helped lift the aviation service standards.[44]
- There are frequent flight cancellations, operations are restricted, and the cost of airline operations is high. International air traffic serving the Port Moresby's Jackson's International Airport, which is the country's international gateway, is very expensive. The unit costs (per passenger, per nautical mile) on PNG's flights to Australia are the most expensive in the Pacific. Air Niugini's unit cost on Asian routes is more than 2.5 times than that of inter-Asian flights (footnote 44).
- PNG's airport sector experiences an acute shortage of skilled manpower, pilots, and maintenance engineers (footnote 44).

ENERGY

Parameter	Value	Unit
Electric power consumption	416	kWh per capita
Share of clean energy	52.5	% of total energy use
Access to electricity	59	% of population
Getting electricity (score out of 100)	65.5	number
Energy imports	UA	% of total energy use
Investment in energy with private participation	65	current $ million
Total number of projects with cumulative lending, grant, and technical assistance commitments in energy sector	29	number
Total amount of cumulative lending, grant, and technical assistance commitments in energy sector	248	$ million

✓ = Yes, × = No, NA = Not Applicable, UA = Unavailable.

Sources: The Economist Intelligence Unit. Papua New Guinea. https://infrascope.eiu.com/; The Global Economy. Share of Clean Energy—Country Rankings. https://www.theglobaleconomy.com/rankings/share_of_clean_energy/; World Bank. Access to Electricity. https://data.worldbank.org/indicator/EG.ELC.ACCS.ZS?locations=PG; Doing Business. Getting Electricity. https://www.doingbusiness.org/en/data/doing-business-score?topic=getting-electricity; The Global Economy. Energy Imports. https://www.theglobaleconomy.com/rankings/energy_imports/; Asian Development Bank. Cumulative Lending, Grant, and Technical Assistance Commitments. https://data.adb.org/dataset/cumulative-lending-grant-and-technical-assistance-commitments.

1. Contracting Agencies in the Energy Sector

The PNG Power Limited (PPL) is a fully integrated power authority. The generation, transmission, distribution, and retailing of electricity throughout Papua New Guinea is done by PPL. It also services individual electricity consumers and industrial, commercial, government, and domestic sector customers in almost all urban centers throughout the country. The services extend to rural communities adjacent to these urban centers wherever possible. It acts as a government contracting agency.[45]

44 Development Asia. Case Study: A Flexible Financing Model for Large-Scale Infrastructure Investments. https://development.asia/case-study/flexible-financing-model-large-scale-infrastructure-investments.

45 Asian Development Bank. Cumulative Lending, Grant, and Technical Assistance Commitments. https://data.adb.org/dataset/cumulative-lending-grant-and-technical-assistance-commitments.

PPL also undertakes a regulatory role on behalf of the Independent Consumer and Competition Commission (ICCC). Some of PPL's responsibilities include approving licenses for electrical contractors, providing certification for models of electrical equipment and appliances to be sold in the country, and providing safety advisory services and checks for major installations.[46]

Section 2.1 (d) of the Third Party Access Code section requires that the Power Purchase Agreement (PPA) first be reviewed and approved by the ICCC before it is signed; therefore PNG Power does not sign any PPA without the approval of the ICCC.

2. Energy Sector Laws and Regulations

PNG's governing laws on the industry include the Constitution of the Independent State of Papua New Guinea, Independent Consumer and Competition Commission Act (2002), Electricity Industry Act (2002), Oil and Gas Act (1998), and Mining Act (1992). Other key supporting pieces of legislation exist in PNG, however, they provide a cumbersome and loose legal framework within which the energy sector operates. The following are the key features of laws and regulations in the energy sector:

- The Electricity Industry Act 2002 regulates the generation, supply, and sale of electricity.[47]
- The Oil and Gas Act 1998 regulates the negotiation and conclusion by the government on petroleum agreements related to petroleum exploration, development, production, and transportation.[48]
- The Geothermal Energy Policy provides the framework for the use and regulation of geothermal resources related to electricity generation from heat and steam.
- The Mining Act 1992 regulates the minerals exploration, development, production, and transportation. Petroleum is excluded from the Act's provisions.[49]
- The ICCC Act 2002 establishes the regime for consumer protection, including promotion and protection of competition and regulation of state-owned monopolies.[50]

The ICCC has published a draft Third Party Access Code. This code provides grid codes and open access rules for private entities to generate and supply electricity in PNG. The code provides open access on the PNG network on its adoption. This may attract independent power producers to participate in the power market and improve supply reliability. However, the areas not served by the grid might have limited access, which may not attract the private sector. PPL exclusively serves its consumers within a 10-kilometer radius of its grid and wheeling of power is denied currently. However, the private sector is free to develop projects and sell power directly to consumers with loads above 10 megawatts (MW) (footnote 46).

PNG has recently created the Ministry for Communication, Information Technology, and Energy. The Ministry of Petroleum and Energy and the Energy Division in particular manages sector policy formulation. PPL performs

[46] Government of Papua New Guinea, Department of Public Enterprises and Department of Petroleum and Energy. 2015. *National Energy Policy*. Port Moresby. http://prdrse4all.spc.int/system/files/national_energy_policy_19.07.2015v5_final_png.pdf; *Papua New Guinea Power Limited News*. PNG Power Complies with Third Party Access Code. http://www.pngpower.com.pg/index.php/news/view/png-power-complies-with-third-party-access-code.

[47] Government of Papua New Guinea. 2002. *Electricity Industry Act*. Port Moresby. http://prdrse4all.spc.int/system/files/electricity_industry_act_chapter_78_consolidated_to_no_10_of_2002.pdf.

[48] Government of Papua New Guinea. 1998. *Oil and Gas Act*. Port Moresby. http://www.paclii.org/pg/legis/consol_act/oaga199894.pdf.

[49] Government of Papua New Guinea. 1992. *Mining Act*. Port Moresby. https://www.ilo.org/dyn/natlex/docs/ELECTRONIC/82401/90191/F973763837/PNG82401.pdf.

[50] Government of Papua New Guinea. 2002. *Independent Consumer and Competition Commission Act 2002*. Port Moresby. http://www.paclii.org/pg/legis/consol_act/icacca2002483.pdf.

the technical regulation of the sector through agreement with the Consumer and Competition Commission. However, the function of technical regulation of the sector should be transferred to the National Energy Authority through the National Energy Policy 2016–2020, although it is intended to be eventually transferred to the Energy Division. In the power sector, the ministry will be in charge of preparing a bill that aims to create a new energy authority and a technical regulator.[51]

Table 11 presents the regulatory authorities in Papua New Guinea's energy sector.

Table 11: Key Agencies Responsible for Regulating the Energy Sector

Agency	Function
Department of Petroleum and Energy	The Department of Petroleum and Energy is the overarching agency in PNG's energy sector. Its functions include energy sector policy and planning. The Electricity Management Committee is headed by this department. It also supervises the technical regulation of the electricity sector, which is presently performed by the Papua New Guinea Power Limited (PPL).
Kumul Consolidated Holdings (KCH)	The KCH is a holding company with ownership in the PPL and other state-owned enterprises. It maintains management oversight of the companies and may take operational actions in companies requiring support. KCH participates in monthly review meetings in the energy sector and supports the PPL.
Independent Consumer and Competition Commission (ICCC)	The ICCC is the regulator for electricity tariffs. It cannot carry out its mandate and take decisions independently as it lacks the capacity required. The ICCC employs a revenue cap regulation principle and sets license conditions for market participants, though the PPL is the only regulated entity at present. The ICCC also issues licenses to independent power producers and mining companies that own generation and distribution facilities.
PNG Power Limited (PPL)	The PPL is a state-owned, vertically integrated electricity utility. It is responsible for generation, transmission, distribution, and retail services in most grid-connected urban areas.
Western Province Power Limited	This is a wholly-owned subsidiary of PNG Sustainable Development Program Limited and provides generation, distribution, and retail electricity services in the Western Province, principally through small-scale power projects.

ICCC = Independent Consumer and Competition Commission, PNG = Papua New Guinea, PPL = Papua New Guinea Power Limited.

Source: Asian Development Bank. 2014. *Energy Sector Assessment*. Manila. https://www.adb.org/sites/default/files/linked-documents/CAPE-PNG-6-Energy-Sector-Assessment.pdf.

2.1 Foreign Investment Restrictions in the Energy Sector

There are no sector-specific restrictions, limitations, or requirements applied to foreign investment.

Business Activity	Maximum % of FDI Allowed
Power generation	100
Power transmission	100
Power distribution	100
Oil and gas	100

FDI = foreign direct investment.

Source: United States Department of State. 2019. *2019 Investment Climate Statements: Papua New Guinea*. Washington, DC. https://www.state.gov/reports/2019-investment-climate-statements/papua-new-guinea/.

[51] Department of Public Enterprises and Department of Petroleum and Energy of Papua New Guinea. 2015. National energy Policy. Papua New Guinea. http://prdrse4all.spc.int/system/files/national_energy_policy_19.07.2015v5_final_png.pdf.

2.2 Standard Contracts in the Energy Sector

Type of contract	Availability
PPP/concession agreement	×
Power purchase agreement	×
Capacity take-or-pay contract	×
Fuel supply agreement	×
Transmission and use of system agreement	×
Performance-based operation and maintenance contract	×
Engineering procurement and construction contract	✓

✓ = Yes, × = No, NA = Not Applicable, UA = Unavailable.

Source: Asian Development Bank. 2019. *Public–Private Partnership Monitor, Second Edition.* Manila. https://www.adb.org/sites/default/files/publication/509426/ppp-monitor-second-edition.pdf.

3. Energy Sector Master Plan

The energy sector currently accounts for 14% of the country's GDP and is a critical enabler for all other sectors to build a modern PNG economy. The installed capacity needs to multiply nearly four times between 2010 and 2030, from 500 MW to 1,970 MW, according to PNG's Strategic Development Plan, 2010–2030. Hydropower would be the leading energy resource, rising from 215 MW to 1,140 MW. Diesel use is expected to nosedive from 160 MW to just 30 MW, or 1.5% of total capacity. On the other hand, the use of other renewables (mainly geothermal) is expected to increase to 380 MW, or 19.2% of the total capacity (footnote 11). It is estimated that PNG has hydropower potential of about 15,000 MW comprising large and small hydro projects.

The energy sector engages in the generation, transmission, distribution, and retail of electricity. Presently, grids in Port Moresby and in the Lae–Madang–Highlands area (the Ramu grid) are the two main stand-alone power grids. A number of smaller grids provides service to the smaller urban centers. Because of the unreliability of grid supply, there is considerable self-generation and back-up generation taking place in urban areas, but maintenance and operation costs are high and efficiencies are low. PNG has about 580 megawatts (MW) of installed generation capacity, including hydropower (230 MW or 39.7%), diesel (217 MW or 37.4%), gas-fired (82 MW or 14.1%), and geothermal (53 MW or 9.1%). PNG has significant underutilized indigenous energy sources, such as hydropower, natural gas, geothermal, and solar.[52]

The government has identified the energy as a key sector in the Papua New Guinea Development Strategic Plan, 2010–2030. The National Energy Plan (NEP) has been approved along with the National Energy Policy. The National Energy Plan promotes the development of appropriate regulatory guidelines and standards to meet the needs of producers, suppliers, and users. The NEP includes the National Electrification Roll-Out Plan, which focuses on grid extension and off-grid stand-alone power supply system and promotes 100% electricity usage from renewable energy sources by 2050 (footnote 11).

Table 12 provides a list of PPP energy projects in the Energy Sector Master Plan.

[52] Asian Development Bank. 2013. *Sector Assessment (Summary): Energy.* Manila. https://www.adb.org/sites/default/files/linked-documents/43197-013-png-ssa.pdf.

Table 12: List of Public–Private Partnership Energy Projects

No.	Project	Implementing Agency	Estimated Project Cost ($ million)	(K million)	Status
1.	National Energy Policy Rollout	Government of PNG	8.67	30.00	UA
2.	Naoro Brown Energy Development	DP	10.20	35.31	UA
3.	Ramu Transmission	Government of PNG/DP	19.09	66.06	UA
4.	Rural Electrification Program	Government of PNG/DP	68.53	237.13	UA
5.	Mt. Hagen–Mendi–Tari Grid	Government of PNG/DP	20.23	70.00	UA
6.	PNG Towns Electrification Investment Program	Government of PNG/DP	47.69	165.00	UA
7.	Port Moresby Grid Development	Government of PNG/DP	31.21	108.00	UA

✓ = Yes, × = No, NA = Not Applicable, UA = Unavailable.

DP = development plan, PNG = Papua New Guinea.

Source: Asian Development Bank. 2013. Sector *Assessment (Summary): Energy*. Manila. https://www.adb.org/sites/default/files/linked-documents/43197-013-png-ssa.pdf.

3.1 Projects under Preparation and Procurement in the Energy Sector

Figure 29 presents the number of PPP projects that are under preparation and procurement in Papua New Guinea's energy sector.

Figure 29: Public–Private Partnership Energy Projects under Preparation and Procurement

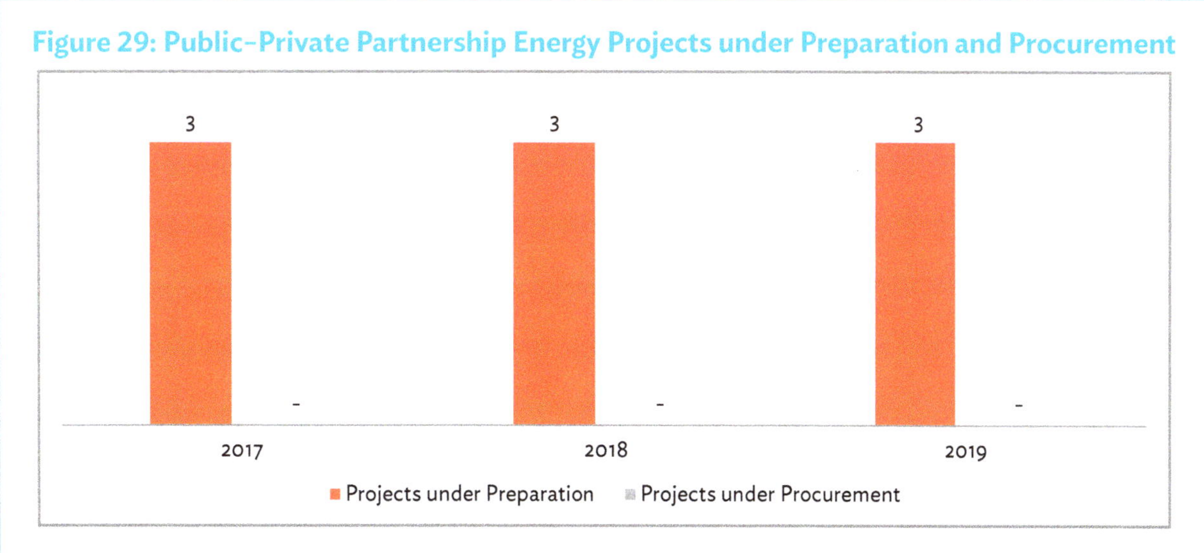

✓ = Yes, × = No, UA = Unavailable, NA = Not Applicable.

Note: "-" includes: no projects, data not available, or not applicable.

Source: Asian Development Bank. 2019. *Public–Private Partnership Monitor. Second Edition. Manila.* https://www.adb.org/sites/default/files/publication/509426/ppp-monitor-second-edition.pdf.

4. Features of Past Public–Private Partnership Projects in the Energy Sector

Figure 30 shows the number of PPP projects procured through various modes including direct appointment, unsolicited bids, and competitive bids in Papua New Guinea's energy sector.

Figure 30: Modes of Procurement for Public–Private Partnership Energy Projects

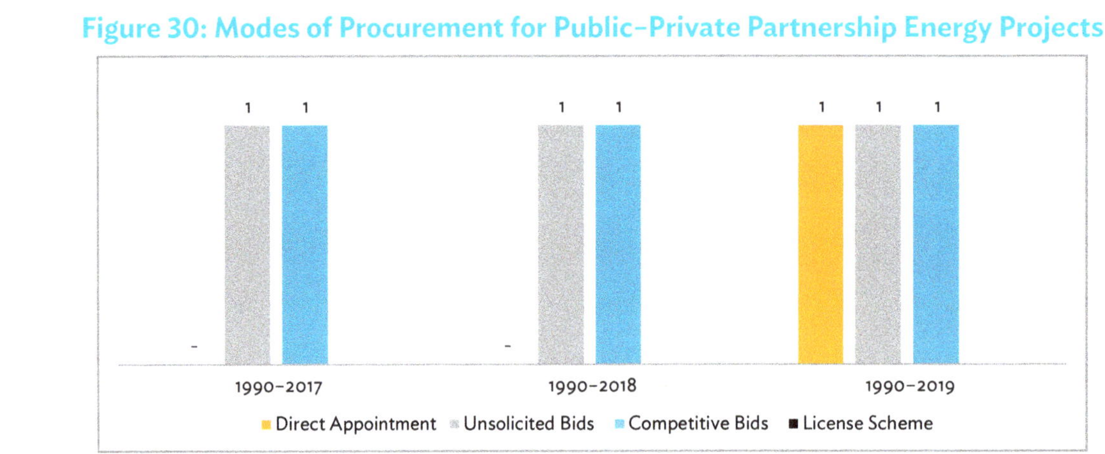

✓ = Yes, × = No, UA = Unavailable, NA = Not Applicable.

Note: Only active and concluded projects are considered in the above graph. "-" includes: no projects, data not available, or not applicable according to the database.

Source: Asian Development Bank. 2019. *Public–Private Partnership Monitor, Second Edition*. Manila. https://www.adb.org/sites/default/files/publication/509426/ppp-monitor-second-edition.pdf.

The actual design of the Port Moresby Power Station was tendered by and awarded to ExxonMobil because they had previously intended to fund and deliver the power station themselves. Plans changed however when the funding model became uncertain, thus the NiuPower stepped into the breach and offered to fund, own, and operate the power station. In 2018, two companies each put up half of the capital to proceed with the development of the power station—the Kumul Petroleum, which is widely viewed as the national oil company of Papua New Guinea, and the Oil Search Limited. The 58.7-megawatt facility was commissioned in November 2019.[53]

Services of Shenzhen Energy Group were procured for RAMU-2 project through competitive bidding.[54]

[53] Energy, Oil and Gas. Profiles. http://www.energy-oil-gas.com/2020/06/10/niupower/.

[54] *Post-Courier*. 2018. Ramu 2 Set to Flood the Country with Energy. 26 September. https://postcourier.com.pg/ramu-2-set-flood-country-energy/.

Figure 31 shows the number of PPP projects that have reached financial closure and the total value of those projects in Papua New Guinea's energy sector.

Figure 31: Independent Power Producer and Public–Private Partnership Energy Projects Reaching Financial Closure

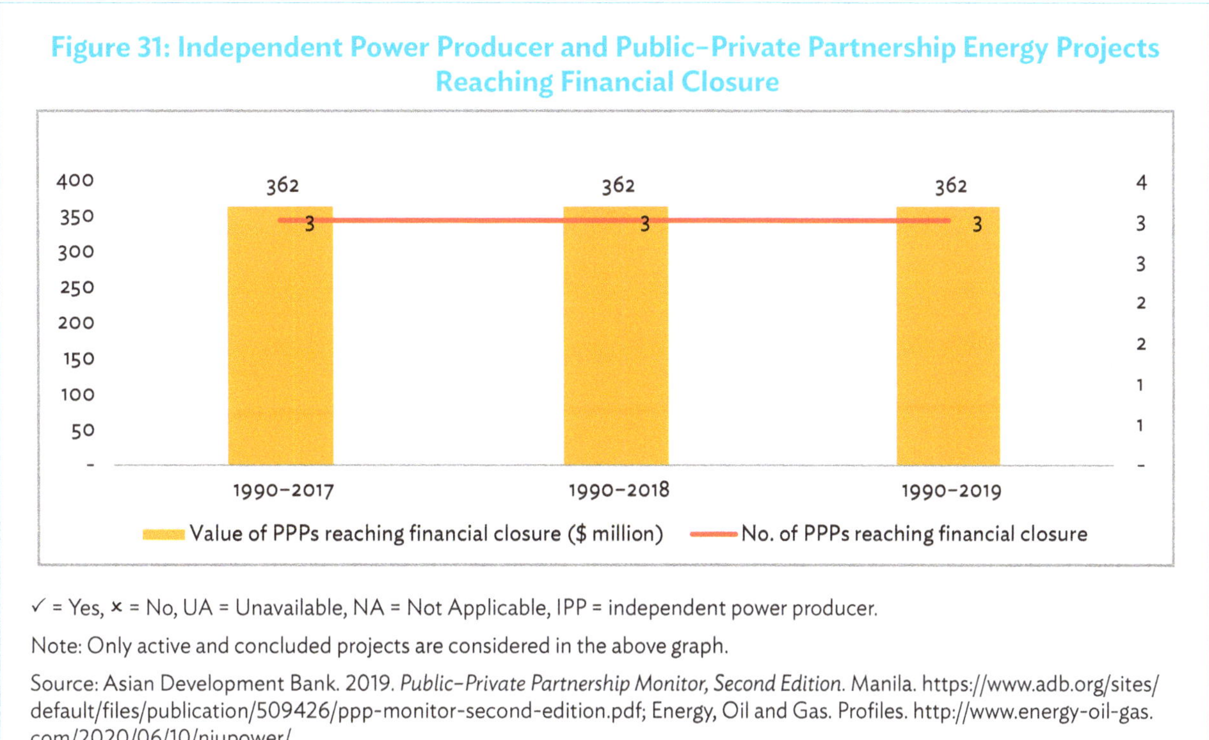

✓ = Yes, × = No, UA = Unavailable, NA = Not Applicable, IPP = independent power producer.

Note: Only active and concluded projects are considered in the above graph.

Source: Asian Development Bank. 2019. *Public–Private Partnership Monitor, Second Edition.* Manila. https://www.adb.org/sites/default/files/publication/509426/ppp-monitor-second-edition.pdf; Energy, Oil and Gas. Profiles. http://www.energy-oil-gas.com/2020/06/10/niupower/.

Three projects have reached financial closure in the energy sector. The first project is the Port Moresby Diesel-Fired Plant which reached financial closure in January 1996. It was a Greenfield PPI project based on a build–operate–transfer mode. The period of the contract was 15 years. It received sponsoring from foreign investors like Hyundai, Hanjung Power, and Daewoo (footnote 7). The second project is the RAMU-2 hydroelectric power plant signed in 2015 with the People's Republic of China's Shenzhen Energy Group. The third project is the Port Moresby Power Station which was commissioned in November 2019, costing $100 million (K340 million as of June 2020).[55]

[55] Oil Search. 2019. *NiuPower and PNG Power Limited Sign Historic Power Purchase Agreement.* Port Moresby. https://www.oilsearch.com/__data/assets/pdf_file/0006/34557/190428-NiuPower-and-PNG-Power-Limited-sign-historic-Power-Purchase-Agreement.pdf.

Figure 32 presents the number of PPP projects that have foreign sponsor participation in Papua New Guinea's energy sector.

Figure 32: Public–Private Partnership Energy Projects with Foreign Sponsor Participation

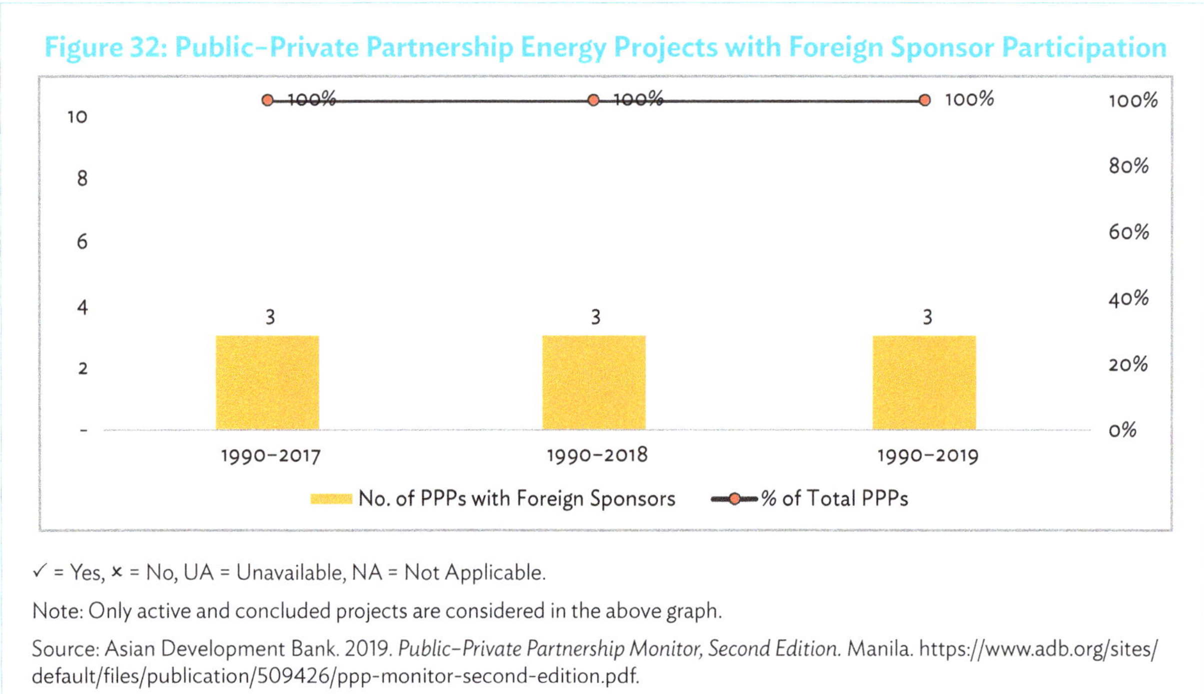

✓ = Yes, × = No, UA = Unavailable, NA = Not Applicable.

Note: Only active and concluded projects are considered in the above graph.

Source: Asian Development Bank. 2019. *Public–Private Partnership Monitor, Second Edition.* Manila. https://www.adb.org/sites/default/files/publication/509426/ppp-monitor-second-edition.pdf.

Figure 33 shows the number of PPP projects that have received government support including viability gap funding (VGF) mechanism, government guarantees, and availability/performance payment in Papua New Guinea's energy sector.

Figure 33: Government Support to Public–Private Partnership Energy Projects

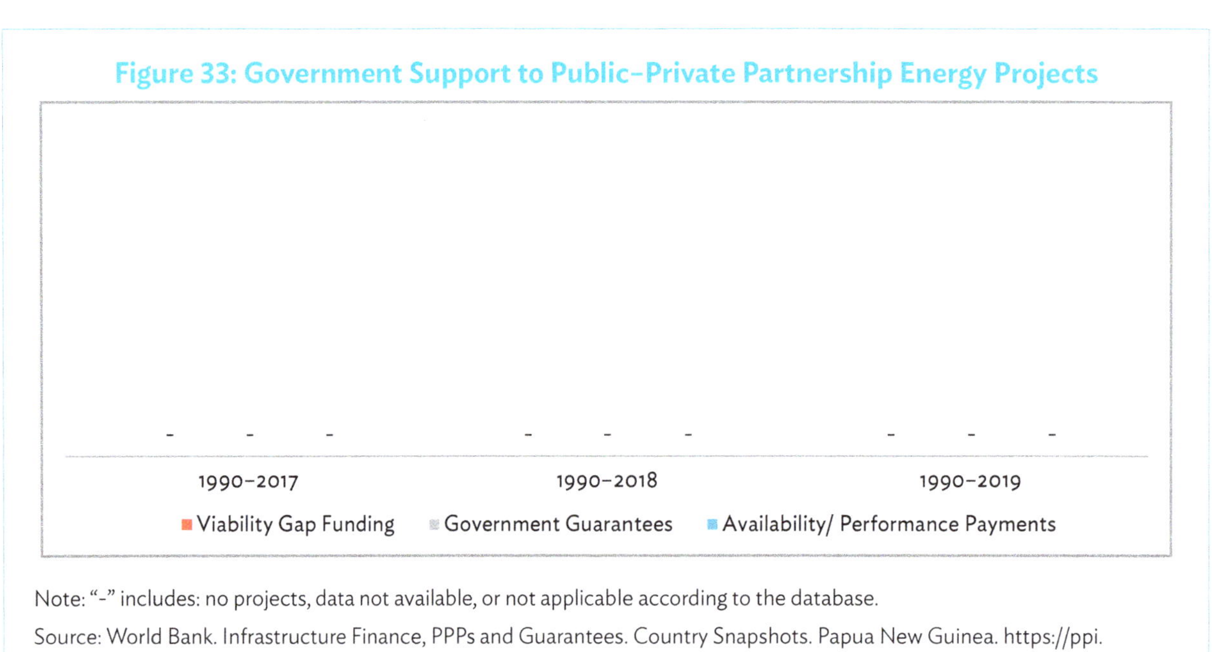

Note: "-" includes: no projects, data not available, or not applicable according to the database.

Source: World Bank. Infrastructure Finance, PPPs and Guarantees. Country Snapshots. Papua New Guinea. https://ppi.worldbank.org/en/snapshots/country/papua-new-guinea (accessed 30 June 2020).

Figure 34 presents the number of PPP projects that have received payment in the form of user charges and government pay (off-take) in Papua New Guinea's energy sector.

Figure 34: Payment Mechanisms for Public–Private Partnership Energy Projects

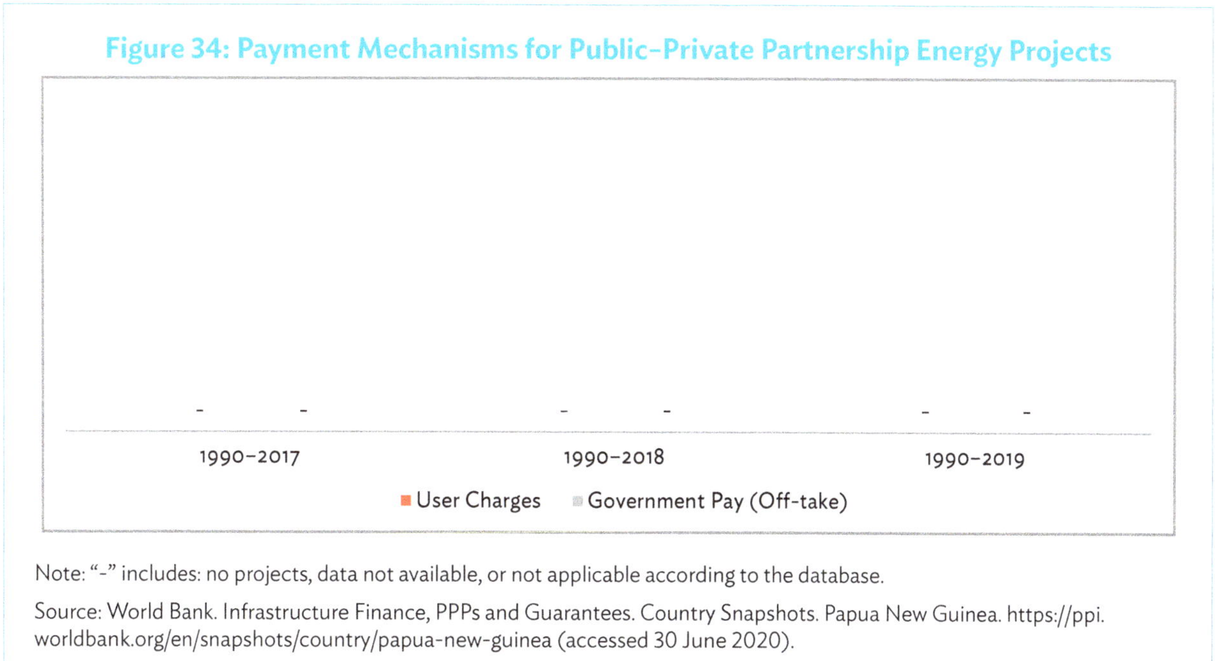

Note: "-" includes: no projects, data not available, or not applicable according to the database.

Source: World Bank. Infrastructure Finance, PPPs and Guarantees. Country Snapshots. Papua New Guinea. https://ppi.worldbank.org/en/snapshots/country/papua-new-guinea (accessed 30 June 2020).

4.1 Tariffs in the Energy Sector

The PPL sends tariff applications to the ICCC every year. Revenue requirements and price caps determine the tariffs. However, the ICCC does not have benchmarks for implementing price cap regulation nor expertise in assessing demand projects and investment plans prepared by the PPL (footnote 11).

Due to inadequate funds, the ICCC posts information on its website and in newspapers instead of conducting hearings on tariff applications. The ICCC earns around 10% of the budget through the license fees paid by entities, while the remainder of its budget is provided by the government. Although the ICCC is an independent entity, the government exercises control over the retail tariffs charged by the PPL (footnote 11).

The uniform retail tariff is not cost reflective. The cost of supply between the cheap hydropower-run main grid-connected regions and the expensive diesel-generation-powered Highlands area is cross-subsidized by the uniform tariff, in the absence of explicit subsidy. The uniform tariff serves as a disincentive for the PPL to make investments for increasing electricity access in rural areas. Yet, it has been politically difficult to move away from uniform tariffs, though the Electricity Industry Policy (EIP) allows for flexible tariff setting (footnote 11).

According to the National Energy Policy (2016–2020), the private sector will be encouraged through feed-in tariff (FIT) to develop potential sites to generate electricity for their own consumption and for export of any surplus to the national grid and neighboring countries. Investors that guarantee purchase of electrical energy on just and reasonable terms will be provided with letters of comfort by the government. The specific details of FIT for renewable energy resources will be captured in the Renewable Energy Policy to be produced by the institution mandated to draw up this sector policy (footnote 11).

4.2 Typical Risk Allocation for Public–Private Partnership Projects in the Energy Sector

The typical risk allocation framework for the energy sector projects is provided in Table 13.

Table 13: Risk Allocations to the Public and Private Sectors for Energy Projects, by Risk Type

Risk Category	Private	Public	Shared	
Demand risk		✓		
Revenue collection risk		✓		
Tariff risk	✓			
Government payment risk		✓		
Environmental and social risk	✓			
Land acquisition risk			✓	
Permits	✓			
Handover risk	✓			
Political risk		✓		
Regulatory risk		✓		
Interconnection risk			✓	
Brownfield risk: asset condition				NA
Grid performance risk	✓			
Hydrology risk	✓			
Exploration and drilling risk	✓			

✓ = Yes, × = No, UA = Unavailable, NA = Not Applicable.

Source: Asian Development Bank. 2019. *Public–Private Partnership Monitor, Second Edition.* Manila. https://www.adb.org/sites/default/files/publication/509426/ppp-monitor-second-edition.pdf.

4.3 Financing Details in the Energy Sector

Parameter	1990–2017	1990–2018	1990–2019
PPP projects with foreign lending participation	UA	UA	UA
PPP projects that received export credit agency/international financing institution support	UA	UA	UA
Typical debt-equity ratio		UA	
Time for financial closure		UA	
Typical concession period		UA	
Typical financial internal rate of return		UA	

✓ = Yes, × = No, UA = Unavailable, NA = Not Applicable.

5. Challenges in the Energy Sector

- The lack of clarity on how to proceed with the implementation plan toward achieving the goals of the strategy documents (MTDP 2011–2015 and PNGDSP) prepared by the government is one of the major challenges to developing the energy sector. PNG also needs to formulate a robust strategy to develop its hydropower resources, which reportedly have the potential to generate about 10,000 MW. Still, only about 215 MW of this capacity has been developed.[56]
- Achieving the strategic goals has been difficult due to lack of funds. The PPL has scarce funds for routine maintenance of the existing electricity infrastructure. This has led to de-rating of equipment and unplanned maintenance, resulting in power shortages and poor reliability and quality of electricity supply (footnote 56).
- Institutional capacity is also a constraint. The inadequacy of trained staff in the Department of Petroleum and Energy (DPE) to undertake all its intended functions has led the department to plan substantial augmentation of its staff. The ICCC is intended to be both the technical and economic regulator, but since it has inadequate technical capacity, the function of technical regulation currently resides with the PPL, which itself is the regulated entity (footnote 56).
- The uniform retail tariff does not reflect the actual cost as it cross-subsidizes the cost of supply between the cheap hydropower-run main grid-connected regions and the expensive diesel-generation-powered Highlands area, in the absence of explicit subsidy. It discourages the PPL investment in rural areas. Although the Electricity Industry Policy (EIP) allows for flexible tariff setting, it has been politically difficult to move away from uniform tariffs (footnote 56).
- Private sector investments are critical for the country. However, attracting private investments will require enabling policies, such as the planned PPP policy, and risk mitigation instruments to overcome the perception of country and utility risk. The utility in PNG remains vertically integrated and the PPL acts as a single buyer to supply the three main grids serving the urban areas, although there are draft policies on open access. This too poses a risk for private investments. Investments by the multilateral banks and other development partners are thus essential to the development of the electricity sector (footnote 36).
- While PNG plans to significantly expand electricity access to urban and rural consumers, the focus is clearly on strengthening and augmenting the grid to supply the urban areas. Another primary challenge to developing the electricity sector is the attitude among PNG's public and private sector stakeholders toward prioritizing the improvement and reliability of electricity supply in urban areas and the expansion of electricity access to rural consumers (footnote 36).
- There have been delays in the implementation of several power projects—the 200-MW Hela hydroelectric power plant in the Highlands being one of them. A 2,500-MW plant on the Purari River, which costs $5 billion and is the PNG's largest hydro project to date, was put on hold. In March 2014, developer Origin Energy announced that it was shelving the plan. The plant's output would have been enough to power PNG several times over, and then sell the excess output to Queensland, Australia via undersea cable. The RAMU-2 project has also witnessed more than 5 years of delay, and the status of the project is unclear (footnote 36).

[56] Asian Development Bank. 2014. *Energy Sector Assessment. Manila.* https://www.adb.org/sites/default/files/linked-documents/CAPE-PNG-6-Energy-Sector-Assessment.pdf.

WATER AND WASTEWATER

Parameter	Value	Unit
Improved water source access	39.70	% of population with access
Improved sanitation facilities access	18.70	% of population with access
Investment in water and sanitation with private participation	71.00	current $ million
Total number of projects with cumulative lending, grant, and technical assistance commitments in water and other urban infrastructure and services	13	number
Total amount of cumulative lending, grant, and technical assistance commitments in water and other urban infrastructure and services	52	$ million

✓ = Yes, × = No, UA = Unavailable, NA = Not Applicable.

Sources: Asian Development Bank. 2015. *Papua New Guinea, 2016–2020—Country Partnership Strategy*. Manila. https://www.adb.org/sites/default/files/institutional-document/157927/cps-png-2016-2020.pdf; The Economist Intelligence Unit. Papua New Guinea. https://infrascope.eiu.com/; Asian Development Bank. Cumulative Lending, Grant, and Technical Assistance Commitments. https://data.adb.org/dataset/cumulative-lending-grant-and-technical-assistance-commitments.

PNG's estimated 8.9 million people are among those with the least access to safe water supply in the world. The government's Water, Sanitation and Hygiene (WASH) Policy 2015–2030 indicates that 89% of people in urban areas and 33% in rural areas have access to safe water, while 57% of urban dwellers and only 13% of the rural population have access to basic sanitation.[57]

1. Contracting Agencies in the Water and Wastewater Sector

According to the National Water Supply and Sanitation Act 2016,[58] the Water Papua New Guinea Limited (Water PNG Ltd.) has the capacity and power to enter into contracts and agreements for the purchase of land or easements in or over land, and the acquisition of any materials or construction of any works (footnote 58).

2. Water and Wastewater Sector Laws and Regulations

The National Water Supply and Sanitation Act 2016 is the legislative framework for water and sanitation in Papua New Guinea. It repeals the National Water Supply and Sewerage Act 1986. Under this act, the Water PNG Ltd. is mandated to comply with the Public Health Act (Chapter 226), the consumer protection provisions of the Independent Consumer and Competition Commission Act 2002, and the Environment Act 2000, and abide by the water quality and sewerage discharge standards that are enforced from time to time.

Parameter	2017	2018	2019
Can the private sector be given water abstraction rights?	UA	UA	UA
Are there regulations in place on raw water extraction?	UA	UA	UA
Are there regulations in place on the release of treated effluents?	UA	UA	UA

✓ = Yes, × = No, NA = Not Applicable, UA = Unavailable.

[57] Government of Papua New Guinea. *WASH Policy 2015–2030*. https://png-data.sprep.org/system/files/WaSH_POLICY04.03.2015.pdf.

[58] Government of Papua New Guinea. 2016. *National Water Supply and Sanitation Act 2016*. Port Moresby. http://extwprlegs1.fao.org/docs/pdf/png177402.pdf.

Water PNG Ltd. is the key agency for regulating the water and wastewater in Papua New Guinea. It has the following functions (footnote 58):

- design, construct, and maintain the water supply systems as may be required for collection, production, supply, and use of water for private and public consumption in and for cities, towns, and rural areas;
- design, construct, and maintain sanitation systems as may be required for the disposal of sewage and wastewater in and for cities, towns, and rural areas;
- secure and provide an adequate supply of water;
- manage, operate, and maintain water supply systems and sanitation systems owned by the company and other installations as may be erected or constructed by the company;
- work with provincial governments and through them, with authorities involved in district administration, and where appropriate, with other state-owned enterprises;
- comply with the Public Health Act (Chapter 226), the consumer protection provisions of the Independent Consumer and Competition Commission Act 2002, and the Environment Act 2000, and abide by water quality and sewerage discharge standards that are enforced from time to time; and
- generally carry out supplementary, incidental, or consequential acts and things that are necessary or convenient for carrying out its functions.

2.1 Foreign Investment Restrictions in the Water and Wastewater Sector

Parameter	2017	2018	2019
Maximum allowed foreign ownership of equity in greenfield projects	UA	UA	UA
• Bulk water supply and treatment	UA	UA	UA
• Water distribution	UA	UA	UA
• Wastewater treatment	UA	UA	UA
• Wastewater collection	UA	UA	UA

✓ = Yes, × = No, NA = Not Applicable, UA = Unavailable.

2.2 Standard Contracts in the Water and Wastewater Sector

Type of contract	
PPP/concession agreement	×
Bulk water supply agreement	×
Performance-based operation and maintenance contract	×
Engineering procurement and construction contract	×

✓ = Yes, × = No, NA = Not Applicable, UA = Unavailable.

3. Water and Wastewater Sector Master Plan

The PNG WASH Policy recognizes the need to substantially improve access to water and sanitation services and hygiene behaviors, particularly among currently underserved rural and peri-urban settlement areas.[59] It is widely perceived as ambitious and aspirational (footnote 59).

[59] Government of Papua New Guinea. 2015. *WASH Policy 2015-2030*. Papua New Guinea. https://png-data.sprep.org/system/files/WaSH_POLICY04.03.2015.pdf.

The WASH Policy has the following targets for 2030: (i) 70% of the rural population, 95% of the urban population, and 100% of educational institutions and medical centers have access to a safe, convenient, and sustainable water supply; (ii) 70% of the rural population, 85% of the urban population, and 100% of educational institutions and medical centers have access to safe, convenient, and sustainable sanitation facilities; (iii) 100% of educational institutions and medical centers have handwashing facilities with running water and soap; and (iv) 100% of households have access to improved water supply and total sanitation (footnote 59).

The government's key strategy is to improve sector coordination and leadership through the National Water, Sanitation and Hygiene Authority (NWSHA), headquartered in Port Moresby and with offices in provinces and districts. The NWSHA board comprises of representatives from the public and private sectors as well as civil society, and supersedes the existing National WASH Coordinating Committee. The NWSHA is mandated to undertake water supply and sanitation service delivery at the national, urban, and rural levels and work together with existing sector institutions and organizations (footnote 59).

The government recognizes the need for private sector participation. The private sector helps deliver water supply and sanitation services to communities through improved program implementation and strengthening of supply chains for improved sanitation marketing and through sustainable provision of essential services. Public–private partnerships (PPPs) will also be considered for private sector engagement. Possible PPP models include the build–own–operate and build–operate–transfer schemes, as well as concessions, leases, and management contracts for system operations (footnote 59).

3.1 Projects under Preparation and Procurement in the Water and Wastewater Sector

Figure 35 presents the number of PPP projects that are under preparation and procurement in Papua New Guinea's water and wastewater sector.

Figure 35: Public–Private Partnership Water and Wastewater Projects under Preparation and Procurement

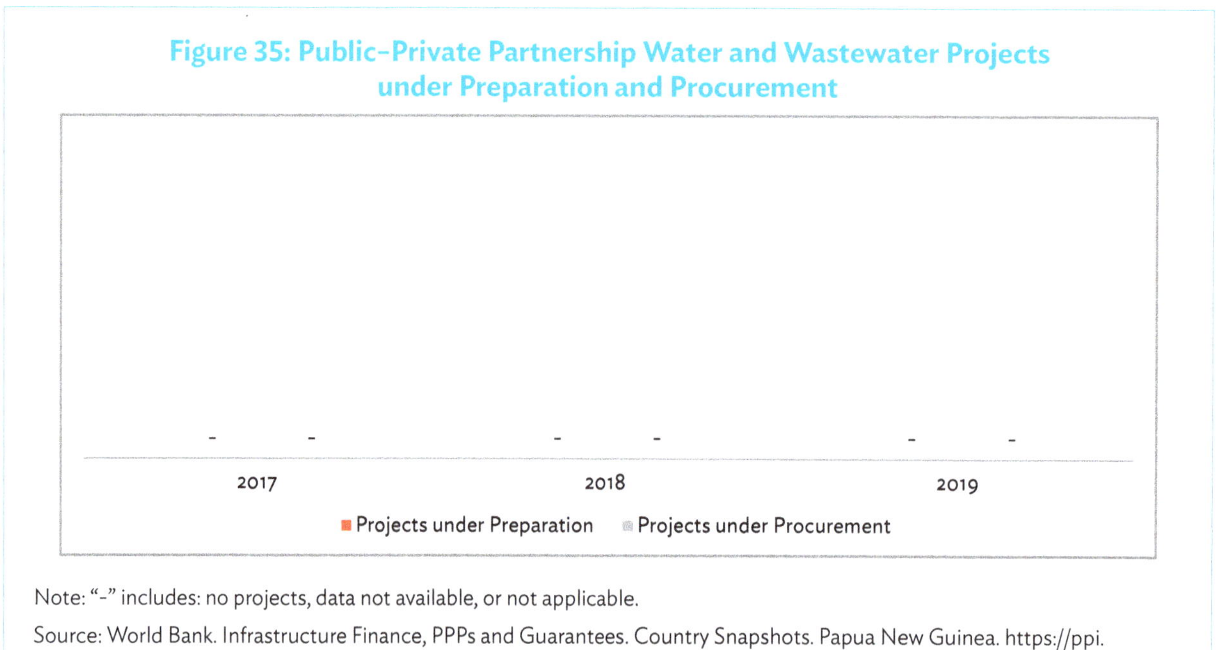

Note: "-" includes: no projects, data not available, or not applicable.

Source: World Bank. Infrastructure Finance, PPPs and Guarantees. Country Snapshots. Papua New Guinea. https://ppi.worldbank.org/en/snapshots/country/papua-new-guinea (accessed 30 June 2020).

4. Features of Past Public–Private Partnership Projects in the Water and Wastewater Sector

Figure 36 shows the number of PPP projects procured through various modes including direct appointment, unsolicited bids, and competitive bids in Papua New Guinea's water and wastewater sector.

Figure 36: Modes of Procurement for Public–Private Partnership Water and Wastewater Projects

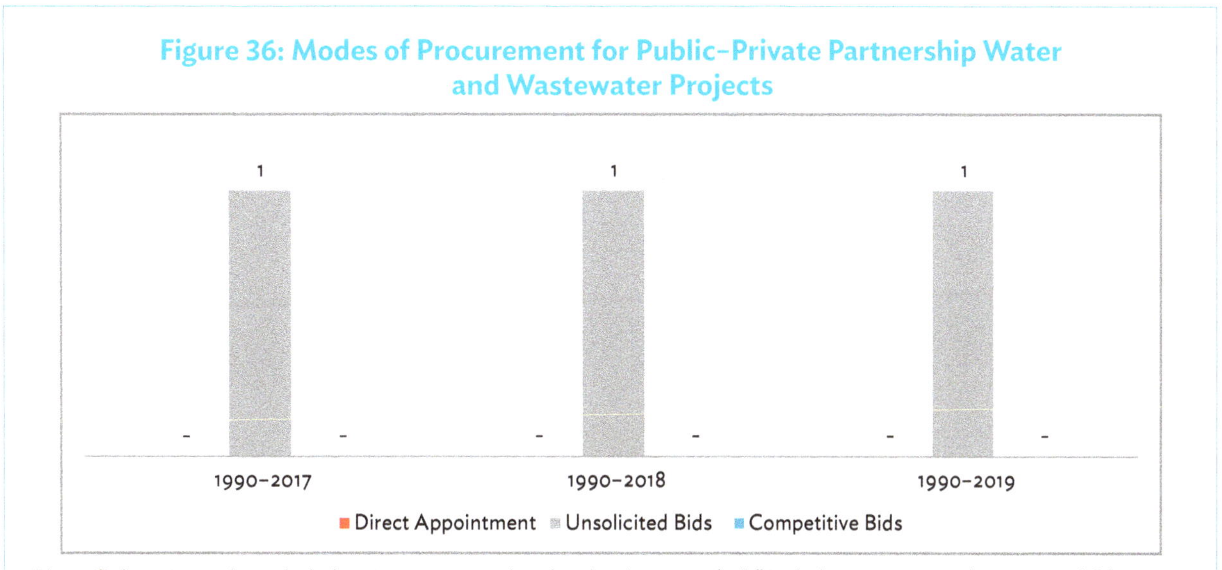

Note: Only active and concluded projects are considered in the above graph. "-" includes: no projects, data not available, or not applicable according to the database.

Source: World Bank. Infrastructure Finance, PPPs and Guarantees. Country Snapshots. Papua New Guinea. https://ppi.worldbank.org/en/snapshots/country/papua-new-guinea (accessed 30 June 2020).

Figure 37 presents the number of PPP projects that have reached financial closure and the total value of those projects in Papua New Guinea's water and wastewater sector.

Figure 37: Public–Private Partnership Water and Wastewater Projects Reaching Financial Closure

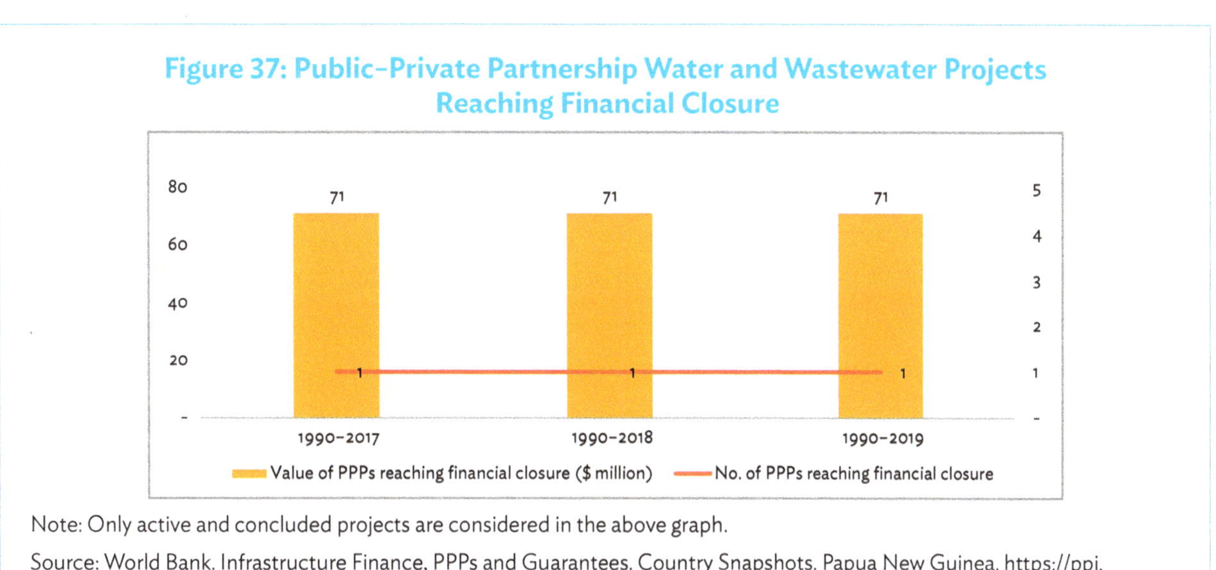

Note: Only active and concluded projects are considered in the above graph.

Source: World Bank. Infrastructure Finance, PPPs and Guarantees. Country Snapshots. Papua New Guinea. https://ppi.worldbank.org/en/snapshots/country/papua-new-guinea (accessed 30 June 2020).

In 1997, the Concessionaire (Contract) Agreement was signed between PNG Water Ltd. (Malaysian Consortium) and Eda Ranu for the treatment and distribution of water in Port Moresby. Eda Ranu is the sole provider of water and sewerage services in the National Capital District. It was founded through the National Capital District Water Supply and Sewerage Act 1996. The build–operate–transfer (BOT) contract runs for a period of 22 years. The concession period ended in June 2019.[60]

Figure 38 shows the number of PPP projects that have foreign sponsor participation in Papua New Guinea's water and wastewater sector.

Figure 38: Public–Private Partnership Water and Wastewater Projects with Foreign Sponsor Participation

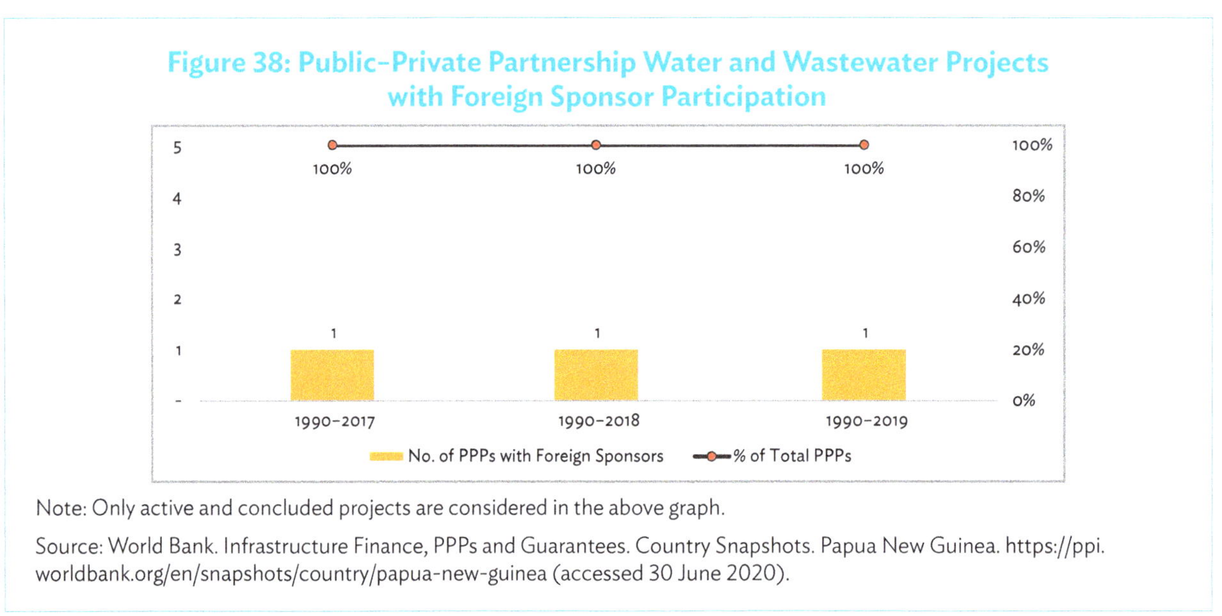

Note: Only active and concluded projects are considered in the above graph.

Source: World Bank. Infrastructure Finance, PPPs and Guarantees. Country Snapshots. Papua New Guinea. https://ppi.worldbank.org/en/snapshots/country/papua-new-guinea (accessed 30 June 2020).

Figure 39 presents the number of PPP projects that have received government support including viability gap funding (VGF) mechanism, government guarantees, and availability/performance payment in Papua New Guinea's water and wastewater sector.

Figure 39: Government Support to Public–Private Partnership Water and Wastewater Projects

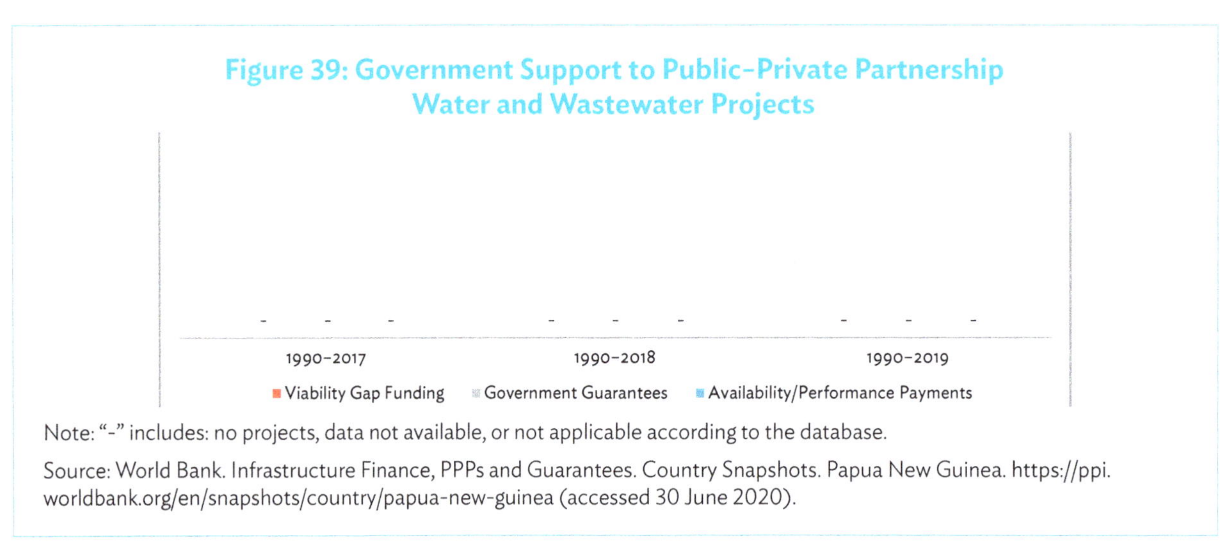

Note: "-" includes: no projects, data not available, or not applicable according to the database.

Source: World Bank. Infrastructure Finance, PPPs and Guarantees. Country Snapshots. Papua New Guinea. https://ppi.worldbank.org/en/snapshots/country/papua-new-guinea (accessed 30 June 2020).

[60] Government of Papua New Guinea, Department of Treasury. 2019. *Infrastructure Financing and Public–Private Partnership Network of Asia and the Pacific.* Presentation for the United Nations Economic and Social Commission for Asia and the Pacific. Ningbo, People's Republic of China. 2–3 September. https://www.unescap.org/sites/default/files/Session%202%20-%20Panelist%20-%202Mr.%20Martin%20Teine_PNG.pdf.

Figure 40 presents the number of PPP projects that have received payment in the form of user charges and government pay (off-take) in Papua New Guinea's water and wastewater sector.

Figure 40: Payment Mechanisms for Public–Private Partnership Water and Wastewater Projects

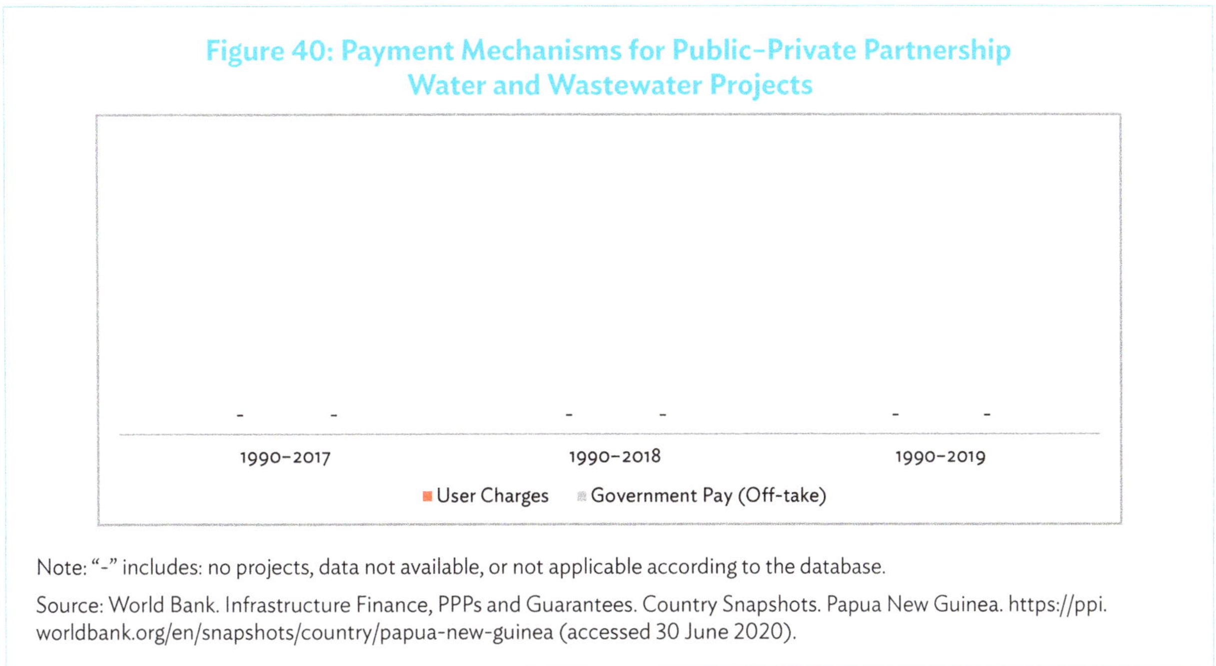

Note: "-" includes: no projects, data not available, or not applicable according to the database.

Source: World Bank. Infrastructure Finance, PPPs and Guarantees. Country Snapshots. Papua New Guinea. https://ppi.worldbank.org/en/snapshots/country/papua-new-guinea (accessed 30 June 2020).

4.1 Tariffs in Water and Wastewater Sector

The Water PNG Ltd. is authorized to impose tariffs, rates, fees, and charges for the water and sanitation services it supplies, and from time to time to vary the quantum (percentages or monetary amounts) of those tariffs, rates, fees, and charges. The nature or quantum of them is published by notice in the National Gazette and takes effect on the date of publication, wherein the tariff, rates, fees, and charges are imposed or varied.[61]

The tariffs, rates, fees, and charges levied or charged by the Water Board prior to the commencement date are those which the company may levy or charge under the National Water Supply and Sanitation Act 2016 until such time when the company sets new tariffs, rates, fees, and charges (footnote 61).

In 2015, the ICCC set a new tariff regime, which has effectively increased the minimum water consumption from 12 to 20 cubic meters (m^3) and decreased the price for this minimum level of water consumption from K1.3 per m^3 to K0.3 per m^3 (footnote 61).

4.2 Typical Risk Allocation for Public–Private Partnership Projects in the Water and Wastewater Sector

According to section 8.2.4 of the PPP Policy, an Outline Business Case prepared for the National Executive Council approval will include a public sector comparator analysis, which is an assessment of the net cost of the PPP project to the country, including the net cost to the government of retained risks to determine whether

[61] World Bank. 2017. *Water Supply and Sanitation Development Project*. Washington, DC. http://documents.worldbank.org/curated/en/591931485443649141/pdf/PAD1746-PNG-Water-Supply-PAD-01232017.pdf.

the PPP represents better value for money than public sector implementation. A risk management manual will be developed to guide this process during the Outline Business Case preparation and the Final Business Case development at the latter stage of procurement. Furthermore, section 8.14 of the PPP Policy states that a preliminary identification and notional allocation of risks will be a part of the concept note that is to be submitted to the PPP Center for review (footnote 1).

Generally the private sector assumes the completion and delivery risks while the public sector will assume approval and regulatory risks. The detailed risk allocation will be determined on a case-by-case basis through negotiation between the government and the private sector service providers (footnote 1).

4.3 Financing Details in the Water and Wastewater Sector

Parameter	1990–2017	1990–2018	1990–2019
PPP projects with foreign lending participation	UA	UA	UA
PPP projects that received export credit agency/international financing institution support	UA	UA	UA
Typical debt–equity ratio	UA	UA	UA
Time for financial close		UA	
Typical concession period		UA	
Typical financial internal rate of return		UA	

✓ = Yes, ✗ = No, NA = Not Applicable, UA = Unavailable.

5. Challenges in the Water and Wastewater Sector

No details are available.

INFORMATION AND COMMUNICATION TECHNOLOGY

Parameter	Value	Unit
Telephone subscribers	1.87	per 100 inhabitants
Cellular phone subscribers	47.62	per 100 inhabitants
Cellular network coverage	UA	% of population covered
Internet subscribers	11.21	per 100 inhabitants
Internet bandwidth per internet user	UA	kbps
Total number of projects with cumulative lending, grant, and technical assistance commitments in ICT sector	UA	number
Total amount of cumulative lending, grant, and technical assistance commitments in ICT sector	UA	$ million

✓ = Yes, ✗ = No, NA = Not Applicable, UA = Unavailable.

ICT = information and communication technology.

Sources: Trading Economics. Papua New Guinea—Mobile and Fixed Line Telephone Subscribers. https://tradingeconomics.com/papua-new-guinea/mobile-and-fixed-line-telephone-subscribers-wb-data.html; World Bank. Cell Phone Subscribers. https://data.worldbank.org/indicator/IT.CEL.SETS.P2?locations=PG-MM; World Bank. Internet Subscribers. https://data.worldbank.org/indicator/IT.NET.USER.ZS?locations=PG-MM.

The ICT sector in Papua New Guinea has seen significant progress in recent years, which has helped ensure expansion of coverage and offerings. An increase in sector investment has helped both local and international companies expand into rural areas, while telecommunication providers have also been able to bring more affordable and faster services to a greater share of the population.

However, isolated parts of this large and sparsely populated country are still having difficulties in achieving connectivity, and unaffordability, despite recent improvements, remains an issue for mobile phone and internet users.

1. Contracting Agencies in the ICT Sector

PNG's ICT sector is governed by an independent regulator, the National Information and Communications Technology Authority (NICTA), formed in 2010, with additional oversight by the Independent Consumer and Competition Commission (ICCC) to ensure fair competition in the telecommunication sector. NICTA is responsible for issuing telecommunication licenses in PNG. The main responsibilities of the authority are to regulate television and radio broadcasting and the internet; manage licensing, both for spectrum and operators; and encourage and promote development. NICTA has the ability to enter into legally binding contracts.

2. ICT Sector Laws and Regulations

The National Information and Communications Technology Act 2009 is the regulatory framework for the ICT sector.[62] This Act is formed to (i) regulate the information and communications technology industry and radio communications and spectrum, (ii) provide for the establishment of the National Information and Communications Technology Authority, and (iii) repeal the Telecommunications Act 1996 and the Radio Spectrum Act 1996 (Table 14).

Table 14: Key Agencies Regulating the ICT Sector in Papua New Guinea

Agency	Function
Ministry of Communication and Information Technology	• Act as the principal government institution in the ICT sector
National Information and Communications Technology Authority	• Enforce the National ICT Act and its regulatory principles • Provide advice to the Minister in formulating government policy in respect of any aspect of the National ICT Act or that otherwise promotes the objective of this Act • Exercise all licensing and regulatory functions in relation to the ICT industry as are contemplated by the National ICT Act • Oversee the performance of ICT licensees and their compliance with the National ICT Act and any mandatory instrument • Assist the ICCC in investigating complaints regarding market conduct for the purposes of the ICCC enforcing compliance with laws relating to market conduct in the ICT industry in Papua New Guinea • Develop and monitor a system for reviewing and responding to complaints by retail customers in relation to ICT services

continued on next page

62 Government of Papua New Guinea. *National Information and Communications Technology Act 2009.* https://www.nicta.gov.pg/legislative/acts/.

continued from previous page

Agency	Function
	• Consult, where appropriate, commercial, industrial, and consumer organizations about any matter relating to the ICT industry or the National ICT Act • Act as the duly appointed representative of the State at all international bodies or authorities which have the purpose of regulating or administering ICT services and radio communications • Develop and monitor procedures for ensuring the safety and quality of ICT services and radio communications • Make available to persons engaged in the ICT industry and other interested persons general information for their guidance with respect to the carrying out of the functions, or the exercise of the powers of NICTA under the National ICT Act • Conduct research in relation to matters affecting the interests of consumers of ICT services • Make available to the public general information in relation to matters affecting the interests of retail customers of ICT services • Perform such other functions as are assigned to or conferred on NICTA under the National ICT Act or any other law.

ICCC = Independent Consumer and Competition Commission, ICT = information and communication technology, NICTA = National Information and Communications Technology Authority.

Source: National Information and Communications Technology Authority. Legislative Acts. https://www.nicta.gov.pg/legislative/acts/.

2.1 Foreign Investment Restrictions in the ICT Sector

Parameter	2017	2018	2019
Maximum allowed foreign ownership of equity in greenfield projects	100%	100%	100%

2.2 Standard Contracts in the ICT Sector

Type of contract	Availability
PPP/concession agreement	×
Performance-based operation and maintenance contract	×
Engineering procurement and construction contract	×

✓ = Yes, × = No, NA = Not Applicable, UA = Unavailable.

3. ICT Sector Master Plan

The government has been targeting continued growth in the ICT sector. This has been emphasized in Vision 2050, PNG's overarching long-term blueprint for addressing infrastructure gaps and maintaining economic stability. The plan calls for the establishment of a technical vocational training institute and widespread implementation of ICT infrastructure.

The state has also launched the PNG Development Strategic Plan 2010–2030, which aims to increase mobile, internet, and television and radio penetration to 80%, 70%, and 100%, respectively. According to the plan, the government will focus on building PPPs with both national and international companies to build the rural satellite network and ensure international best practices are adopted in the sector.

In March 2018, the media reported that a taskforce, including the PNG Digital Commerce Association, was working with the government on a National ICT Roadmap to solidify policies for the rollout of more advanced technologies, providing businesses with a clear path forward. Launched in May 2018, the plan aims to develop six key areas: infrastructure, governance, services, skills, business environment, and safety.

Both short- and long-term measures are being taken to improve affordability of ICT services, a lack of which stems partly from low international internet bandwidth and limited high-speed domestic infrastructure, as well as the challenges associated with having a widely dispersed population.

No.	Project	Implementing Agency	Estimated Project Cost ($ million)	Estimated Project Cost (K million)	Status
1.	UA	UA	UA	UA	UA

✓ = Yes, × = No, NA = Not Applicable, UA = Unavailable.

3.1 Projects under Preparation and Procurement in the ICT Sector

Figure 41 presents the number of PPP projects that are under preparation and procurement in Papua New Guinea's ICT sector.

Figure 41: Public–Private Partnership ICT Projects under Preparation and Procurement

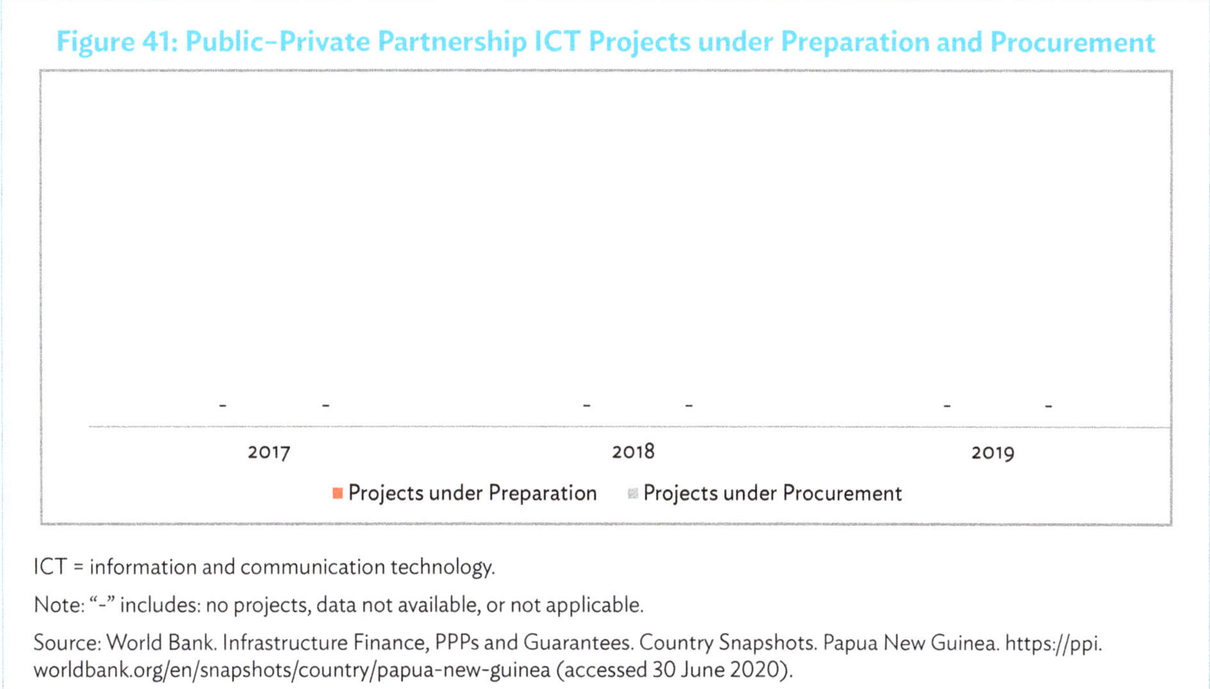

ICT = information and communication technology.

Note: "-" includes: no projects, data not available, or not applicable.

Source: World Bank. Infrastructure Finance, PPPs and Guarantees. Country Snapshots. Papua New Guinea. https://ppi.worldbank.org/en/snapshots/country/papua-new-guinea (accessed 30 June 2020).

4. Features of Past Public–Private Partnership Projects in the ICT Sector

Figure 42 shows the number of PPP projects procured through various modes including direct appointment, unsolicited bids, and competitive bids in Papua New Guinea's ICT sector.

Figure 42: Modes of Procurement for Public–Private Partnership ICT Projects

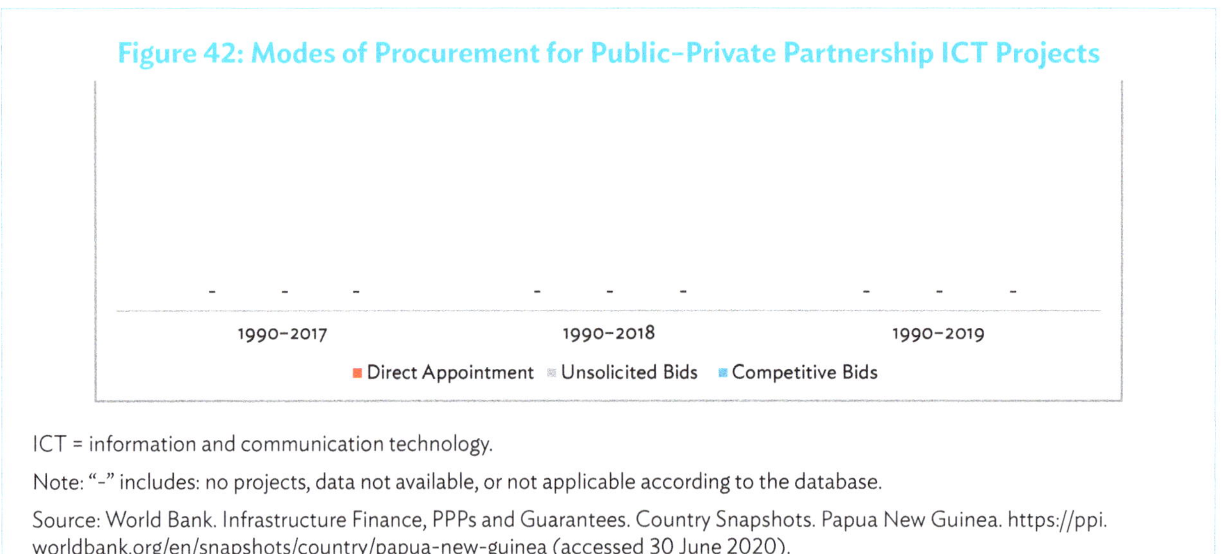

ICT = information and communication technology.

Note: "-" includes: no projects, data not available, or not applicable according to the database.

Source: World Bank. Infrastructure Finance, PPPs and Guarantees. Country Snapshots. Papua New Guinea. https://ppi.worldbank.org/en/snapshots/country/papua-new-guinea (accessed 30 June 2020).

Bemobile builds, operates, and ultimately owns the telecommunication network under a BOO contract. The Independent Consumer and Competition Commission (ICCC) granted the Bemobile a value-added services license for a period of 15 years. The project was also supported and partly financed by ADB. Other sponsors include Telikom PNG and General Enterprise Management Services (GEMS), a private equity fund based in Hong Kong, China.[63]

Figure 43 shows the number of PPP projects that have reached financial closure and the total value of those projects in Papua New Guinea's ICT sector.

Figure 43: Public–Private Partnership ICT Projects Reaching Financial Closure

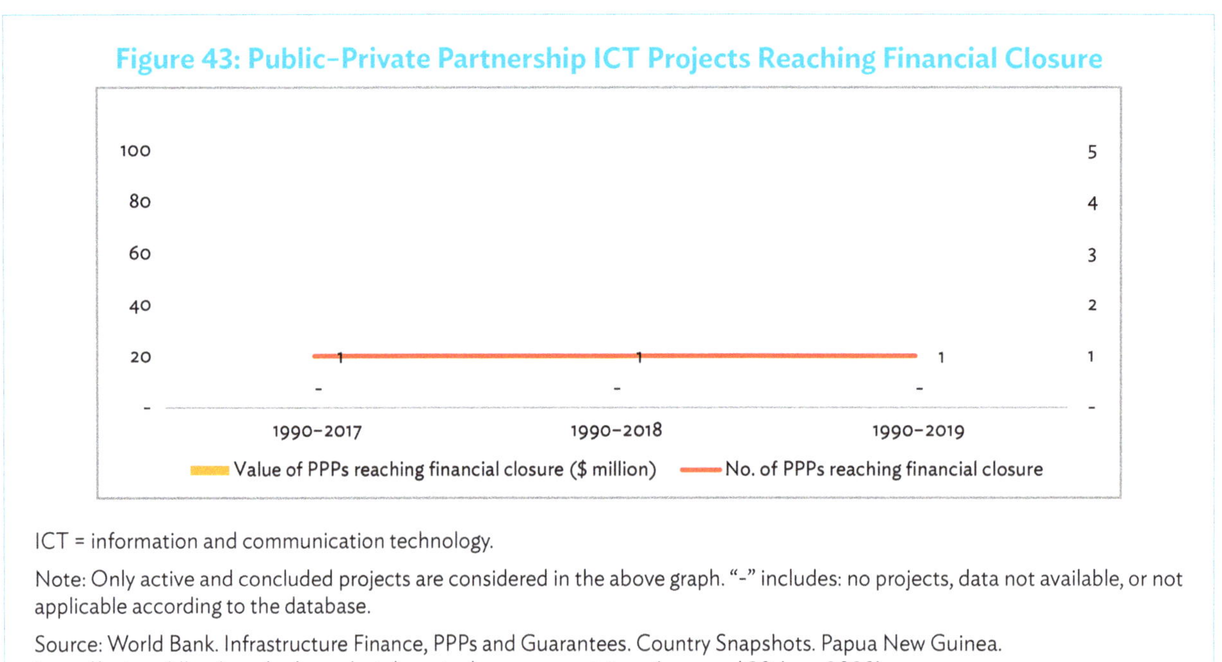

ICT = information and communication technology.

Note: Only active and concluded projects are considered in the above graph. "-" includes: no projects, data not available, or not applicable according to the database.

Source: World Bank. Infrastructure Finance, PPPs and Guarantees. Country Snapshots. Papua New Guinea. https://ppi.worldbank.org/en/snapshots/country/papua-new-guinea (accessed 30 June 2020).

[63] Universal Postal Union. 2018. *Guide to PPP for eServices in Postal Sector, Papua New Guinea.*

Figure 44 presents the number of PPP projects that have foreign sponsor participation in Papua New Guinea's ICT sector.

Figure 44: Public–Private Partnership ICT Projects with Foreign Sponsor Participation

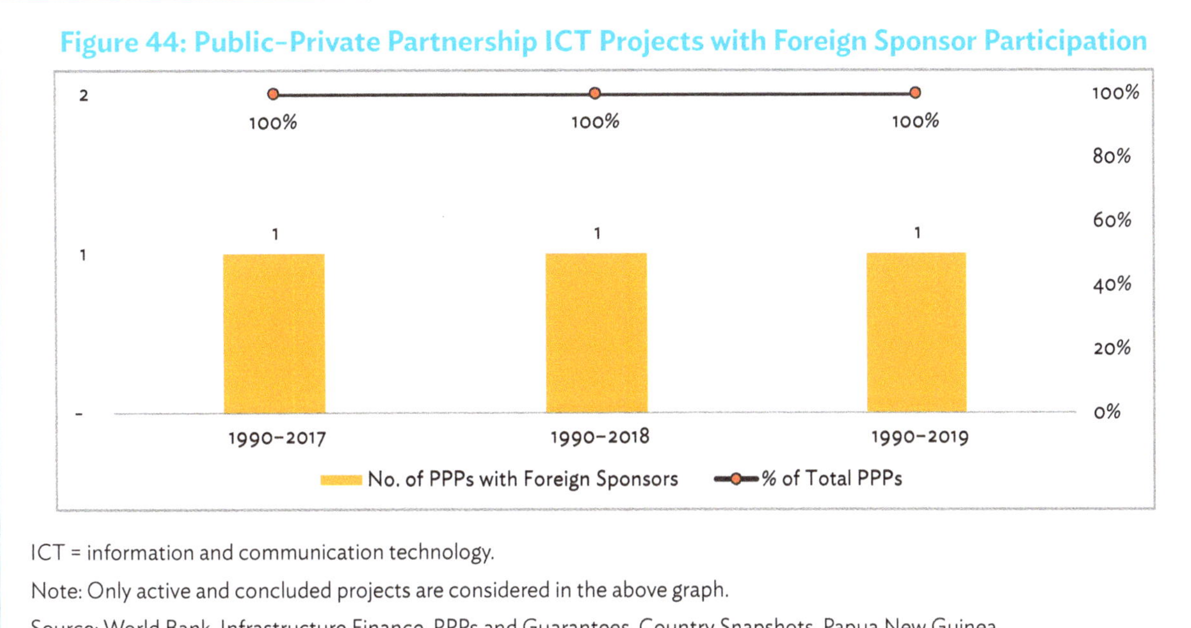

ICT = information and communication technology.

Note: Only active and concluded projects are considered in the above graph.

Source: World Bank. Infrastructure Finance, PPPs and Guarantees. Country Snapshots. Papua New Guinea. https://ppi.worldbank.org/en/snapshots/country/papua-new-guinea (accessed 30 June 2020).

Figure 45 shows the number of PPP projects that have received government support including viability gap funding (VGF) mechanism, government guarantees, and availability/performance payment in Papua New Guinea's ICT sector.

Figure 45: Government Support for Public–Private Partnership ICT Projects

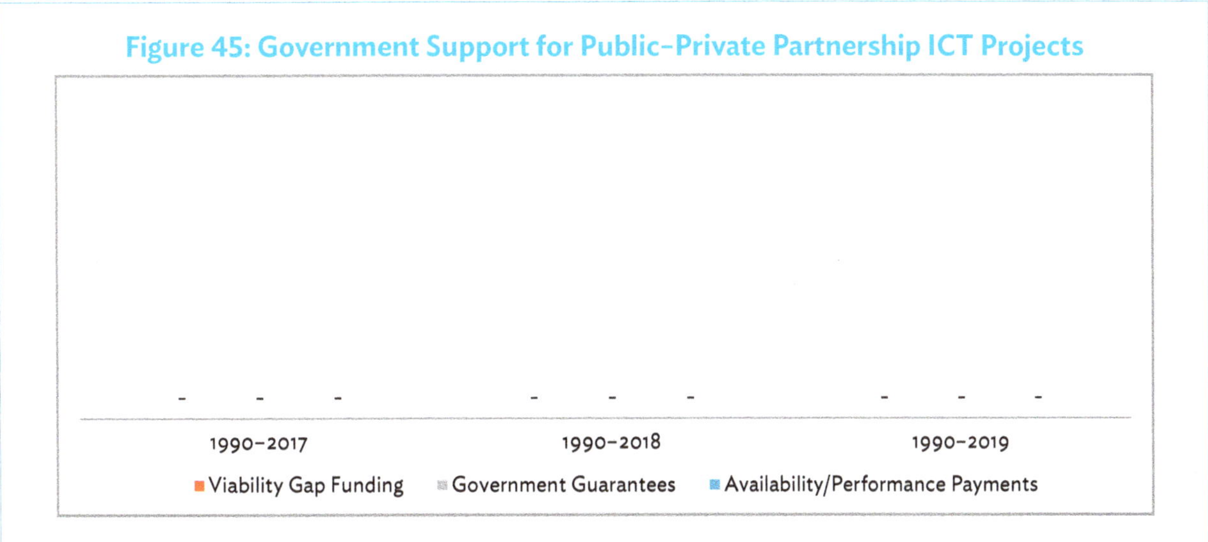

ICT = information and communication technology.

Note: "-" includes: no projects, data not available, or not applicable according to the database.

Source: World Bank. Infrastructure Finance, PPPs and Guarantees. Country Snapshots. Papua New Guinea. https://ppi.worldbank.org/en/snapshots/country/papua-new-guinea (accessed 30 June 2020).

Figure 46 presents the number of PPP projects that have received payment in the form of user charges and government pay (off-take) in Papua New Guinea's ICT sector.

Figure 46: Payment Mechanisms for Public–Private Partnership ICT Projects

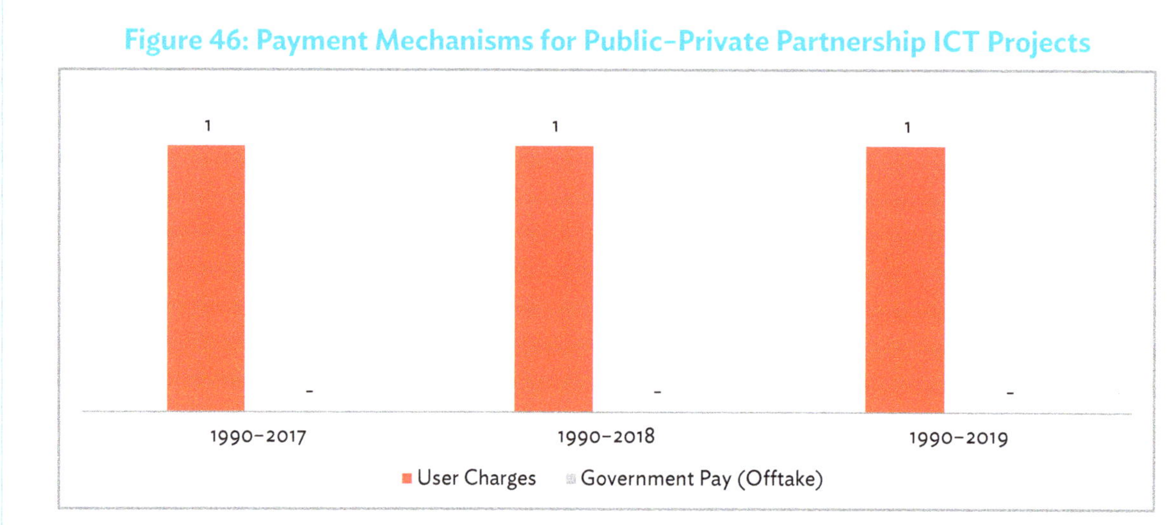

ICT = information and communication technology.

Note: Only active and concluded projects are considered in the above graph. "-" includes: no projects, data not available, or not applicable according to the database.

Source: World Bank. Infrastructure Finance, PPPs and Guarantees. Country Snapshots. Papua New Guinea. https://ppi.worldbank.org/en/snapshots/country/papua-new-guinea (accessed 30 June 2020).

4.1 Tariffs in the ICT Sector

NICTA may recommend to the Minister that a retail service supplied by an operator licensee should be subject to a retail service determination. An operator licensee that is subject to a retail service determination is required to comply with the terms of that retail service determination in relation to the supply of the retail service to retail customers. A retail service determination may regulate prices for the supply of the retail service, over its given term.[64]

4.2 Typical Risk Allocation for Public–Private Partnership Projects in the ICT Sector

No details are available.

4.3 Financing Details in the ICT Sector

Parameter	1990–2017	1990–2018	1990–2019
PPP projects with foreign lending participation	UA	UA	UA
PPP projects that received export credit agency/international financing institution support	UA	UA	UA
Typical debt–equity ratio	UA	UA	UA

continued on next page

64 National Information and Communications Technology Authority. Acts. https://www.nicta.gov.pg/legislative/acts/.

continued from previous page

Parameter	1990-2017	1990-2018	1990-2019
Time for financial close		UA	
Typical concession period		UA	
Typical financial internal rate of return		UA	

✓ = Yes, × = No, NA = Not Applicable, UA = Unavailable.

5. Challenges in the ICT Sector

No details are available.

SOCIAL INFRASTRUCTURE

Parameter	Value	Unit
Government expenditure on education	1.93	% of GDP
Education spending as % of government spending	10.70	%
Primary school gross enrollment	60.10	%
Adult literacy rate	62.40	%
Total number of projects with cumulative lending, grant, and technical assistance commitments in education sector	11.00	number
Total amount of cumulative lending, grant, and technical assistance commitments in education sector	63.29	$ million
Total health expenditure	4.30	% of GDP
Health spending per capita	61.46	$
Maternal mortality ratio (modelled estimates per 100,000 live births)	220.00	(per 100,000 live births)
Infant mortality rate	48.40	(below 1 year/per 1,000 live births)
Life expectancy at birth	62.30	(years)
Child malnutrition	18.10	(% below 5 years old)
Total number of projects with cumulative lending, grant, and technical assistance commitments in health sector	37	number
Total amount of cumulative lending, grant, and technical assistance commitments in health sector	423	$ million
Existing number of affordable housing units	UA	number
Affordable housing gap	UA	

✓ = Yes, × = No, NA = Not Applicable, UA = Unavailable.

Sources: World Bank. Papua New Guinea Government Expenditure on Education. https://data.worldbank.org/indicator/SE.XPD.TOTL.GD.ZS?locations=PG; The Global Economy. Education Spending, Percent of Government Spending—Country Rankings. https://www.theglobaleconomy.com/rankings/Education_spending_percent_of_government_spending/; Asian Development Bank. 2015. *Papua New Guinea, 2016–2020 — Country Partnership Strategy*. Manila. https://www.adb.org/sites/default/files/institutional-document/157927/cps-png-2016-2020.pdf ; The Economist Intelligence Unit. Papua New Guinea. https://infrascope.eiu.com/; The Global Economy. Health Spending per Capita—Country Rankings. https://www.theglobaleconomy.com/rankings/Health_spending_per_capita/; Asian Development Bank. Cumulative Lending, Grant, and Technical Assistance Commitments. https://data.adb.org/dataset/cumulative-lending-grant-and-technical-assistance-commitments.

1. Contracting Agencies in the Social Infrastructure Sector

The following institutions are responsible for implementing projects in the social infrastructure sector:

- Education sector
  - Ministry of Education
  - National Department of Education (NDoE)
- Healthcare sector
  - Ministry of Health
  - National Department of Health
- Housing sector
  - National Housing Corporation

2. Social Infrastructure Sector Laws and Regulations

2.1 Education Sector Regulations

Education Act 1983 is the regulatory framework for the education sector in Papua New Guinea.[65] Under this Act (consolidated in 1995, p. 9), administration of the national education system is vested in the following authorities (see also Table 15):

- the Minister for Education,
- the National Education Board (NEB),
- the departmental head (Secretary for Education),
- the Teaching Service Commission (TSC),
- provincial governments,
- education boards,
- local-level governments (LLGs),
- education agencies, and
- the governing bodies of schools (footnote 65).

[65] Government of Papua New Guinea. 1983. *Education Act 1983*. Port Moresby. https://www.education.gov.pg/TISER/documents/legislation/ea1983104.pdf.

Table 15: Key Agencies Regulating the Education Sector in Papua New Guinea

Agency	Function
Ministry for Education	• The Minister for Education acts as the political head responsible for the overall management of education
National Department of Education	• Determines national policies and standards and supports their implementation by the provinces, with services such as planning, research, training, and staff development • Responsible for teacher education, inspection, and registration; the national curriculum; curriculum materials; and examinations. It is also responsible for national institutions, namely teachers' colleges, technical colleges, national high schools, special education resource centers, flexible open and distance education centers, and schools in the National Capital District
Office of Libraries and Archives	• Coordinates the planning and development of libraries and archives throughout the country • Preserves all documents on Papua New Guinea's life and society in the national collection for all Papua New Guineans to enjoy and learn from
Teaching Service Commission	• Acts as the agent of the state for the employment of teachers • Oversees teachers' terms and conditions of service, salaries, allowances, and welfare. It also supports the rights of teachers
The National Education Board	• Oversees the development and functioning of the education system and the implementation of the National Education Plan (NEP) • Advises the minister, in consultation with provincial governments, the Teaching Service Commission, and education boards and agencies
Departmental head	• The head of the Department of Education is the Secretary for Education. The Secretary also chairs the National Education Board
Provincial governments	• Responsible for establishing, building and maintaining schools; deploying teachers; and employing provincial and district education officers
Education boards	• The Provincial Education Board is the highest education decision-making body in a province
Local-level governments	• Responsible for funding and maintenance of elementary and primary schools and helping districts develop district education plans consistent with provincial education plans
Education agencies	• Education agencies are key partners in the delivery of education services in Papua New Guinea
Governing boards of member schools	• Governing boards are Boards of Management in elementary and primary schools and Boards of Governors in secondary and other post-primary schools. They are the schools' highest decision-making bodies and have financial and management powers

Source: United Nations Educational, Scientific and Cultural Organization. 2016. *Papua New Guinea National Education Plan 2015–2019*. Papua New Guinea. https://planipolis.iiep.unesco.org/sites/planipolis/files/ressources/papua_new_guinea_nep_2015-2019_doe.pdf.

2.2 Healthcare Sector Regulations

The Ministry of Health has the portfolio responsibility for health as determined by the Prime Minister. The Ministry executes government health policy and is assisted by the National Department of Health (NDoH) to discharge that responsibility.[66]

[66] J. Grundy et al. 2019. *Independent State of Papua New Guinea Health System Review*. 9 (1). New Delhi: World Health Organization, Regional Office for South-East Asia. https://apps.who.int/iris/bitstream/handle/10665/280088/9789290226741-eng.pdf?sequence=5&isAllowed=y.

The NDoH has statutory responsibility to oversee the establishment, maintenance, and development of the healthcare system in Papua New Guinea. It also sets the policy and standards for improving the health of the population. It provides technical advice and support for operating health facilities and delivering health services, and maintains the national health information system. The NDoH also oversees the management of public hospitals in accordance with the Public Hospitals Act of 1994 and the rollout of the recent legislative changes in the Provincial Health Authorities Act, 2007.[67]

The main legislations governing the regulation and governance of third parties, providers, human resource, pharmaceuticals, and equipment are as follows:

- Medical Registration Act, 1980;
- Medical Registration By-laws and Nursing Registration By-laws, 1984;
- Public Services (Management) Act, 1995;
- National Health Administration Act of 1997; and the
- Provincial Health Authorities Act, 2007 (footnote 67).

Table 16 describes these Acts' role in governance and regulation and their influence. The related policies and guidelines developed in the specific areas of focus (e.g., facilities, human resource, financing) appear in other parts of the *Independent State of Papua New Guinea Health System Review* (footnote 67).

Table 16: Key Agencies Regulating the Health Sector in Papua New Guinea

Agency	Function
National Government	• Oversee the healthcare system • Coordinate and provide technical advice and support to lower levels of the government • Oversee management of public hospitals
National Health Board	• Endorse the National Health Plan and recommend its adoption to the National Executive Council • Approve standards and monitor progress against the National Health Plan • May be requested or directed to carry out inquiries
National Department of Health	• Provide assistance and support to the National Health Board in discharging its functions • Develop standards and monitor and ensure compliance to standards, and provide technical assistance to the provinces in implementing the National Health Plan and in meeting relevant standards • Maintain the National Health Service Standards

Source: J. Grundy et al. 2019. *Independent State of Papua New Guinea Health System Review*. 9 (1). New Delhi: World Health Organization, Regional Office for South-East Asia. https://apps.who.int/iris/bitstream/handle/10665/280088/9789290226741-eng.pdf?sequence=5&isAllowed=y.

2.3 Social Housing Sector Regulations

The National Housing Corporation Act 1990 is the regulatory framework for the housing sector in Papua New Guinea. The National Housing Corporation (NHC) is established under this Act as the commercial statutory authority, with the following functions:[68]

[67] Asia Pacific Observatory on Health System and Policies. 2019. *Independent State of Papua New Guinea Health System Review*. Papua New Guinea. https://apps.who.int/iris/bitstream/handle/10665/280088/9789290226741-eng.pdf?sequence=5&isAllowed=y.

[68] International Labour Organization. Papua New Guinea. https://www.ilo.org/dyn/natlex/natlex4.detail?p_lang=en&p_isn=88036.

- Act as an agent or an instrumentality of the State in matters relating to residential development for its employees on such terms and conditions as to payment of commission, or otherwise, as are agreed on
- Perform and do such other acts, matters, or things in relation to such housing on behalf of a body referred to in paragraph (a) of National Housing Corporation Act 1990, on such terms and conditions as are agreed on

2.4 Foreign Investment Restrictions in the Social Infrastructure Sector

Parameter	2017	2018	2019
Maximum allowed foreign ownership of equity in greenfield projects	UA	UA	UA
• Healthcare infrastructure	UA	UA	UA
• Healthcare services	UA	UA	UA
• Education infrastructure	UA	UA	UA
• Education services	UA	UA	UA

✓ = Yes, × = No, NA = Not Applicable, UA = Unavailable.

2.5 Standard Contracts in the Social Infrastructure Sector

Parameter	2017	2018	2019
What standardized contracts are available and used in the market?			
• PPP/concession agreement?	UA	UA	UA
• Performance-based operation and maintenance contract?	UA	UA	UA
• Engineering procurement and construction contract?	UA	UA	UA

✓ = Yes, × = No, NA = Not Applicable, UA = Unavailable.

3. Social Infrastructure Sector Master Plan

Education Sector

The Department of Education has prepared the National Education Plan (NEP) 2015–2019.[69] An important part of this plan is the monitoring and evaluation system that will be conducted in parallel with the plan's strategies. Effective monitoring and evaluation will inform the government's decisions, specifically on what works and what does not, and provide the opportunity to make changes in the NEP (footnote 45).

The NEP 2015–2019 builds on the NEP 2005–2014 and the Education Sector Strategic Plan 2010–2030,[70] while complementing the Universal Basic Education (UBE) Plan 2010–2019.[71] The Education Sector Strategic Plan 2010–2030 covers the following:

[69] Government of Papua New Guinea, Department of Education. 2016. *National Education Plan 2015–2019*. Port Moresby. https://planipolis.iiep.unesco.org/sites/planipolis/files/ressources/papua_new_guinea_nep_2015-2019_doe.pdf.

[70] Government of Papua New Guinea, Department of Education. 2012. *Education Sector Strategic Plan 2011–2030*. Port Moresby. http://wbgfiles.worldbank.org/documents/hdn/ed/saber/supporting_doc/EAP/Papua%20New%20Guinea/SAA/DoE_2012_Education_Sector_Strategic_Plan_2011_-_2030.pdf.

[71] Government of Papua New Guinea, National Executive Council and Department of Education. 2009. *Universal Basic Education Plan 2010–2019*. Port Moresby. https://planipolis.iiep.unesco.org/sites/planipolis/files/ressources/papua_new_guinea_ube_2010-2019.pdf.

- **Access to education.** All children complete 9 years of basic education and have the opportunity for education or training beyond the primary and secondary education.
- **Teachers and teacher education.** All teachers are well-trained and resourced and are accepted by the community as professionals.
- **Curriculum.** All curricula are sensitive to local needs and students' aspirations.
- **System management and planning.** All institutions are managed effectively and transparently, and are accountable to their local communities.
- **Technical and vocational education and training.** A national system of public and private institutions offers short- and full-time skills development courses, leading to diploma and technical qualifications.

The NEP 2015–2019 has six focus areas, namely, access and equity, teachers and teaching, learning, alternate pathways, local management, and system strengthening, which together will contribute toward achieving the ultimate goal of quality learning for all.

Healthcare Sector

The National Health Plan 2011–2020 places an emphasis on the PNG healthcare system, focusing on providing basic care for the country's poor and rural population. The plan aligns with the PNG Development Strategic Plan 2010–2030, as well as the nation's Vision 2050 goals—one of which is to be among the top 50 countries in the United Nations Development Programme's (UNDP) human development index by 2050. PNG also measures its progress against the UN Sustainable Development Goals, previously UN Millennium Development Goals.[72]

Complementing the National Health Plan, the National Health Service Standards 2011 outlines a seven-level model of health service delivery. For the first time, the minimum standards for health facility infrastructure and staffing levels were defined, standard equipment lists for each level of service delivery compiled, and an accreditation system for hospitals and health centers implemented. Recognizing that improvements in health care service delivery are required at all levels, the plan targets better integration between hospitals and rural health services such as community health posts. It also calls for the construction of new hospitals, including at the district level, as well as the need for regional specialists and national referral mechanisms.[73]

The National Health Plan's primary objective is to provide universal health coverage and equal access for the country's rural population and the urban poor. At the national level, the National Department of Health formulates and administers health policy, but the management of the National Health Plan is devolved to the provincial, district, and local levels of government under a system of decentralization. The central government administers the national referral hospital, Port Moresby General Hospital, along with specialist, regional, and provincial public hospitals. Health services can be accessed at public hospitals and clinics, as well as at church-run health centers, which supply about half of all rural health services, and at aid posts staffed by community health workers and run by local governments and NGOs.

The National Health Plan also emphasizes the importance of PPPs. It aims to implement the National Public–Private Partnerships Policy and introduce innovative and cost-effective options for delivering health services. The Plan's strategies involve establishing PPPs with relevant major mining and agriculture ventures and setting up of health sector monitoring and coordination mechanisms for PPPs.

---

72 Government of Papua New Guinea, Ministry of Health. Acts and Policies. https://www.health.gov.pg/subindex.php?acts=1.

73 Government of Papua New Guinea. 2011. *National Health Service Standards for Papua New Guinea 2011–2020*. Port Moresby. https://hwfsmspng.net/publications/NHSS_PNG_2011-2020_Vol1&2/national_health_service_standards_for_png_2011-2020_Vol1.pdf.

Social Housing Sector

The NHC has implemented a flagship build–sell–share, which aims to profitably develop low-cost housing. Under the scheme, private developers will build homes on NHC-registered land, which will then be sold at reduced and affordable prices. The NHC plans to subsidize the bulk of the cost of developing land and civil works, making homes affordable for the average citizen and offering a more promising forecast for mid-tier and affordable housing growth.[74]

No.	Project	Implementing Agency	Estimated Project Cost		Status
			$ million	(K million)	
1.	UA	UA	UA	UA	UA

✓ = Yes, × = No, NA = Not Applicable, UA = Unavailable.

3.1 Projects under Preparation and Procurement in the Social Infrastructure Sector

Figure 47 shows the number of PPP projects that are under preparation and procurement in Papua New Guinea's social infrastructure sector.

Figure 47: Public–Private Partnership Social Infrastructure Projects under Preparation and Procurement

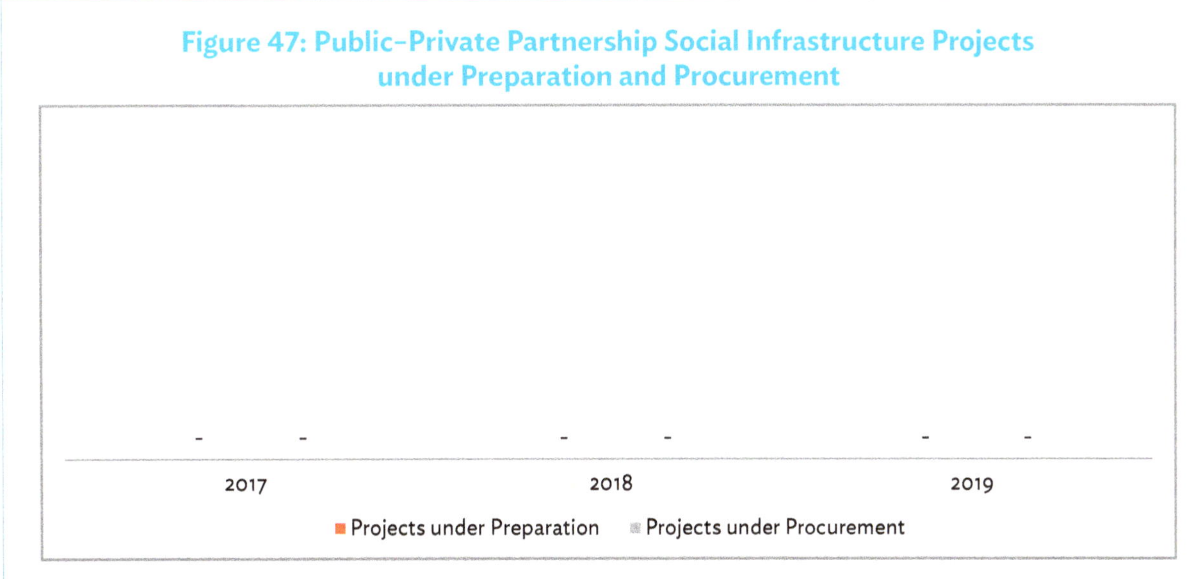

Note: "-" includes: no projects, data not available, or not applicable.

Source: World Bank. Infrastructure Finance, PPPs and Guarantees. Country Snapshots. Papua New Guinea. https://ppi.worldbank.org/en/snapshots/country/papua-new-guinea (accessed 30 June 2020).

[74] The National Research Institute. 2018. *Potential Public–Private Partnership Strategy for Promoting Effective Housing Delivery in Papua New Guinea.* Discussion Paper No.165. Port Moresby. November. https://pngnri.org/images/Publications/DP165.pdf.

4. Features of Past Public–Private Partnership Projects in the Social Infrastructure Sector

Figure 48 presents the number of PPP projects procured through various modes including direct appointment, unsolicited bids, and competitive bids in Papua New Guinea's social infrastructure sector.

Figure 48: Modes of Procurement for Public–Private Partnership Social Infrastructure Projects

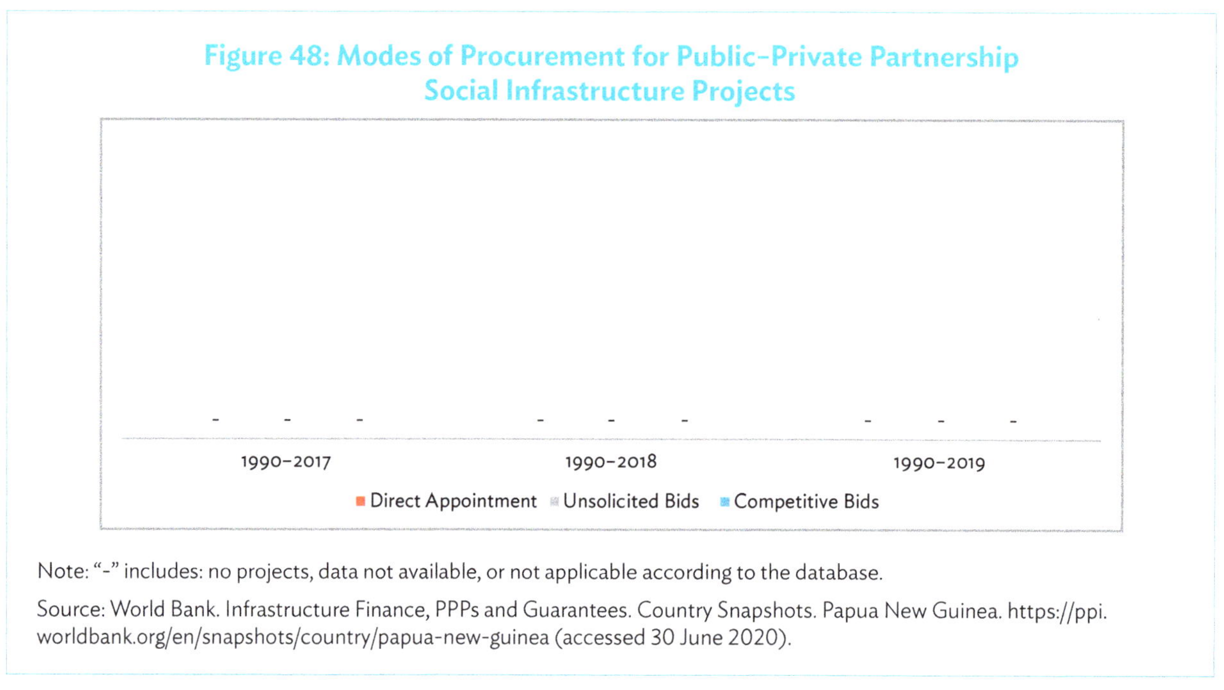

Note: "-" includes: no projects, data not available, or not applicable according to the database.

Source: World Bank. Infrastructure Finance, PPPs and Guarantees. Country Snapshots. Papua New Guinea. https://ppi.worldbank.org/en/snapshots/country/papua-new-guinea (accessed 30 June 2020).

Figure 49 provides the number of PPP projects that have reached financial closure and the total value of those projects in Papua New Guinea's social infrastructure sector.

Figure 49: Public–Private Partnership Social Infrastructure Projects Reaching Financial Closure

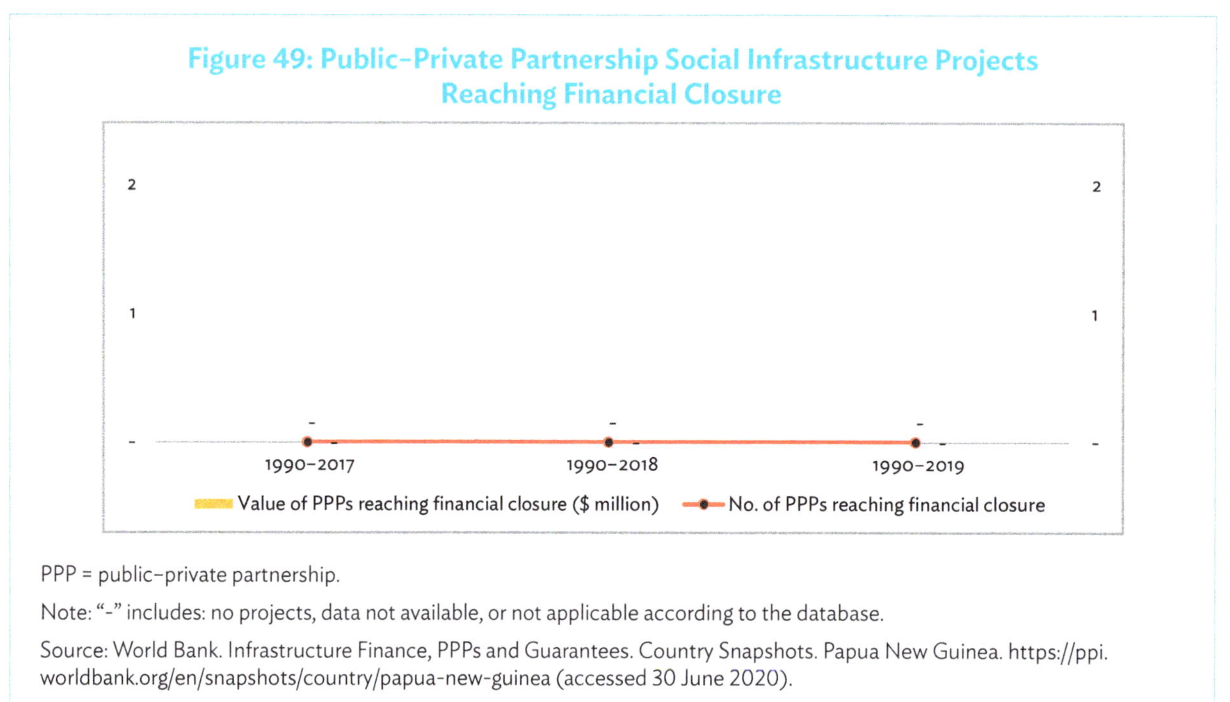

PPP = public–private partnership.

Note: "-" includes: no projects, data not available, or not applicable according to the database.

Source: World Bank. Infrastructure Finance, PPPs and Guarantees. Country Snapshots. Papua New Guinea. https://ppi.worldbank.org/en/snapshots/country/papua-new-guinea (accessed 30 June 2020).

Figure 50 shows the number of PPP projects that have foreign sponsor participation in Papua New Guinea's social infrastructure sector.

Figure 50: Public–Private Partnership Social Infrastructure Projects with Foreign Sponsor Participation

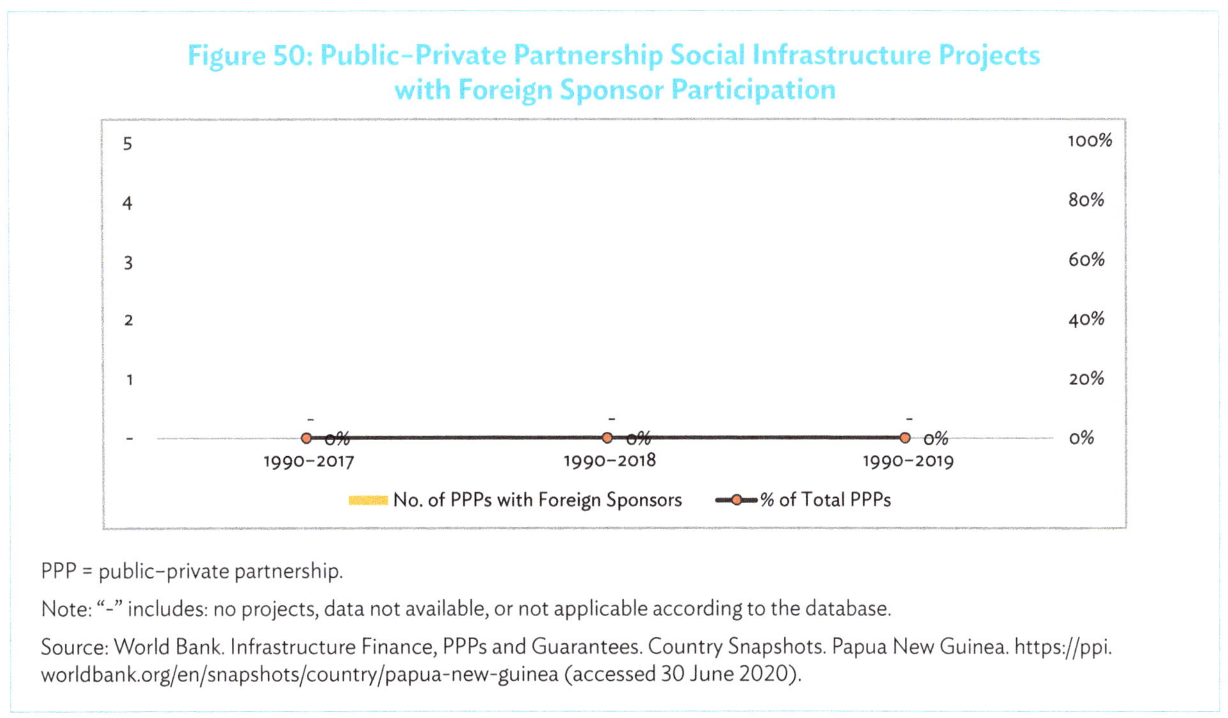

PPP = public–private partnership.

Note: "-" includes: no projects, data not available, or not applicable according to the database.

Source: World Bank. Infrastructure Finance, PPPs and Guarantees. Country Snapshots. Papua New Guinea. https://ppi.worldbank.org/en/snapshots/country/papua-new-guinea (accessed 30 June 2020).

Figure 51 presents the number of PPP projects that have received government support including Viability Gap Funding (VGF) mechanism, government guarantees, and availability/performance payment in Papua New Guinea's social infrastructure sector.

Figure 51: Government Support to Public–Private Partnership Social Infrastructure Projects

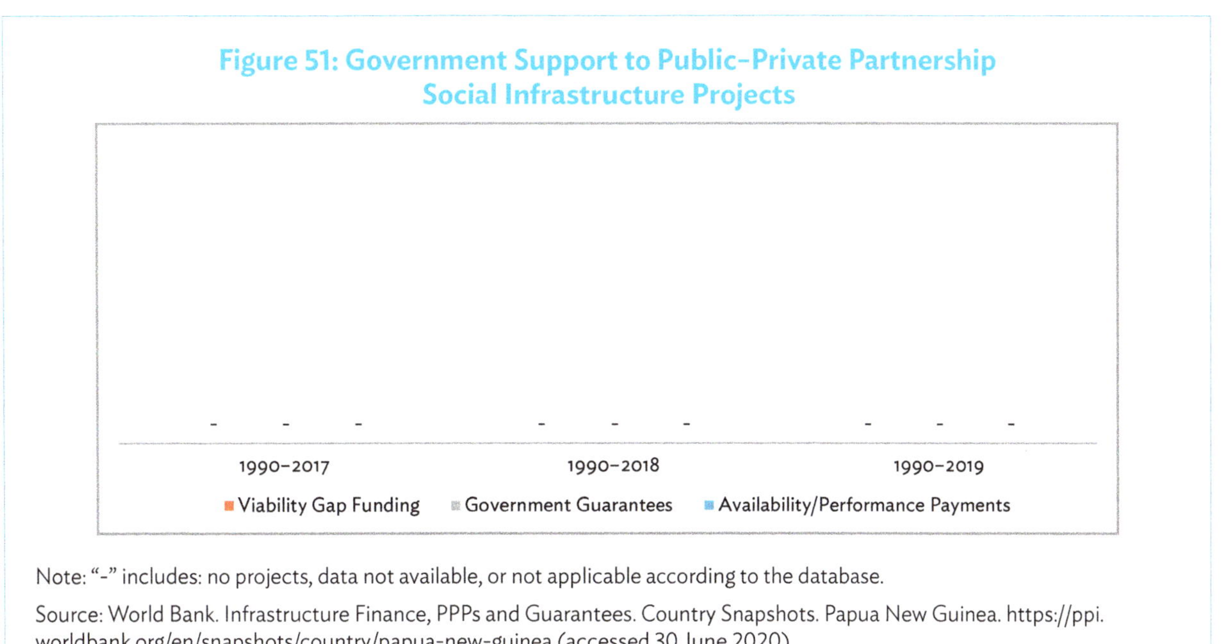

Note: "-" includes: no projects, data not available, or not applicable according to the database.

Source: World Bank. Infrastructure Finance, PPPs and Guarantees. Country Snapshots. Papua New Guinea. https://ppi.worldbank.org/en/snapshots/country/papua-new-guinea (accessed 30 June 2020).

Figure 52 shows the number of PPP projects that have received payment in the form of user charges and government pay (off-take) in Papua New Guinea's social infrastructure sector.

Figure 52: Payment Mechanisms for Public–Private Partnership Social Infrastructure Projects

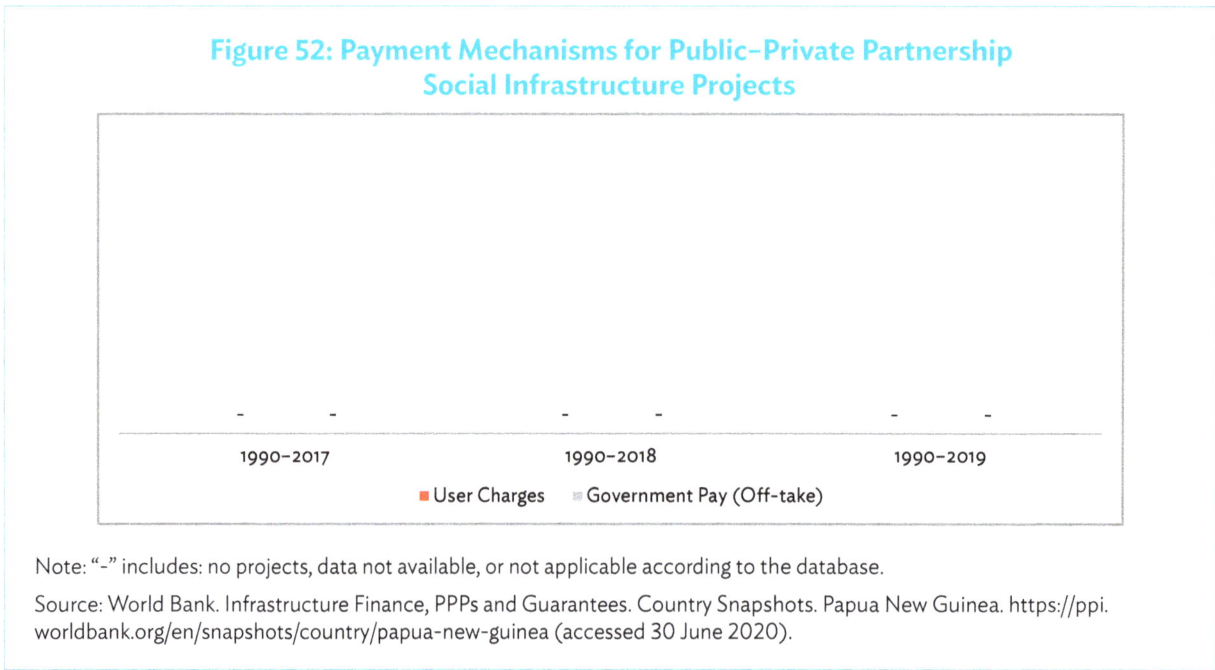

Note: "-" includes: no projects, data not available, or not applicable according to the database.

Source: World Bank. Infrastructure Finance, PPPs and Guarantees. Country Snapshots. Papua New Guinea. https://ppi.worldbank.org/en/snapshots/country/papua-new-guinea (accessed 30 June 2020).

4.1 Tariffs in the Social Infrastructure Sector

No information on the tariffs for social infrastructure projects is available.

4.2 Typical Risk Allocation for Public–Private Partnership Projects in the Social Infrastructure Sector

No details are available.

4.3 Financing Details in the Social Infrastructure Sector

Parameter	1990–2017	1990–2018	1990–2019
PPP projects with foreign lending participation	UA	UA	UA
PPP projects that received export credit agency/international financing institution support	UA	UA	UA
Typical debt-equity ratio	UA	UA	UA
Time for financial close		UA	
Typical concession period		UA	
Typical financial internal rate of return		UA	

✓ = Yes, × = No, NA = Not Applicable, UA = Unavailable.

5. Challenges in the Social Infrastructure Sector

No details are available.

IV. Local Government Public–Private Partnership Landscape

Parameter	Value	Unit
Number of Subnational Governments (SNGs)		
- Municipal level	UA	number
- Intermediate level	UA	number
- Regional or state level	UA	number
Total number of SNGs	UA	number
SNG Expenditure Profile		
Total SNG Expenditure as % of GDP	UA	%
- SNG Current Expenditure as % of GDP	UA	%
- SNG Staff Expenditure as % of GDP	UA	%
- SNG Investment as % of GDP	UA	%
Total SNG Expenditure as % of the Total General Government (% of Total Public Expenditure)	UA	%
- SNG Current Expenditure as a % of Total Current Expenditure of the General Government	UA	%
- SNG Staff Expenditure as a % of Total Staff Expenditure of the General Government	UA	%
- SNG Investment as a % of Total Investment of the General Government	UA	%
Current Expenditure of SNG as a % of Total SNG Expenditure	UA	%
Staff Expenditure of SNG as a % of Total SNG Expenditure	UA	%
Investments of SNG as a % of Total SNG Expenditure	UA	%
SNG Expenditure by Function		
- General public services	UA	%
- Defense	UA	%
- Security and public order	UA	%
- Economic affairs	UA	%
- Environmental protection	UA	%
- Housing and community amenities	UA	%
- Health	UA	%
- Recreation, culture, and religion	UA	%
- Education	UA	%
- Social protection	UA	%

continued on next page

continued from previous page

Parameter	Value	Unit
SNG Revenue Profile		
Total SNG Revenue as a % of GDP	UA	%
- *SNG Tax Revenue as a % of GDP*	UA	%
- *SNG Grants and Subsidies as a % of GDP*	UA	%
- *SNG Other Revenues as a % of GDP*	UA	%
Total SNG Revenue as % of Total General Government Revenue	UA	%
- *SNG Tax Revenue as a % of Total General Government Tax Revenue*	UA	%
- *SNG Grants and Subsidies as a % of Total General Government Grants and Subsidies*	UA	%
- *SNG Other Revenues as a % of Total Other Revenues*	UA	%
SNG Tax Revenue as a % of Total SNG Revenue	UA	%
SNG Grants and Subsidies as a % of Total SNG Revenue	UA	%
SNG Other Revenues as a % of Total SNG Revenue	UA	%
SNG Debt Profile		
Outstanding SNG Debt as % of GDP	UA	%
Outstanding SNG Debt as % of Total Outstanding Debt of General Government	UA	%
Parameters for transfers to the Subnational Governments from the National Government		
Score on transfers to Subnational Governments	B	
- *Score on system for allocating transfers*	B	
- *Score on timeliness of information on transfers*	A	
- *Score on extent of collection and reporting of consolidated fiscal data for general government*	D	
Value of Central Government transfers to Subnational Governments	UA	% of the GDP
Value of actual budgetary allocation to Subnational Governments from National Government	UA	% of total expenditure
Value of deviation of actual against the budgeted transfers to Subnational Governments	UA	% of budgeted transfers

✓ = Yes, × = No, NA = Not Applicable, UA = Unavailable.

GDP = gross domestic product, SNG = subnational government.

Source: UCLG. 2016. Subnational Governments around the World—Structure and Finance. https://www.uclg.org/sites/default/files/global_observatory_of_local_finance-part_iii.pdf; International Monetary Fund. 2015. *Papua New Guinea Public Expenditure and Financial Accountability Assessment.* Washington, DC. https://www.pefa.org/sites/pefa/files/assessments/reports/PNG-Aug15-PFMPR-Testing-version-Public-with-PEFA-Check.PDF.

Local Governance System in Papua New Guinea

Papua New Guinea is a federal constitutional monarchy. National, provincial, and local are the three levels of government in Papua New Guinea. It consists of 20 provinces, the national capital area of Port Moresby, the autonomous region of Bougainville, and 89 districts.

There are a total of 318 local governments also known as local-level governments (LLGs) consisting of 31 urban LLGs and 265 rural LLGs. The composition or the functions and responsibilities of the urban LLGs and rural LLGs have a slight difference. The main governing legislation is the Organic Law on Provincial Governments and Local-Level Governments 1995 and the Local-Level Governments Administration Act 1997.[75]

The statutory responsibility for all matters relating to local government lies with the Department of Provincial and Local Government Affairs (DPLGA) within the Ministry of Inter-Government Relations. Local governments may levy a variety of local taxes and charges. Government transfers are available to cover staff salaries as well as specific development projects.[76]

In 2016, the local government expenditure reached approximately 1.6% of the total government expenditure. LLGs are responsible for water supply, and are jointly responsible for provinces in matters of roads, waste disposal, health and environmental protection, and economic promotion and tourism (footnote 76).

Infrastructure Development Plan of Local Governments

In each province, LLGs compile their plans and budgets for submission to a district development authority. The provincial governments, working with LLGs, are primarily responsible for the implementation and oversight of the resulting 5 years development plan (footnote 76). Each LLG creates their own plan using the plan of their respective wards, incorporating it into the district plan. The district's key role is to integrate the "top-down" planning of the province and country with the "bottom-up" planning of the LLGs.[77]

Sectors in Which Local Governments Can Implement Public–Private Partnerships

The national government provides most of the public services with support from the provinces and LLGs. Local governments are responsible for the road and parks development, collection and disposal of refuse, health and environmental protection, economic promotion and tourism, and water supply. LLGs are empowered to enter into public–private partnerships and church partnerships (footnote 76).

Government Contracting Agency (GCA)	Preparation Agency	Project Title	Estimated Project Cost		Estimated Concession Period	Status
			($)	(K)		
UA	UA	UA	UA	UA	UA	UA

✓ = Yes, × = No, UA = Unavailable, NA = Not Applicable.

Revenues for Local Governments

Most LLGs are dependent on national government for funding their recurrent and development budgets. Only a few urban LLGs collect fees and rates. Hence, it is difficult to provide an accurate report on income and expenditure (footnote 75).

75 Government of Papua New Guinea. 1998. *Organic Law on Provincial Governments and Local-level Governments*. Port Moresby. https://www.ilo.org/dyn/natlex/docs/ELECTRONIC/88035/100550/F518409/PNG88035.pdf; Government of Papua New Guinea. 1997. *Local-level Administration Act 1997*. Port Moresby. http://www.paclii.org/pg/legis/consol_act/lgaa1997403/#:~:text=Local%2Dlevel%20Governments%20Administration%20Act%201997%2C,Governments%20and%20for%20their%20administration.

76 Commonwealth Local Government Forum. 2019. *The Local Government System in Papua New Guinea*. http://www.clgf.org.uk/default/assets/File/Country_profiles/Papua_New_Guinea.pdf.

77 United Nations Development Programme. 2016. *Community Development in Papua New Guinea*. https://www.pg.undp.org/content/dam/papua_new_guinea/docs/MDG/MDG%20high%20res/019UNDP%20CDM_DIGITAL%20(3).pdf.

Local governments may levy:

- taxes, fees, and charges for community services;
- public entertainment taxes;
- general trading license fees;
- domestic animal license fees;
- billboard fees;
- fees for small-scale logging; and
- other charges, fees, and fines (footnote 76).

The DPLGA supervises locally raised taxes through budget approval and reporting.

The standard grants available for local governments include

- administration support grant (unconditional),
- staffing grant,
- development grants, and
- town and urban services grants (footnote 76).

LLGs are given a direct allocation of K10,000 annually, made to each of the 6,186 council wards. They are also given K500,000 annually for service improvements (footnote 76).

As legitimate governments, LLGs can apply for loans to assist in delivering services. However, commercial banks hesitate to lend to them due to the lack of steady income flows to repay the loans. Some well-established business arms of LLGs do take out commercial loans (footnote 76).

Borrowings by Local Governments

Consolidated Loans and Advances from Commercial Banks ($ million):

	2011	2012	2013	2014	2015	2016	2017
Agriculture	UA	UA	UA	UA	UA	UA	UA
Industry	UA	UA	UA	UA	UA	UA	UA
Services	UA	UA	UA	UA	UA	UA	UA
Finance	UA	UA	UA	UA	UA	UA	UA
Total	UA	UA	UA	UA	UA	UA	UA

✓ = Yes, × = No, NA = Not Applicable, UA = Unavailable.

	2015	2016	2017	2018	2019 (up to May 2019)
Total regional loans realization (K)	UA	UA	UA	UA	UA
Total regional loans realization ($ billion)	UA	UA	UA	UA	UA
Regions (number)	UA	UA	UA	UA	UA
Utilization	UA	UA	UA	UA	UA

✓ = Yes, × = No, UA = Unavailable, NA = Not Applicable.

Budgetary Allocation to Local Governments

The Public Expenditure and Financial Accountability (PEFA) framework (2015) gave Papua New Guinea an overall rating of B (on a four-point rating scale A [best] to D [worst]) for the transfers to the subnational governments from the national government.[78]

In 2016, the local government expenditure reached approximately 1.6% of the total government expenditure (footnote 51).

The function grants have dropped by 2% between 2017 and 2018—a decrease of approximately $5.12 million (K18 million as of June 2020) from $163.29 million (K565 million as of June 2020) in 2017 to $158.17 million (K547.3 million as of June 2020) in 2018. The Reform on Intergovernmental Financing Arrangements (RIGFA) methodology allows for an inbuilt stability in the system by providing provinces and local-level governments with the ability to effectively plan for service delivery. The current declining economic activity, including goods and services tax, is likely to see a fall in function grants. The National Economic and Fiscal Commission (NEFC) is currently undertaking a modelling exercise to determine the overall impact of declining revenue on grant allocations in the near future.[79]

According to Budget 2020, approximately $1,066.24 million (K3,689.4 million as of June 2020) from the total expenditure is allocated to the provinces.[80] In 2017, this amount was approximately $918.56 million (K3,178.4 million as of June 2020), which increased to $1,029.11 million (K3,560.9 million as of June 2020) in 2018.[81]

Credit Rating of Local Governments

Papua New Guinea does not have a domestic credit rating agency and the local governments are not being rated.

Case Study

No details are available.

---

78 International Monetary Fund. 2015. *Public Expenditure and Financial Accountability Assessment*. Washington, DC. https://www.pefa.org/sites/pefa/files/assessments/reports/PNG-Aug15-PFMPR-Testing-version-Public-with-PEFA-Check.PDF.

79 National Economic and Fiscal Commission. 2018. *2018 Budget Fiscal Report*. Port Moresby. https://www.nefc.gov.pg/documents/publications/fiscalReports/2018Fiscal_Report.pdf.

80 Deloitte. 2020. *Papua New Guinea Budget 2020*. Port Moresby. https://www2.deloitte.com/content/dam/Deloitte/pg/Documents/financial-services/deloitte-pg-fs-papua-new-guinea-budget-281119.pdf.

81 Government of Papua New Guinea. 2018. *Final Budget Outcome 2018*. Port Moresby. https://www.treasury.gov.pg/html/national_budget/files/2013/budget_documents/Related%20Budget%20Documents/2018%20Final%20Budget%20Outcome.pdf.

Appendixes

Appendix 1: Methodology

Research Period

The research was carried out in 2020.

List of Indicators

Table A1.1 through Table A1.6 present a list of indicators for each major topic, including the definition and/or explanation of certain indicators where it is deemed necessary.

Table A1.1: Overview

Subcategory	Supporting Indicators	Units	Definition
Overview	None	Description	• Overview of the PPP legal and regulatory framework • Number of PPP projects reaching financial close from 1990 until the end of 2019 across sectors • Total investment made in PPPs from 1990 to 2019 across sectors • Features of past PPP projects including the number of PPPs procured through various modes of PPP procurement • Number of PPP projects under preparation and procurement • Number of PPP projects supported by the government • Payment mechanism for PPPs • Foreign sponsor participation in PPPs from 1990 to 2019 • Major sponsors active in the country's infrastructure sector • Challenges associated with the PPP landscape in the country

Table A1.2: National Public-Private Partnership Landscape

Subcategory	Supporting Indicators	Units	Definition
National PPP legal and regulatory framework	Does the country have—		Details on the legal and regulatory framework applicable to PPPs and its evolution since the introduction of PPPs in the country Details on other supporting laws and regulations governing PPPs in the country
	• National PPP laws and regulations?	Yes/No/Not Applicable/ Unavailable	
	• Public financial management laws and regulations?	Yes/No/Not Applicable/ Unavailable	
	• Sector-specific laws and regulations?	Yes/No/Not Applicable/ Unavailable	
	• Procurement laws and regulations?	Yes/No/Not Applicable/ Unavailable	
	• Environmental laws and regulations?	Yes/No/Not Applicable/ Unavailable	
	• Laws and regulations for social compliance?	Yes/No/Not Applicable/ Unavailable	
	• Laws and regulations governing land acquisition and ownership?	Yes/No/Not Applicable/ Unavailable	
	• Taxation laws and regulations?	Yes/No/Not Applicable/ Unavailable	
	• Employment laws and regulations?	Yes/No/Not Applicable/ Unavailable	
	• Licensing requirements?	Yes/No/Not Applicable/ Unavailable	
	Evolution of the PPP legal and regulatory framework in the country?	Description	
	What are the other components of the PPP legal and regulatory framework?	Description	
PPP types	Number of PPP types defined in the PPP regulations	Number	Details on the PPP types allowed to be used as per PPP legal and regulatory framework. In case the PPP legal and regulatory framework does not specify the PPP types, this section provides the details on the specific PPP types which have been adopted for various PPP projects at various stages of the PPP lifecycle.
Eligible sectors	Transportation infrastructure	Yes/No/Not Applicable/ Unavailable	Details on various infrastructure sectors for which projects could be procured through the PPP route as per the PPP legal and regulatory framework
	• Road infrastructure	Yes/No/Not Applicable/ Unavailable	
	• Water resources and irrigation infrastructure	Yes/No/Not Applicable/ Unavailable	

continued on next page

continued from previous page

Subcategory	Supporting Indicators	Units	Definition
	• Water supply infrastructure	Yes/No/Not Applicable/ Unavailable	
	• Infrastructure for centralized water waste management systems	Yes/No/Not Applicable/ Unavailable	
	• Infrastructure for local water waste management system	Yes/No/Not Applicable/ Unavailable	
	• Infrastructure for waste management system	Yes/No/Not Applicable/ Unavailable	
	• Telecommunication and informatics infrastructure	Yes/No/Not Applicable/ Unavailable	
	• Energy and electricity infrastructure including renewable energy	Yes/No/Not Applicable/ Unavailable	
	• Energy conservation infrastructure	Yes/No/Not Applicable/ Unavailable	
	• Urban facilities infrastructure	Yes/No/Not Applicable/ Unavailable	
	• Zone infrastructure	Yes/No/Not Applicable/ Unavailable	
	• Tourism infrastructure (e.g., tourism information center)	Yes/No/Not Applicable/ Unavailable	
	• Education facilities, research and development infrastructure	Yes/No/Not Applicable/ Unavailable	
	• Health infrastructure	Yes/No/Not Applicable/ Unavailable	
	• Public housing infrastructure	Yes/No/Not Applicable/ Unavailable	
Public-private partnership institutional framework	Does the country have a national PPP unit?	Yes/No/Not Applicable/ Unavailable	Details on the PPP institutional framework including availability of a PPP Unit, functions of the PPP Unit, principal public entities associated with PPPs and their respective functions, and details of public entities responsible for PPP project identification, appraisal, approval, oversight, and monitoring
	What are the functions of the national PPP unit?		
	Supporting the design and operationalization of the National PPP Enabling Framework?	Yes/No/Not Applicable/ Unavailable	
	Helping develop a national PPP pipeline?	Yes/No/Not Applicable/ Unavailable	
	Supporting the arrangement of funding for project preparation (budgetary allocations, technical assistance funding from multilateral development agencies, operating a dedicated project preparation/ project development fund)?	Yes/No/Not Applicable/ Unavailable	

continued on next page

continued from previous page

Subcategory	Supporting Indicators	Units	Definition
	• Guidance for project preparation to and coordination with the government agencies responsible for sponsoring the projects?	Yes/No/Not Applicable/ Unavailable	
	• Making recommendations to the PPP Committee and/or other approving authorities to provide approvals associated with various stages of the PPP process?	Yes/No/Not Applicable/ Unavailable	
Entities responsible for PPP project identification, approval, and oversight	Who is responsible for identifying, preparing, and procuring the PPP projects?	Description	
	Is there a PPP Committee for providing approvals at various stages of PPP projects?	Yes/No/Not Applicable/ Unavailable	
	Who are the approving authorities other than the PPP Committee for the PPP projects?		
	Does the country have an independent think tank for various PPP planning, budgeting, and policy decisions?	Yes/No/Not Applicable/ Unavailable	
	Is there a legislature for the PPP program oversight?	Yes/No/Not Applicable/ Unavailable	
Entities responsible for PPP project monitoring	Is there an entity for monitoring of PPP projects post commercial close?	Yes/No/Not Applicable/ Unavailable	
	Is there an entity for monitoring and management of fiscal risks and liabilities from PPP projects for the Ministry of Finance (MOF)?	Yes/No/Not Applicable/ Unavailable	
The public-private partnership process	Does the PPP legal and regulatory framework provide for a PPP implementation process covering the entire PPP lifecycle?	Yes/No/Not Applicable/ Unavailable	Details on various stages of the PPP process including PPP project identification, preparation, structuring, procurement, and management as per the PPP legal and regulatory framework in the country
	Does the Feasibility Assessment Stage cover—	Yes/No/Not Applicable/ Unavailable	
	Technical feasibility?	Yes/No/Not Applicable/ Unavailable	
	Socioeconomic feasibility?	Yes/No/Not Applicable/ Unavailable	
	Environmental sustainability?	Yes/No/Not Applicable/ Unavailable	
	Financial feasibility?	Yes/No/Not Applicable/ Unavailable	
	Fiscal affordability assessment?	Yes/No/Not Applicable/ Unavailable	
	Legal assessment?	Yes/No/Not Applicable/ Unavailable	

continued on next page

continued from previous page

Subcategory	Supporting Indicators	Units	Definition
	• Risk assessment and PPP project structuring?	Yes/No/Not Applicable/ Unavailable	
	• Value for Money assessment?	Yes/No/Not Applicable/ Unavailable	
	• Market sounding with stakeholders?	Yes/No/Not Applicable/ Unavailable	
	Is the PPP procurement plan required?	Yes/No/Not Applicable/ Unavailable	
	Is there a need to set up a separate PPP procurement committee?	Yes/No/Not Applicable/ Unavailable	
	Is competitive bidding the only method for selection of PPP private developer?	Yes/No/Not Applicable/ Unavailable	
	Is the prequalification stage necessary? Or does the PPP legal and regulatory framework allow flexibility to skip the pre-qualification stage?	Yes/No/Not Applicable/ Unavailable	
	Does the PPP legal and regulatory process provide the option to the preferred bidder for contract negotiations?	Yes/No/Not Applicable/ Unavailable	
	Does the PPP Legal and Regulatory Framework allow unsuccessful bidders to challenge the award/ submit complaints?	Yes/No/Not Applicable/ Unavailable	
	What is the maximum time allowed for submitting a complaint/challenging the award by unsuccessful bidders from the announcement of the preferred bidder?	Yes/No/Not Applicable/ Unavailable	
	Does the PPP legal and regulatory framework provide for transparency?	Yes/No/Not Applicable/ Unavailable	
	Which of the following are required to be published?	Yes/No/Not Applicable/ Unavailable	
	• Findings from the feasibility assessment?	Yes/No/Not Applicable/ Unavailable	
	• Procurement notice?	Yes/No/Not Applicable/ Unavailable	
	• Outcome of stakeholder consultations from market sounding?	Yes/No/Not Applicable/ Unavailable	
	• Clarifications to prequalification queries?	Yes/No/Not Applicable/ Unavailable	
	• Prequalification results?	Yes/No/Not Applicable/ Unavailable	
	• Clarifications to pre-bid queries?	Yes/No/Not Applicable/ Unavailable	
	• Results for the bid stage and selection of preferred bidder?	Yes/No/Not Applicable/ Unavailable	

continued on next page

continued from previous page

Subcategory	Supporting Indicators	Units	Definition
	Final concession agreement to be entered between the government agency and the preferred bidder? And other PPP project agreements executed between government agency and preferred bidder?	Yes/No/Not Applicable/ Unavailable	
	Confidentiality?	Yes/No/Not Applicable/ Unavailable	
PPP standard operating procedures, toolkits, templates, and model bidding documents	Does the country have PPP Guidelines/PPP Guidance Manual?	Yes/No/Not Applicable/ Unavailable	Details on standard operating procedures and standard templates or model bidding documents available for PPPs, if any. Details on the key clauses in a PPP agreement based on the review of select PPP Agreements already executed, and/or the review of the PPP legal and regulatory framework
	Does the PPP Guidelines/PPP Guidance Manual adequately cover the process, entities involved, roles and responsibilities of various entities, approvals required at various stages, and the timelines for the various stages of the PPP project lifecycle?	Yes/No/Not Applicable/ Unavailable	
	What are the templates and checklists available in the PPP Guidelines/PPP Guidance Manual?	Yes/No/Not Applicable/ Unavailable	
	• Project Needs Assessment and Options Analysis checklist?	Yes/No/Not Applicable/ Unavailable	
	• Project Due Diligence checklist?	Yes/No/Not Applicable/ Unavailable	
	• Technical Assessment checklist?	Yes/No/Not Applicable/ Unavailable	
	• Environmental Assessment checklist?	Yes/No/Not Applicable/ Unavailable	
	• PPP Procurement Plan template?	Yes/No/Not Applicable/ Unavailable	
	Does the country have standardized/model bidding documents for PPPs?	Yes/No/Not Applicable/ Unavailable	
	• Model Request for Qualification (RFQ) document?	Yes/No/Not Applicable/ Unavailable	
	• Model Request for Proposal (RFP) document?	Yes/No/Not Applicable/ Unavailable	
	• Model PPP/Concession Agreement?	Yes/No/Not Applicable/ Unavailable	
	• State Support Agreement?	Yes/No/Not Applicable/ Unavailable	
	• VGF Agreement?	Yes/No/Not Applicable/ Unavailable	
	• Guarantee Agreement?	Yes/No/Not Applicable/ Unavailable	
	• Power Purchase Agreement?	Yes/No/Not Applicable/ Unavailable	

continued on next page

continued from previous page

Subcategory	Supporting Indicators	Units	Definition
	• Capacity Take-or-Pay Contract?	Yes/No/Not Applicable/ Unavailable	
	• Fuel Supply Agreement?	Yes/No/Not Applicable/ Unavailable	
	• Transmission and Use of System Agreement?	Yes/No/Not Applicable/ Unavailable	
	• Performance-based Operations and Maintenance Contract?	Yes/No/Not Applicable/ Unavailable	
	• Engineering, Procurement and Construction Contract?	Yes/No/Not Applicable/ Unavailable	
	Does the country have standardized PPP agreement terms?	Yes/No/Not Applicable/ Unavailable	
	• PPP Family Indicator?	Yes/No/Not Applicable/ Unavailable	
	• PPP Mode Validity Indicator?	Yes/No/Not Applicable/ Unavailable	
	• PPP Suitability Filter?	Yes/No/Not Applicable/ Unavailable	
	• PPP Screening Tool?	Yes/No/Not Applicable/ Unavailable	
	• Financial Viability Indicator Model?	Yes/No/Not Applicable/ Unavailable	
	• Economic Viability Indicator Model?	Yes/No/Not Applicable/ Unavailable	
	• VFM Indicator Tool?	Yes/No/Not Applicable/ Unavailable	
	• Readiness Filter?	Yes/No/Not Applicable/ Unavailable	
	Is there a framework for monitoring fiscal risks from PPPs including the following?	Yes/No/Not Applicable/ Unavailable	
	• Process for assessing fiscal commitments?	Yes/No/Not Applicable/ Unavailable	
	• Process for approving fiscal commitments?	Yes/No/Not Applicable/ Unavailable	
	• Process for monitoring fiscal commitments?	Yes/No/Not Applicable/ Unavailable	
	• Process for reporting fiscal commitments?	Yes/No/Not Applicable/ Unavailable	
	• Process for budgeting fiscal commitments?	Yes/No/Not Applicable/ Unavailable	
	Are there fiscal prudence norms/thresholds to limit fiscal exposure to PPPs?	Yes/No/Not Applicable/ Unavailable	
	Is there a process for assessing and budgeting contingent liabilities from PPPs?	Yes/No/Not Applicable/ Unavailable	

continued on next page

continued from previous page

Subcategory	Supporting Indicators	Units	Definition
Lender's security rights	Does the law specifically enable lenders the following rights:	Yes/No/Not Applicable/ Unavailable	The rights of a lender including the charge of project assets
	• Security over the project assets?	Yes/No/Not Applicable/ Unavailable	
	• Security over the land on which they are built (land use right)?	Yes/No/Not Applicable/ Unavailable	
	• Security over the shares of a PPP project company?	Yes/No/Not Applicable/ Unavailable	
	• Can there be a direct agreement between the government and lenders?	Yes/No/Not Applicable/ Unavailable	
	• Do lenders get priority in the case of insolvency?	Yes/No/Not Applicable/ Unavailable	
	• Can lenders be given step-in rights?	Yes/No/Not Applicable/ Unavailable	
Termination and compensation	Does the law specifically enable compensation payment to the private partner in case of early termination due to:		Definition on whether the private player is eligible for compensation in case of PPP project termination due to various reasons
	• Public sector default or termination for reasons of public interest?	Yes/No/Not Applicable/ Unavailable	
	• Private sector default?	Yes/No/Not Applicable/ Unavailable	
	• Force majeure?	Yes/No/Not Applicable/ Unavailable	
	• Does the law enable the concept of economic/financial equilibrium?	Yes/No/Not Applicable/ Unavailable	
	Does the law enable compensation payment to the private partner due to:	Yes/No/Not Applicable/ Unavailable	
	• Material adverse government action	Yes/No/Not Applicable/ Unavailable	
	• Force majeure	Yes/No/Not Applicable/ Unavailable	
	• Change in law	Yes/No/Not Applicable/ Unavailable	
Unsolicited PPP proposals	Does the PPP legal and regulatory framework allow submission and acceptance of unsolicited proposals?	Yes/No/Not Applicable/ Unavailable	Details on possibility of submission of unsolicited PPP proposals, and their treatment including, potential advantages provided to the unsolicited PPP proposal proponent at the PPP procurement stage
	What are the advantages provided to the project proponent for an unsolicited bid?		
	• Competitive advantage at bid evaluation?	Yes/No/Not Applicable/ Unavailable	
	• Swiss Challenge?	Yes/No/Not Applicable/ Unavailable	

continued on next page

continued from previous page

Subcategory	Supporting Indicators	Units	Definition
	• Compensation of the project development costs?	Yes/No/Not Applicable/ Unavailable	
	• Government support for land acquisition and resettlement cost?	Yes/No/Not Applicable/ Unavailable	
	• Government support in the form of viability gap funding and guarantees?	Yes/No/Not Applicable/ Unavailable	
Foreign investor participation restrictions	Is there any restriction for foreign investors on:		Definition of whether there are any statutory restrictions on foreign equity investments and ownership in PPP projects
	• Land use/ownership rights as opposed to similar rights of local investors	Yes/No/Not Applicable/ Unavailable	
	• Currency conversion	Yes/No/Not Applicable/ Unavailable	
Dispute resolution	Does the country have a dispute resolution tribunal (DRT)?	Yes/No/Not Applicable/ Unavailable	Definition of the dispute resolution process and mechanisms available in the country
	Does the country have an institutional arbitration mechanism?	Yes/No/Not Applicable/ Unavailable	
	Can a foreign law be chosen to govern PPP contracts?	Yes/No/Not Applicable/ Unavailable	
	What dispute resolution mechanisms are available for PPP agreements?		
	• Court litigation	Yes/No/Not Applicable/ Unavailable	
	• Local arbitration	Yes/No/Not Applicable/ Unavailable	
	• International arbitration	Yes/No/Not Applicable/ Unavailable	
	Has the country signed the New York Convention on the Recognition and Enforcement of Foreign Arbitral Awards?	Yes/No/Not Applicable/ Unavailable	
Environmental and social issues	Is there a local regulation establishing a process for environmental impact assessment?	Yes/No/Not Applicable/ Unavailable	Details on whether the legal and regulatory framework governing PPPs stipulates a mechanism for managing the environmental impact of a PPP project, including the potential environmental issues which could be caused by a PPP project

continued on next page

continued from previous page

Subcategory	Supporting Indicators	Units	Definition
	Is there a legal mechanism for the private partner to limit environmental liability for what is outside of its control or caused by third parties?	Yes/No/Not Applicable/ Unavailable	Deliberation on whether a private partner can limit the circumstances where it is penalized for breaching environmental standards where such a breach is not within its control. For example, a wastewater treatment plant operator will wish to avoid prosecution or even liability for pollution caused by a pollutant in the influent which the treatment plant cannot treat, or will at least want to have the power to pursue the polluter to stop the pollution and/or obtain compensation.
	Is there a local regulation establishing a process for social impact assessment?	Yes/No/Not Applicable/ Unavailable	Details on whether the legal and regulatory framework governing PPPs stipulates a mechanism for managing the social impact of a PPP project, including the potential social issues which could be caused by a PPP project
	Is there involuntary land clearance for PPP projects?	Yes/No/Not Applicable/ Unavailable	Deliberation on whether land expropriation is possible for PPP projects
Land rights	Which of the following is permitted to the private partner:		Definition of various mechanisms through which landownership and/or land use rights could be provided to the private partner in respect of the project site for a PPP project
	• Transfer land lease/use/ownership rights to third party	Yes/No/Not Applicable/ Unavailable	
	• Use leased/owned land as collateral	Yes/No/Not Applicable/ Unavailable	
	• Mortgage leased/owned land	Yes/No/Not Applicable/ Unavailable	Details on land records and registration which could be provided to the private partner
	Is there a legal mechanism for granting wayleave rights, for example, laying water pipes or fiber cables over land occupied by persons other than the government or the private partner?	Yes/No/Not Applicable/ Unavailable	
	Is there a land registry/cadastre with public information on land plots?	Yes/No/Not Applicable/ Unavailable	

continued on next page

continued from previous page

Subcategory	Supporting Indicators	Units	Definition
	Which of the following information on land plots is available to the private partner:	Yes/No/Not Applicable/ Unavailable	
	• Appraisal of land value	Yes/No/Not Applicable/ Unavailable	
	• Landowners	Yes/No/Not Applicable/ Unavailable	
	• Land boundaries	Yes/No/Not Applicable/ Unavailable	
	• Utility connections	Yes/No/Not Applicable/ Unavailable	
	• Immovable property on land	Yes/No/Not Applicable/ Unavailable	
	• Plots classification	Yes/No/Not Applicable/ Unavailable	
Government financial support for PPP projects	Is there a dedicated government financial support mechanism for PPP projects?	Yes/No/Not Applicable/ Unavailable	Details on various mechanisms of government financial support available to make PPP projects financially viable Salient features of government financial support mechanisms available
	What are the instruments of government financial support available under this government financial support mechanism?		
	• Capital grant	Yes/No/Not Applicable/ Unavailable	
	• Operations grant	Yes/No/Not Applicable/ Unavailable	
	• Annuity/availability payments	Yes/No/Not Applicable/ Unavailable	
	• Guarantees to cover	Yes/No/Not Applicable/ Unavailable	
	– Currency inconvertibility and transfer risk	Yes/No/Not Applicable/ Unavailable	
	– Foreign exchange risk	Yes/No/Not Applicable/ Unavailable	
	– War and civil disturbance risk	Yes/No/Not Applicable/ Unavailable	
	– Breach of contract risk	Yes/No/Not Applicable/ Unavailable	
	– Regulatory risk	Yes/No/Not Applicable/ Unavailable	
	– Expropriation risk	Yes/No/Not Applicable/ Unavailable	
	– Government payment obligation risk	Yes/No/Not Applicable/ Unavailable	
	– Credit risk	Yes/No/Not Applicable/ Unavailable	

continued on next page

continued from previous page

Subcategory	Supporting Indicators	Units	Definition
	– Minimum demand/revenue risk	Yes/No/Not Applicable/ Unavailable	
	– Risk of making annuity/availability payments in a timely manner	Yes/No/Not Applicable/ Unavailable	
	What are the caps/ceilings for the government financial support under each of the abovementioned government financial support instruments?		
	Is there a minimum PPP project size (investment) for a PPP project to be eligible for receiving government financial support?	Yes/No/Not Applicable/ Unavailable	
	Are there minimum financial commitment requirements for the private developer equity before the government support could be drawn?	Yes/No/Not Applicable/ Unavailable	
	Is the government financial support required, and an allowed bid parameter for PPP projects?	Yes/No/Not Applicable/ Unavailable	
	Are unsolicited PPP proposals eligible to receive government financial support?	Yes/No/Not Applicable/ Unavailable	
	Are there standard operating procedures for providing government financial support to PPP projects?	Yes/No/Not Applicable/ Unavailable	
	• Appraisal and approval process	Yes/No/Not Applicable/ Unavailable	
	• Budgeting process	Yes/No/Not Applicable/ Unavailable	
	• Disbursement process	Yes/No/Not Applicable/ Unavailable	
	• Monitoring process	Yes/No/Not Applicable/ Unavailable	
	• Accounting, auditing, and reporting process	Yes/No/Not Applicable/ Unavailable	
	Who are the signatories to the Government Financial Support Agreement?		
	Who is responsible for monitoring the performance of PPP projects availing government financial support?	Yes/No/Not Applicable/ Unavailable	
	• Independent engineer?	Yes/No/Not Applicable/ Unavailable	
	• Government agency?	Yes/No/Not Applicable/ Unavailable	
	• Ministry of Finance?	Yes/No/Not Applicable/ Unavailable	

continued on next page

continued from previous page

Subcategory	Supporting Indicators	Units	Definition
	What are the other forms of government support available for PPP projects?	Yes/No/Not Applicable/ Unavailable	
	• Land acquisition funding support?	Yes/No/Not Applicable/ Unavailable	
	• Funding support for resettlement and rehabilitation of affected parties?	Yes/No/Not Applicable/ Unavailable	
	• Tax holidays/exemptions?	Yes/No/Not Applicable/ Unavailable	
	• Real estate development rights?	Yes/No/Not Applicable/ Unavailable	
	• Advertising and marketing rights?	Yes/No/Not Applicable/ Unavailable	
	• Interest rate/cost of debt subventions?	Yes/No/Not Applicable/ Unavailable	
	• Other subsidies and subventions?	Yes/No/Not Applicable/ Unavailable	
	Can the other forms of government support be availed over and above the government financial support through various instruments listed above?	Yes/No/Not Applicable/ Unavailable	
Project development funding support	What are the various sources of funds for PPP project preparation?		Details on various sources through which funding could be availed for the development activities (preparation, structuring, and procurement) for a PPP project Details on stages of the PPP project development stage during which such funding could be availed and utilized, including payments to transaction advisors
	• Budgetary allocations?	Yes/No/Not Applicable/ Unavailable	
	• Dedicated project preparation/project development fund?	Yes/No/Not Applicable/ Unavailable	
	• Technical assistance from multilateral, bilateral, and donor agencies?	Yes/No/Not Applicable/ Unavailable	
	• Recovery of project preparation funding from the preferred bidder?	Yes/No/Not Applicable/ Unavailable	
	At what stage of the PPP project can the project preparation/development funding be availed by the government agency?		
	• Pre-feasibility stage	Yes/No/Not Applicable/ Unavailable	
	• Detailed feasibility stage	Yes/No/Not Applicable/ Unavailable	
	• Transaction stage	Yes/No/Not Applicable/ Unavailable	
	Is there a list of project preparation/project development activities toward which the project development funding can be utilized?	Yes/No/Not Applicable/ Unavailable	

continued on next page

continued from previous page

Subcategory	Supporting Indicators	Units	Definition
	Can the project development funding be utilized to appoint transaction advisors for PPP projects?	Yes/No/Not Applicable/ Unavailable	
	Is there a specific process to be followed by government agencies to appoint transaction advisors?	Yes/No/Not Applicable/ Unavailable	
	What are the payment mechanisms for making payments to transaction advisors?	Yes/No/Not Applicable/ Unavailable	
	• Time-sheet based	Yes/No/Not Applicable/ Unavailable	
	• Milestone based	Yes/No/Not Applicable/ Unavailable	
	Are there standard agreements and documents to avail project development funding?	Yes/No/Not Applicable/ Unavailable	
	Who are the signatories to the project development funding agreements?		
PPP project statistics	Is there a National PPP database for the country?	Yes/No/Not Applicable/ Unavailable	Details on the key PPP statistics in the country, such as (i) availability of a PPP database showing distribution of PPP projects across sectors and across various stages of the PPP lifecycle, and (ii) availability of a national PPP project pipeline and its alignment with the National Infrastructure Plan for the country
	Is the distribution of PPP projects across infrastructure sectors available?	Yes/No/Not Applicable/ Unavailable	
	Is the distribution of PPP projects across various stages of the PPP lifecycle available?	Yes/No/Not Applicable/ Unavailable	
	Does the country publish a national PPP project pipeline?	Yes/No/Not Applicable/ Unavailable	
	At what frequency is the national PPP project pipeline published?		
	Is the national PPP project pipeline based on the National Infrastructure Plan for the country?	Yes/No/Not Applicable/ Unavailable	
Sources of PPP financing	Who are the typical entities financing PPP projects in the country?	Yes/No/Not Applicable/ Unavailable	Details on the sources of financing for PPP projects in the country Details on typical key financing terms for various sources of financing, banks active in project finance for the last 24 months, active PPP project sponsors in the country for the last 24 months, availability of derivatives market, and availability of credit rating agencies in the country
	• Private developers	Yes/No/Not Applicable/ Unavailable	
	• Construction contractors	Yes/No/Not Applicable/ Unavailable	
	• Institutional/financial/private equity investors	Yes/No/Not Applicable/ Unavailable	
	• Pension funds	Yes/No/Not Applicable/ Unavailable	
	• Insurance companies	Yes/No/Not Applicable/ Unavailable	

continued on next page

continued from previous page

Subcategory	Supporting Indicators	Units	Definition
	Banks?	Yes/No/Not Applicable/ Unavailable	
	Non-banking financial corporation/ financial institutions?	Yes/No/Not Applicable/ Unavailable	
	Donor agencies?	Yes/No/Not Applicable/ Unavailable	
	Government agencies and state-owned enterprises?	Yes/No/Not Applicable/ Unavailable	
	What is the distribution of financing among these entities financing PPP projects?		
	Does the country have the history/track record of issuing bonds by infrastructure projects?	Yes/No/Not Applicable/ Unavailable	
	How many infrastructure projects/private developers for infrastructure projects have raised funding through bond issuances?	Number	
	What is the value of funding raised through capital markets by PPPs?	Number	
	Does the country have a matured derivatives market to hedge certain risks associated with PPPs?	Yes/No/Not Applicable/ Unavailable	
	Does the country have a national development bank?	Yes/No/Not Applicable/ Unavailable	
	Does the country have credit rating agencies to rate infrastructure projects?	Yes/No/Not Applicable/ Unavailable	
	Typically, what are the credit ratings achieved/received by infrastructure projects?	Yes/No/Not Applicable/ Unavailable	
	Is there a threshold credit rating for infrastructure PPPs below which institutional investors, pension funds, and insurance companies would not invest in infrastructure PPPs?	Yes/No/Not Applicable/ Unavailable	
	What is the typical funding model for infrastructure PPPs—corporate finance or project finance?		
	Are there regulatory limits/restrictions for the maximum exposure that can be taken by banks to infrastructure projects?	Yes/No/Not Applicable/ Unavailable	

Table A1.3: Sector-Specific Public–Private Partnership Landscape

Subcategory	Supporting Indicators	Units	Definition
Contracting agencies in the sector	None	Description	Details on which government agencies could act as the contracting agencies for a PPP project
Sector laws and regulations	None	Description	Details on the applicable sector laws and regulations for PPP projects including the sector regulators and their respective functions
Foreign investment restrictions in the sector	Maximum allowed foreign ownership of equity in greenfield projects	%	Details on the maximum allowed foreign equity investment in greenfield PPP projects in a particular sector
Standard contracts in the sector	PPP/concession agreement	Yes/No/Not Applicable/ Unavailable	Specifics of whether standard contracts are available for PPP projects in a particular sector
	Performance-based operation and maintenance contract	Yes/No/Not Applicable/ Unavailable	
	Engineering procurement and construction contract	Yes/No/Not Applicable/ Unavailable	
Sector master plan	None	Description	Details on the master plan and/or roadmap adopted for infrastructure development in the sector by the national government and the corresponding line ministry Details on the pipeline of PPP projects for the sector aligned with the sector master plan and/or roadmap Details on the PPP projects under preparation and procurement in the sector
Features of past PPP projects	Number of PPP projects procured through various modes of PPP procurement—Direct Appointment, Unsolicited Bids, and Competitive Bids	Number	Features of past PPP projects based on supporting indicators in terms of the number and value (where applicable) of PPP projects for each supporting indicator
	Number and value of PPP projects reaching financial closure	Number	
	Number of PPP projects with foreign sponsor participation in absolute terms, and as a percentage of total number of PPP projects	Number	

continued on next page

continued from previous page

Subcategory	Supporting Indicators	Units	Definition
	Number of PPP projects supported with various forms of government financial support—Viability Gap Funding, Government Guarantees, and Availability/ Performance Payments	Number	
	Number of PPP projects based on various types of payment mechanisms—User Charges, and Government Pay (Off-take)	Number	
Tariffs applicable to the sector	None	Description	Details on the indicative tariffs applicable in the sector based on the examples of select PPP or other projects operational in the sector
Typical risk allocation for PPP projects in the sector	Traffic risk	Yes/No/Not Applicable/ Unavailable	Details on the typical risk allocation between the government contracting agency and the private partner based on examples of select PPP projects which have achieved commercial close
	Collection risk	Yes/No/Not Applicable/ Unavailable	
	Competition risk	Yes/No/Not Applicable/ Unavailable	
	Government payment risk	Yes/No/Not Applicable/ Unavailable	
	Environmental and social risk	Yes/No/Not Applicable/ Unavailable	
	Land acquisition risk	Yes/No/Not Applicable/ Unavailable	
	Permits	Yes/No/Not Applicable/ Unavailable	
	Geotechnical risk	Yes/No/Not Applicable/ Unavailable	
	Brownfield risk: inventories studies, property boundaries, project scope	Yes/No/Not Applicable/ Unavailable	
	Political risk	Yes/No/Not Applicable/ Unavailable	
	Force majeure	Yes/No/Not Applicable/ Unavailable	
	Foreign exchange risk	Yes/No/Not Applicable/ Unavailable	
	Construction risk	Yes/No/Not Applicable/ Unavailable	
Financing details for PPP projects in the sector	PPP projects with foreign lending participation	Number	Typical financing details based on past PPP projects on the lines of the supporting indicators
	PPP projects that received export credit agency/international financing institution support	Number	

continued on next page

continued from previous page

Subcategory	Supporting Indicators	Units	Definition
	Typical debt–equity ratio	Ratio	
	Time for financial closure	Months	
	Typical concession period	Years	
	Typical financial internal rate of return	%	
Challenges associated with PPPs in the sector	None	Description	Details on the PPP-related and sector-specific challenges faced by PPP projects in the sector

Table A1.4: Typical Sector-Specific Infrastructure Indicators for the Country

Subcategory	Supporting Indicators	Units	Definition
Roads	Length of the total road network	kilometers	
	Quality of road infrastructure	1(low) – 7(high)	
Railways	Length of total railway network	total route-km	
	Total number of passengers carried	Million passenger-km	
	Total volume of freight carried	Million ton-km	
	Quality of railways infrastructure	1(low) – 7(high)	
Ports	Total number of ports	Number	
	Total freight capacity of all ports	MTPA	
	Total container traffic at ports	TEUs	
	Quality of port infrastructure	1(low) – 7(high)	
	Quality of trade and transport-related infrastructure index	1=low to 5=high	
Airports	No. of airports	Number	
	Total passenger capacity	million passengers	
	Quality of air transport infrastructure	1 (low) – 7 (high)	
	Total number of projects with cumulative lending, grant, and technical assistance commitments in the transport sector	Number	
	Total amount of cumulative lending, grant, and technical assistance commitments in the transport sector	$ million	
Energy	Electric power consumption	kilowatt-hour per capita	
	Share of clean energy	% of total energy use	
	Access to electricity	% of population	
	Getting electricity (score out of 100)	Number	
	Energy imports	% of total energy use	
	Investment in energy with private participation	current $ million	

continued on next page

continued from previous page

Subcategory	Supporting Indicators	Units	Definition
	Total number of projects with cumulative lending, grant, and technical assistance commitments in the energy sector	Number	
	Total amount of cumulative lending, grant, and technical assistance commitments in the energy sector	$ million	
Water and wastewater	Improved water source access	% of population with access	
	Improved sanitation facilities access	% of population with access	
	Investment in water and sanitation with private participation	current $ million	
	Total number of projects with cumulative lending, grant, and technical assistance commitments in water and other urban infrastructure and services	Number	
	Total amount of cumulative lending, grant, and technical assistance commitments in water and other urban infrastructure and services	$ million	
ICT	Telephone subscribers	per 100 inhabitants	
	Cellular Phone Subscribers	per 100 inhabitants	
	Cellular Network Coverage	% of population covered	
	Internet Subscribers	per 100 inhabitants	
	Internet Bandwidth per Internet User	kbps	
	Total number of projects with Cumulative Lending, Grant, and Technical Assistance Commitments in ICT sector	Number	
	Total amount of Cumulative Lending, Grant, and Technical Assistance Commitments in ICT sector	$ million	
Social infrastructure	Government Expenditure on Education	% of GDP	
	Education spending as % of government spending	%	
	Primary School Gross Enrollment	%	
	Adult Literacy Rate	%	
	Total number of projects with Cumulative Lending, Grant, and Technical Assistance Commitments in education sector	Number	
	Total amount of Cumulative Lending, Grant, and Technical Assistance Commitments in education sector	$ million	
	Total Health Expenditure	% of GDP	
	Health spending per capita	USD	
	Maternal Mortality Ratio (modelled estimates per 100,000 live births)	(per 100,000 live births)	
	Infant Mortality Rate	(below 1 year/per 1,000 live births)	

continued on next page

continued from previous page

Subcategory	Supporting Indicators	Units	Definition
	Life Expectancy at Birth	(years)	
	Child Malnutrition	(% below 5 years old)	
	Total number of projects with Cumulative Lending, Grant, and Technical Assistance Commitments in health sector	Number	
	Total amount of Cumulative Lending, Grant, and Technical Assistance Commitments in health sector	$ million	
	Existing No. of Affordable Housing Units	No.	
	Affordable Housing Gap		

Table A1.5: Local Government Public–Private Partnership Landscape

Subcategory	Supporting Indicators	Units	Definition
Key indicators related to local governments in the country	Number of Subnational Governments (SNGs)		Details on the local governments using select key indicators on (i) the number and levels of local governments, (ii) the typical expenditure profile and heads, (iii) the typical revenue profile and heads, (iv) the typical debt profile and heads, and (v) grants and transfers from the higher levels of government
	– Municipal Level	Number	
	– Intermediate Level	Number	
	– Regional or State Level	Number	
	Total number of SNGs	Number	
	SNG Expenditure Profile	SNG Expenditure Profile	
	Total SNG Expenditure as % of GDP	%	
	– SNG Current Expenditure as % of GDP	%	
	– SNG Staff Expenditure as % of GDP	%	
	– SNG Investment as % of GDP	%	
	Total SNG Expenditure as % of the Total General Government (% of Total Public Expenditure)	%	
	– SNG Current Expenditure as a % of Total Current Expenditure of the General Government	%	
	– SNG Staff Expenditure as a % of Total Staff Expenditure of the General Government	%	
	– SNG Investment as a % of Total Investment of the General Government	%	
	Current Expenditure of SNG as a % of Total SNG Expenditure	%	
	Staff Expenditure of SNG as a % of Total SNG Expenditure	%	
	Investments of SNG as a % of Total SNG Expenditure	%	

continued on next page

continued from previous page

Subcategory	Supporting Indicators	Units	Definition
	SNG Expenditure by Function	SNG Expenditure by Function	
	– General Public Services	%	
	– Defense	%	
	– Security and Public Order	%	
	– Economic Affairs	%	
	– Environmental Protection	%	
	– Housing and Community Amenities	%	
	– Health	%	
	– Recreation, Culture, and Religion	%	
	– Education	%	
	– Social Protection	%	
	SNG Revenue Profile	SNG Revenue Profile	
	Total SNG Revenue as a % of GDP	%	
	– SNG Tax Revenue as a % of GDP	%	
	– SNG Grants and Subsidies as a % of GDP	%	
	– SNG Other Revenues as a % of GDP	%	
	Total SNG Revenue as % of Total General Government Revenue	%	
	– SNG Tax Revenue as a % of Total General Government Tax Revenue	%	
	– SNG Grants and Subsidies as a % of Total General Government Grants and Subsidies	%	
	– SNG Other Revenues as a % of Total Other Revenues	%	
	SNG Tax Revenue as a % of Total SNG Revenue	%	
	SNG Grants and Subsidies as a % of Total SNG Revenue	%	
	SNG Other Revenues as a % of Total SNG Revenue	%	
	SNG Debt Profile	SNG Debt Profile	
	Outstanding SNG Debt as % of GDP	%	
	Outstanding SNG Debt as % of Total Outstanding Debt of General Government	%	
	Parameters for transfers to the Subnational Governments from the National Government	Parameters for transfers to the Subnational Governments from the National Government	

continued on next page

continued from previous page

Subcategory	Supporting Indicators	Units	Definition
	Score on transfers to Subnational Governments		
	– Score on system for allocating transfers		
	– Score on timeliness of information on transfers		
	– Score on extent of collection and reporting of consolidated fiscal data for general government		
	Value of Central Government transfers to Subnational Governments	% of the GDP	
	Value of Actual budgetary allocation to Subnational Governments from National Government	% of total expenditure	
	Value of Deviation of actual against the budgeted transfers to Subnational Governments	% of budgeted transfers	
Local governance system	None	Description	Details on the local governance system in the country, including the various levels of local governments; their roles, responsibilities and functions; and the devolution of powers from the higher levels of government to these various levels of local governments.
Infrastructure development plan for local governments	None	Description	Details on the infrastructure development plans prepared by the local governments based on their capital investment projects in the pipeline, and the coverage of such infrastructure development plans.
PPP enabling framework for local governments	None	Description	Details on the PPP enabling framework applicable to local government PPP projects, including PPP legal and regulatory framework, PPP policy framework, and PPP institutional framework

continued on next page

continued from previous page

Subcategory	Supporting Indicators	Units	Definition
Eligible sectors for PPPs for local governments	None	Description	Details on the eligible sectors in which PPPs could be undertaken by local government as government contracting agency
Revenues for local governments	None	Description	Details on the typical sources of revenue for local governments
Borrowings by local governments	None	Description	Details on the typical sources of debt financing available for local governments, the purpose for which borrowed funds could be used, the terms of such borrowings, and the borrowing exposure of select local governments
Budgetary allocation to local governments	None	Description	Details on the budgetary allocations and transfers to the local governments from the higher levels of government
Credit rating of local governments	None	Description	Details on the precedence of local governments being rated by credit rating agencies in the country Details of credit ratings obtained by select local governments in the past
Case study on a local government PPP	None	Description	A case of a PPP project undertaken by a local government in the past, which covers details on project background, project assets, PPP structure for the project, risk allocation among the parties for the project, project finance and project revenue details, and key learnings from the PPP project

Table A1.6: Critical Macroeconomic and Infrastructure Sector Indicators for the Country

Subcategory	Supporting Indicators	Units	Definition
Critical macroeconomic and infrastructure sector indicators	Total population	million	Details of major macroeconomic indicators for the country
	Average annual population growth rate	%	
	Population density	persons per square kilometer (km^2) of surface area	
	Urban population	% of total population	
	Surface area	'000 km^2	
	Unemployment rate	%	
	Proportion of population below $1.90 purchasing power parity (PPP) a day	%	
	Nominal gross domestic product (GDP)	$ billion	
		%	
	Annual growth rate of GDP (2019)	%	
	Annual growth rate of GDP (2020 forecast)	%	
	Annual growth rate of GDP (2021 forecast)	%	
	GDP at purchasing power parity (PPP) per capita	$ at PPP	
	GDP at current market prices	$ billion	
	Gross fixed investment at current market prices	% of GDP	
	Per capita gross national income (GNI), Atlas Method	$	
	Inflation rate (2019)	%	
	Inflation rate (2020 forecast)	%	
	Inflation rate (2021 forecast)	%	
	Current account (2019)	% of GDP	
	External trade, goods, value of imports, CIF (2018)	$ billion	
	External trade, goods, value of exports, FOB (2018)	$ billion	
	CPI % change over 2018	% of CPI in 2018	
	Real effective exchange rate		
	Investment in energy with private sector participation	Current $ million	
	Investment in transport with private sector participation	Current $ million	
	Investment in water and sanitation with private sector participation	Current $ million	
	Logistics Performance Index (LPI) rank	number	
	Logistics Performance Index (LPI) score	number	
	Customs rank	number	
	Customs score	number	

continued on next page

continued from previous page

Subcategory	Supporting Indicators	Units	Definition
	Infrastructure rank	number	
	Infrastructure score	number	
	International shipments rank	number	
	International shipments score	number	
	Logistics competence rank	number	
	Logistics competence score	number	
	Tracking and tracing rank	number	
	Tracking and tracing score	number	
	Timeliness rank	number	
	Timeliness score	number	
	Structure of Output (% of GDP at current producer | basic prices)		
	Agriculture	%	
	Industry	%	
	Services	%	
	Consumer price index (national)	% annual change	
	Producer price index	% annual change	
	Wholesale price index (national)	% annual change	
	Retail price index	% annual change	
	Exchange rates (End of period)	Local currency - $	
	ADF Portfolio		
	Total number of loans	Number	
	1. Sovereign	Number	
	2. Nonsovereign	Number	
	Net loan amount	$ million, cumulative	
	1. Sovereign	$ million, cumulative	
	2. Nonsovereign	$ million, cumulative	
	Disbursed amount	$ million, cumulative	
	1. Sovereign	$ million, cumulative	
	2. Nonsovereign	$ million, cumulative	
	Net foreign direct investment (FDI) inflows	% of GDP	
	Sovereign debt risk rating	Letter rating	
	Central government debt	% of GDP	
	CPIA quality of budgetary and financial management rating	1=low to 6=high	

continued on next page

continued from previous page

Subcategory	Supporting Indicators	Units	Definition
	Ease of Doing Business		
	Ease of doing business rank	number	
	Starting a business (rank)	number	
	Dealing with construction permits (rank)	number	
	Getting electricity (rank)	number	
	Registering property (rank)	number	
	Getting credit (rank)	number	
	Protecting minority investors (rank)	number	
	Paying taxes (rank)	number	
	Trading across borders (rank)	number	
	Enforcing contracts (rank)	number	
	Resolving insolvency (rank)	number	
	Corruption and Sustainable Development Index		
	Corruption Perceptions Index rank (out of 180)	number	
	Corruption Perceptions Index score (out of 100)	number	
	Sustainable Development Index rank	number	
	Sustainable Development Index score	number	
	Cumulative Lending, Grant, and Technical Assistance Commitments		
	Number of projects	number	
	Total lending	$ million	
	GCI infrastructure score	out of 7	
	EIU Infrascope Index Score		
	PPP regulations score (out of 100)	number	
	PPP regulations rank	number	
	PPP institutions score (out of 100)	number	
	PPP institutions rank	number	
	PPP market maturity score (out of 100)	number	
	PPP market maturity rank	number	
	PPP financing score (out of 100)	number	
	PPP financing rank	number	
	Investment and business climate score (out of 100)	number	
	Investment and business climate rank	number	

continued on next page

continued from previous page

Subcategory	Supporting Indicators	Units	Definition
Ease of Doing Business	Score of starting a business	(0–100)	Details on the various *Ease of Doing Business* parameters for the country based on the World Bank's *Ease of Doing Business* publication
	• Procedures	(number)	
	• Time	(days)	
	• Cost	(number)	
	• Paid-in min. capital	(% of income per capita)	
	Score of dealing with construction permits	(0–100)	
	• Procedures	(number)	
	• Time	(days)	
	• Cost	(% of warehouse value)	
	• Building quality control index	(0–15)	
	Score of getting electricity	(0–100)	
	• Procedures	(number)	
	• Time	(days)	
	• Cost	(% of income per capita)	
	• Reliability of supply and transparency of tariff index	(0–8)	
	Score of registering property	(0–100)	
	• Procedures	(number)	
	• Time	(days)	
	• Cost	(% of property value)	
	• Quality of the land administration index	(0–30)	
	Score of getting credit	(0–100)	
	• Strength of legal rights index	(0–12)	
	• Depth of credit information index	(0–8)	
	• Credit registry coverage	(% of adults)	
	• Credit bureau coverage	(% of adults)	
	Score of protecting minority investors	(0–100)	
	• Extent of disclosure index	(0–10)	
	• Extent of director liability index	(0–10)	
	• Ease of shareholder suits index	(0–10)	
	• Extent of shareholder rights index	(0–6)	
	• Extent of ownership and control index	(0–7)	
	• Extent of corporate transparency index	(0–7)	
	Score of paying taxes	(0–100)	
	• Payments	(number per year)	
	• Time	(hours per year)	
	• Total tax and contribution rate	(% of profit)	
	• Postfiling index	(0–100)	

continued on next page

continued from previous page

Subcategory	Supporting Indicators	Units	Definition
	Score of trading across borders	(0–100)	
	Time to export		
	• Documentary compliance	(hours)	
	• Border compliance	(hours)	
	Cost to export		
	• Documentary compliance	($)	
	• Border compliance	($)	
	Time to export		
	• Documentary compliance	(hours)	
	• Border compliance	(hours)	
	Cost to export		
	• Documentary compliance	($)	
	• Border compliance	($)	
	Score of enforcing contracts	(0–100)	
	• Time	(days)	
	• Cost	(% of claim value)	
	• Quality of judicial processes index	(0–18)	
	Score of resolving insolvency	(0–100)	
	• Recovery rate	(cents on the dollar)	
	• Time	(years)	
	• Cost	(% of estate)	
	• Outcome	(0 as piecemeal sale and 1 as going concern)	
	• Strength of insolvency framework index	(0–16)	

Comment of Financial Indicators

In regard to indicative loan terms presented in this publication, it should be noted that it is very difficult to generalize the loan terms as the data are dynamic. The data vary from one sector to another, and in a particular sector, the loan terms differ from one project to another depending on the project cash flows and the creditworthiness of the project sponsors. The loan terms are also driven by market forces, monetary policy, fiscal policy, and other macroeconomic variables. Generally, international banks provide project finance in internationally convertible currency and the terms are broadly consistent across countries, given other risk factors are held constant, as country risk is the only risk factor. In general, some of the factors that determine pricing are:

- exposure to market/revenue risk,
- exposure to foreign exchange risk,
- credibility of off-taker,
- credibility of sovereign,

- availability of export credit/multilateral support,
- "proven-ness" of sector and underlying technology, and
- financing market (such as global macroeconomic events) and regulations (i.e., Basel III).

It is understood in project finance that lenders take all securities including security over the "rights" of the concessionaire to operate the asset and collect revenue. The stability of the revenue stream is most important, and most international lenders will require a sovereign guarantee from the Ministry of Finance for the paying authority's obligations. In addition, from a commercial bank's perspective, such sovereign guarantee has to be further guaranteed/insured by export credit agencies and/or multilateral lending agencies.

In general, local banks lending in local currency will have less stringent requirements on a project; however, they will also offer a higher financing cost. From previous market sounding, local banks can generally cope with higher debt–equity ratios, lower debt-service coverage ratio, and no explicit sovereign guarantee where international lenders would require it. They can also cope with some level of revenue and fare risk where international banks demand a guaranteed off-take for greenfield projects. Also, very often banks have the appetite and capacity to finance PPP projects; however, the lack of well-prepared and structured projects limits the progress.

Capital markets are expected to play a major role in financing infrastructure PPPs, but are relatively underdeveloped in majority of the DMCs covered. Capital markets have played a muted role in project financing in such DMCs. DMCs with a relatively matured PPP market and a relatively developed capital market have witnessed some PPPs issuing bonds and raising financing from capital markets. Institutional investors such as insurance companies and pension funds are restricted from taking exposure to PPP projects during construction period due to their internal investment norms and regulatory requirements to invest in investment grade projects and investment avenues, which majority of infrastructure PPPs do not attain during the construction period. Hence majority of such institutional investors take exposure to infrastructure PPPs during the operations period by buying out a part of the equity investment (as allowed by the PPP Agreement) of the project sponsors, or by retiring out bank financing for the project.

Comments on Data Sources

The research was carried out using publicly available sources, including:

- government websites, reports, and publications, including national government line ministries and government contracting agencies;
- annual reports of national government line ministries and government contracting agencies;
- applicable laws and regulations (where regulations were available only in the local language, unofficial translations were used);
- websites and annual reports of sector regulators;
- Asian Development Bank (ADB) reports and publications;
- online publications of other multilateral development agencies;
- industry publications and databases such as *Inframation News* and *IJGlobal Project Finance & Infrastructure Journal*;
- publications and websites of reputable consultancy companies and law firms; and
- other publicly available reports, publications, and documents from authentic and globally acceptable sources.

Some of the widely used databases included

- World Bank Private Participation in Infrastructure (PPI) Database, https://ppi.worldbank.org/en/ppi;
- Inframation database https://www.inframationnews.com/;
- IJGlobal database, https://ijglobal.com/;
- PPP Knowledge Lab, https://pppknowledgelab.org/;
- The Economist Intelligence Unit (EIU) Infrascope Index, https://infrascope.eiu.com/;
- Global Infrastructure Hub, https://www.gihub.org/;
- Organisation for Economic Co-operation and Development (OECD), https://www.oecd.org/;
- TheGlobalEconomy.com, https://www.theglobaleconomy.com/;
- International Monetary Fund (IMF), https://data.imf.org/?sk=388dfa60-1d26-4ade-b505-a05a558d9a42;
- Doing Business, https://www.doingbusiness.org/;
- World Bank Public-Private-Partnership Legal Resource Center, https://ppp.worldbank.org/public-private-partnership/;
- World Economic Forum, The Global Competitiveness Report, http://www3.weforum.org/docs/WEF_TheGlobalCompetitivenessReport2019.pdf;
- Global Infrastructure Outlook, https://outlook.gihub.org/; and
- Trading Economics, https://tradingeconomics.com/.

Some of the other major sources used included

- Asian Development Bank Country Partnership Strategy, 2016–2020: Papua New Guinea. https://www.adb.org/documents/papua-new-guinea-country-partnership-strategy-2016-2020
- Papua New Guinea Public-Private Partnership Act, 2010. http://wk.ixueshu.com/file/27bbf54642ea6319.html
- Papua New Guinea Public-Private Partnership Act, 2014. https://www.treasury.gov.pg/html/legislation/files/acts/2014/Public.Private.Partnership.(PPP).Act.2014.pdf
- Papua New Guinea National Public-Private Partnership Policy 2014. https://www.treasury.gov.pg/html/misc/Special%20Projects/PPP/PNG%20National%20PPP%20Policy%202014.pdf
- Department of Transport and Infrastructure. http://www.transport.gov.pg/
- 2019 Investment Climate Statements: Papua New Guinea. https://www.state.gov/reports/2019-investment-climate-statements/papua-new-guinea/
- Commonwealth Local Government Forum: The Local Government System in Papua New Guinea. http://www.clgf.org.uk/default/assets/File/Country_profiles/Papua_New_Guinea.pdf

A detailed list of sources is provided in the References section of this publication.

In addition to the abovementioned sources, the research for this report was informed by the internal knowledge of CRISIL Infrastructure Advisory, based on various ongoing and completed PPP consultancy assignments in Indonesia; public sector officials; the ADB team from the Office of Public–Private Partnership (OPPP); the ADB

Resident Mission for Indonesia; consultants to the ADB Resident Mission in Indonesia; various government agencies; and contributing legal firms and commercial banks.

It should be noted that, as the research relied primarily on information reported in public sources that have not been verified by the authors and may not be accurate or contain all the required information, there is the risk of inaccuracy and incompleteness, depending on the reliability of sources and the validity of the information used.

For quantitative indicators relating to the number of projects, where there were gaps the total number of cases has been reported based on the limited information available. Therefore, reported numbers of projects in this publication may be an underestimate or overestimate the actual numbers.

Further, for various indicators, this publication captures information based on the provisions of the laws, regulations, policies, and government publications associated with the PPP legal, regulatory, policy, and institutional frameworks in the country. This publication does not provide details on the existing status regarding the adoption or application of such PPP laws, regulations, and policies, and the existing challenges being faced in such applications.

Appendix 2: Critical Macroeconomic and Infrastructure Sector Indicators for Papua New Guinea

The various macroeconomic and infrastructure sector indicators for Papua New Guinea are as provided in the table below:

Table A2: Critical Macroeconomic and Infrastructure Sector Indicators for Papua New Guinea

Parameter	Value	Unit
Total Population (2020)	8.9	(million)
Average Annual Population Growth Rate	2.24	(%)
Population Density	19	(persons per km^2 of surface area)
Urban population	13.17	(% of total population)
Surface Area	462.84	('000 km^2)
Unemployment rate	2.37	(%)
Proportion of Population below $1.90 Purchasing Power Parity (PPP) a Day	UA	(%)
Nominal Gross Domestic Product (GDP)	24.87	($ billion)
	4.8	(%)
Annual Growth Rate of GDP (2019)	5	(%)
Annual Growth Rate of GDP (2020 forecast)	-2	(%)
Annual Growth Rate of GDP (2021 forecast)	3	(%)
GDP at purchasing power parity (PPP) per capita (2018)	4,336	$ at PPP
GDP at current market prices (2018)	20.8	$ billion
Gross fixed investment at current market prices	10.2	% of GDP
Per Capita Gross National Income (GNI), Atlas Method	2,570	($)
Inflation Rate (2019)	4	(%)
Inflation Rate (2020 forecast)	3	(%)
Inflation Rate (2021 forecast)	4	(%)
Current Account (2019)	24.88	% of GDP
External Trade, Goods, Value of Imports, CIF (2018)	5,054.79	$ billion
External Trade, Goods, Value of Exports, FOB (2018)	6,568.90	$ billion
CPI % change over 2018	3.64	% of CPI in 2018
Real Effective Exchange Rate	129.62	
Investment in energy with private participation	65	Current $ million
Investment in transport with private participation	UA	Current $ million
Investment in water and sanitation with private participation	71	Current $ million

continued on next page

continued from previous page

Parameter	Value	Unit
LPI Rank	148	number
LPI Score	2.17	number
Customs Rank	116	number
Customs Score	2.32	number
Infrastructure Rank	144	number
Infrastructure Score	1.97	number
International shipments Rank	150	number
International shipments Score	2.15	number
Logistics competence Rank	160	number
Logistics competence Score	1.88	number
Tracking and tracing Rank	138	number
Tracking and tracing Score	2.26	number
Timeliness Rank	150	number
Timeliness Score	2.44	number
Structure of Output (% of GDP at current producer | basic prices)		
Agriculture	17.88	(%)
Industry	40.50	(%)
Services	41.62	(%)
Consumer price index (national)	4.50	(% annual change)
Producer price index	UA	(% annual change)
Wholesale price index (national)	UA	(% annual change)
Retail price index	UA	(% annual change)
Exchange rates (End of period)	3.37	(Local Currency – $)
ADF Portfolio		
Total number of loans	18.00	number
1. Sovereign	UA	number
2. Nonsovereign	UA	number
Net loan amount	503.00	($ million, cumulative)
1. Sovereign	UA	($ million, cumulative)
2. Nonsovereign	UA	($ million, cumulative)
Disbursed amount	203.00	($ million, cumulative)
1. Sovereign	UA	($ million, cumulative)
2. Nonsovereign	UA	($ million, cumulative)

continued on next page

continued from previous page

Parameter	Value	Unit
Net Foreign direct investment (FDI) inflows	4.80	% of GDP
Sovereign debt risk rating	50.00	letter rating
Central government debt	30.80	% of GDP
CPIA quality of budgetary and financial management rating	3.00	1=low to 6=high
Ease of Doing Business		
EODB Rank	120.00	number
Starting a Business (rank)	142.00	number
Dealing with Construction Permits (rank)	122.00	number
Getting Electricity (rank)	118.00	number
Registering Property (rank)	127.00	number
Getting Credit (rank)	48.00	number
Protecting Minority Investors (rank)	72.00	number
Paying Taxes (rank)	118.00	number
Trading across Borders (rank)	125.00	number
Enforcing Contracts (rank)	173.00	number
Resolving Insolvency (rank)	144.00	number
Corruption and Sustainable Development Index		
Corruption Perceptions Index Rank (out of 180)	137	number
Corruption Perceptions Index Score (out of 100)	28	number
Sustainable Development Index Rank	155.00	number
Sustainable Development Index Score	51.66	number
Cumulative Lending, Grant, and Technical Assistance Commitments		
Number of Projects	272.00	number
Total Lending	3,049.59	$ million
GCI Infrastructure Score	UA	(out of 7)
EIU Infrascope Index Score		
PPP Regulations Score (out of 100)	27	number
PPP Regulations Rank	15	number
PPP Institutions Score (out of 100)	0	number
PPP Institutions Rank	15	number
PPP Market Maturity Score (out of 100)	31	number

continued on next page

continued from previous page

Parameter	Value	Unit
PPP Market Maturity Rank	15	number
PPP Financing Score (out of 100)	28	number
PPP Financing Rank	15	number
Investment and Business Climate Score (out of 100)	60	number
Investment and Business Climate Rank	10	number

CIF = cost, insurance, and freight; CPI = Consumer Price Index; FDI = foreign direct investment; FOB = freight on board; GCI = Global Competitive Index, GDP = Gross Domestic Product, GNI = Gross National Income, LPI = Logistics Performance Index; PPP = purchasing power parity; UA = unavailable.

Sources: The Economist Intelligence Unit. Papua New Guinea. https://infrascope.eiu.com/; Worldometer. Papua New Guinea Population. https://www.worldometers.info/world-population/papua-new-guinea-population/#:~:text=Papua%20New%20Guinea%202020%20population,(and%20dependencies)%20by%20population; Asian Development Bank. 2020. *Basic Statistics 2020*. Manila. https://www.adb.org/publications/basic-statistics-2020; Asian Development Bank. 2019. *Key Indicators for Asia and the Pacific 2019*. Manila. https://www.adb.org/publications/key-indicators-asia-and-pacific-2019; World Bank. *GDP – Papua New Guinea*. https://data.worldbank.org/indicator/NY.GDP.MKTP.KD?locati ons=PG; Asian Development Bank. Inflation Rate in Asia and the Pacific, Asian Development Outlook (ADO). https://data.adb.org/dataset/inflation-rate-asia-and-pacific-asian-development-outlook; International Monetary Fund. https://data.imf.org/?sk=85b51b5a-b74f-473a-be16-49f1786949b3; IMF. Exchange Rate, Selected Indicators. https://data.imf.org/regular.aspx?key=61545850; World Bank. LPI Rankings 2018. https://lpi.worldbank.org/international/global?sort=asc&order=LPI%20Score#datatable; Asian Development Bank. 2015. *Country Partnership Strategy: Papua New Guinea 2016-2020*. Manila. https://www.adb.org/sites/default/files/institutional-document/157927/cps-png-2016-2020.pdf; Doing Business. Ease of Doing Business Rankings. https://www.doingbusiness.org/en/rankings; Transparency International. Countries. https://www.transparency.org/en/countries/papua-new-guinea; Asian Development Bank. Cumulative Lending, Grant, and Technical Assistance Commitments. https://data.adb.org/dataset/cumulative-lending-grant-and-technical-assistance-commitments; PPP Knowledge Lab. Papua New Guinea. https://pppknowledgelab.org/countries/papua-new-guinea.

Appendix 3: World Bank's Ease of Doing Business Parameters for Papua New Guinea

The snapshot of the World Bank Ease of Doing Business parameters for Papua New Guinea are as follows:

Ease of Doing Business in Papua New Guinea			DB Rank - 120	DB Score - 59.8
	Region	East Asia and Pacific		
	Income Category	Lower middle income		
	Population	8,944,922[a]		
	City covered	Port Moresby		

[a] Worldometer. Papua New Guinea Population. https://www.worldometers.info/world-population/papua-new-guinea-population/#:~:text=Papua%20New%20Guinea%202020%20population,(and%20dependencies)%20by%20population.

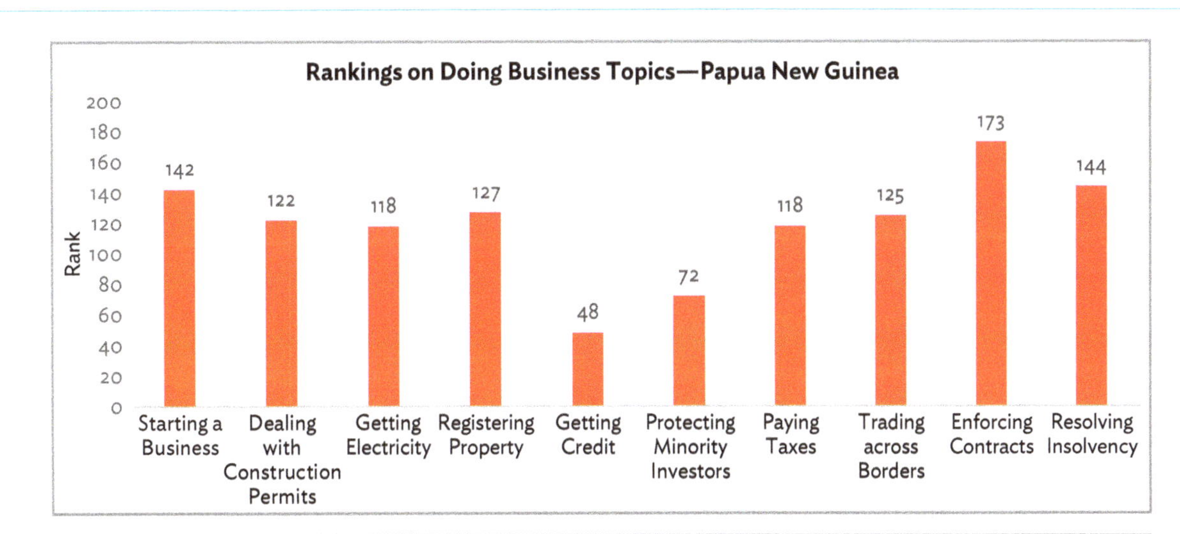

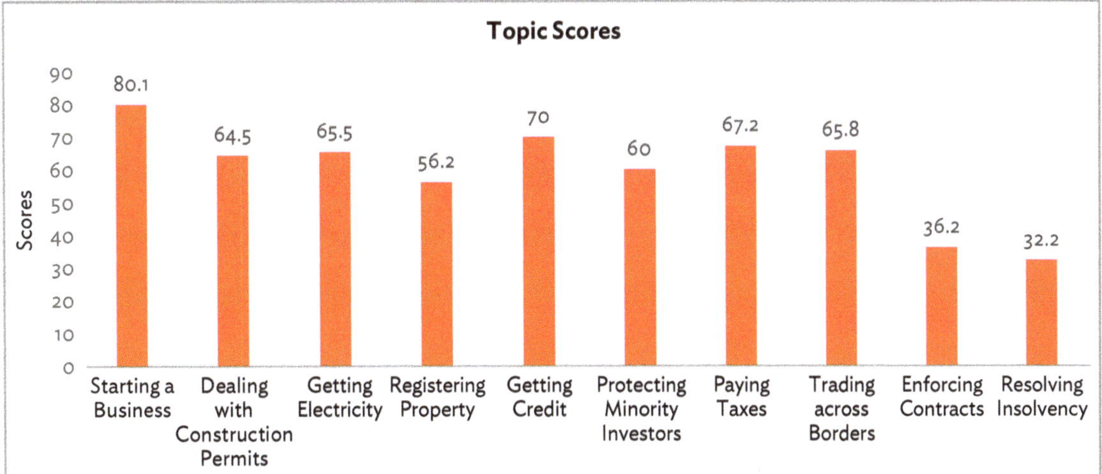

Source: World Bank Group. Doing Business 2020: Economy Profile, Papua New Guinea. https://www.doingbusiness.org/content/dam/doingBusiness/country/p/papua-new-guinea/PNG-LITE.pdf.

Starting a Business (rank)	142	Dealing with Construction Permits (rank)	122	Getting Electricity (rank)	118	Registering Property (rank)	127
Score of starting a business (0–100)	80.1	Score of dealing with construction permits (0–100)	64.5	Score of getting electricity (0–100)	65.5	Score of registering property (0–100)	56.2
Procedures (number)	6	Procedures (number)	17	Procedures (number)	4	Procedures (number)	4
Time (days)	41	Time (days)	217	Time (days)	66	Time (days)	72
Cost (number)	18.6	Cost (% of warehouse value)	1.1	Cost (% of income per capita)	25.6	Cost (% of property value)	5.2
Paid-in minimum capital (% of income per capita)	0	Building quality control index (0–15)	10	Reliability of supply and transparency of tariff index (0–8)	0	Quality of the land administration index (0–30)	5.5

Getting Credit (rank)	48	Protecting Minority Investors (rank)	72	Paying Taxes (rank)	118
Score of getting credit (0–100)	70	Score of protecting minority investors (0–100)	60	Score of paying taxes (0–100)	67.2
Strength of legal rights index (0–12)	9	Extent of disclosure index (0–10)	5	Payments (number per year)	45
Depth of credit information index (0–8)	5	Extent of director liability index (0–10)	5	Time (hours per year)	207
Credit registry coverage (% of adults)	0	Ease of shareholder suits index (0–10)	9	Total tax and contribution rate (% of profit)	37.1
Credit bureau coverage (% of adults)	7.5	Extent of shareholder rights index (0–6)	6	Postfiling index (0–100)	78.5
		Extent of ownership and control index (0–7)	2		
		Extent of corporate transparency index (0–7)	3		

Trading across Borders (rank)	125	Enforcing Contracts (rank)	173	Resolving Insolvency (rank)	144
Score of trading across borders (0–100)	65.8	Score of enforcing contracts (0–100)	36.2	Score of resolving insolvency (0–100)	32.2
Time to export		Time (days)	591	Recovery rate (cents on the dollar)	24.9
Documentary compliance (hours)	48	Cost (% of claim value)	110.3	Time (years)	3
Border compliance (hours)	42	Quality of judicial processes index (0–18)	8.5	Cost (% of estate)	23
Cost to export				Outcome (0 as piecemeal sale and 1 as going concern)	0

continued on next page

continued from previous page

Trading across Borders (rank)	125	Enforcing Contracts (rank)	173	Resolving Insolvency (rank)	144
Documentary compliance ($)	75			Strength of insolvency framework index (0–16)	6
Border compliance ($)	700				
Time to export					
Documentary compliance (hours)	48				
Border compliance (hours)	72				
Cost to export					
Documentary compliance ($)	85				
Border compliance ($)	940				

Appendix 4: Assessment of the Public Financial Management System in Papua New Guinea, 2015

Based on the latest assessment of the Public Financial Management System (PFMS) in Papua New Guinea based on the Public Expenditure and Financial Accountability (PEFA) framework, Papua New Guinea has an **overall rating of B** [on a four-point rating scale A (best) to D (worst)] for the transfers to the Subnational Governments from the National Government (footnote 52).

Parameter / Sub-Parameter	Score	Justification for score
Transfers to Subnational Governments	**B**	**Almost two-thirds of central government's transfers to subnational governments are based on transparent and rules-based systems. The process by which SNGs receive information on their annual transfers is managed through the regular budget calendar, which is generally adhered to and provides clear and sufficiently detailed information. However, Reports that consolidate fiscal information for central governments entities and SNGs are not prepared by the government**
• System for allocating transfers	B	Horizontal allocation of roughly 65% of transfers from central government is determined by a transparent and rules-based system
• Timeliness of information on transfers	A	Provinces are provided with reliable information via a budget circular in June/ July
• Extent of collection and reporting of consolidated fiscal data for general government	D	Information on provinces, districts and local-level governments is collected by Department of Finance, but data on general government finances are not consolidated

Source: International Monetary Fund. 2015. *Papua New Guinea Public Expenditure and Financial Accountability Assessment.* Washington, DC. https://www.pefa.org/sites/pefa/files/assessments/reports/PNG-Aug15-PFMPR-Testing-version-Public-with-PEFA-Check.PDF.

PEFA Assessment of PFMS in Papua New Guinea, 2015

Parameter	Value	Unit
Central Government transfers to Subnational Governments	UA	% of the GDP
Actual budgetary allocation to Subnational Governments from National Government	UA	% of total expenditure
Deviation of actual against the budgeted transfers to Subnational Governments	UA	% of budgeted transfers

✓ = Yes, × = No, UA= Unavailable, NA = Not Applicable, PEFA = public expenditure and financial accountability,

PFMS = public financial management system.

Source: International Monetary Fund. 2015. *Papua New Guinea Public Expenditure and Financial Accountability Assessment.* Papua New Guinea. https://www.pefa.org/sites/pefa/files/assessments/reports/PNG-Aug15-PFMPR-Testing-version-Public-with-PEFA-Check.PDF.

References

Asian Development Bank (ADB). 2013. *Sector Assessment (Summary): Energy*. Manila. https://www.adb.org/sites/default/files/linked-documents/43197-013-png-ssa.pdf.

ADB. 2014. *Energy Sector Assessment*. Manila. https://www.adb.org/sites/default/files/linked-documents/CAPE-PNG-6-Energy-Sector-Assessment.pdf.

ADB. 2016–2020. *Sector Assessment (Summary): Transport*. Manila. https://www.adb.org/sites/default/files/linked-documents/cps-png-2016-2020-ssa-01.pdf.

ADB. 2019. *Public–Private Partnership Monitor, Second Edition*. Manila. https://www.adb.org/sites/default/files/publication/509426/ppp-monitor-second-edition.pdf.

ADB. Cumulative Lending, Grant, and Technical Assistance Commitments. https://data.adb.org/dataset/cumulative-lending-grant-and-technical-assistance-commitments.

ADB. News. https://www.adb.org/news/adb-helps-png-expand-port-moresby-international-airport-using-ppp.

Civil Aviation Safety Authority, Papua New Guinea. *About Us*. https://casapng.gov.pg/about-us/.

Commonwealth Local Government Forum. 2019. *The Local Government System in Papua New Guinea*. http://www.clgf.org.uk/default/assets/File/Country_profiles/Papua_New_Guinea.pdf.

Deloitte. 2020. *Papua New Guinea Budget 2020*. https://www2.deloitte.com/content/dam/Deloitte/pg/Documents/financial-services/deloitte-pg-fs-papua-new-guinea-budget-281119.pdf.

Development Asia. 2017. *Case Study: A Flexible Financing Model for Large-Scale Infrastructure Investments*. https://development.asia/case-study/flexible-financing-model-large-scale-infrastructure-investments.

Energy, Oil and Gas. Profiles. http://www.energy-oil-gas.com/2020/06/10/niupower/.

Government of Australia, Department of Foreign Affairs and Trade. 2018. *Road Management in Papua New Guinea: An Evaluation of a Decade of Australian Support 2007–2017*. Canberra. http://www.oecd.org/derec/australia/australia-ode-evaluation-road-management-in-papua-new-guinea.pdf.

Government of Papua New Guinea, Department of Public Enterprises and Department of Petroleum and Energy. 2015. *National Energy Policy*. http://prdrse4all.spc.int/system/files/national_energy_policy_19.07.2015v5_final_png.pdf.

Government of Papua New Guinea, Department of Transport. *Air Projects*. http://www.transport.gov.pg/113-investment/air-projects.

Government of Papua New Guinea. 2012. *Education Sector Strategic Plan 2011–2030*. Port Moresby. http://wbgfiles.worldbank.org/documents/hdn/ed/saber/supporting_doc/EAP/Papua%20New%20Guinea/SAA/DoE_2012_Education_Sector_Strategic_Plan_2011_-_2030.pdf.

Government of Papua New Guinea, Department of Transport. *Air Projects*. http://www.transport.gov.pg/113-investment/air-projects?start=1.

Government of Papua New Guinea, Department of Transport. *Air Transport*. http://www.transport.gov.pg/air-transport.

Government of Papua New Guinea, Department of Transport. *Civil Aviation Legislation*. http://www.transport.gov.pg/air-transport/civil-aviation-legislation.

Government of Papua New Guinea, Department of Transport. *Civil Aviation Institutions*. http://www.transport.gov.pg/air-transport/civil-aviation-institutions.

Government of Papua New Guinea, Department of Transport. *Land Transport*. http://www.transport.gov.pg/land-transport.

Government of Papua New Guinea, Department of Transport. *Maritime Projects*. http://www.transport.gov.pg/projects/maritime-projects.

Government of Papua New Guinea, Department of Transport. *Maritime Sector Institutions*. http://www.transport.gov.pg/maritime-transport/maritime-sector-institutions.

Government of Papua New Guinea, Department of Transport. *Maritime Sector Legislations*. http://www.transport.gov.pg/maritime-transport/maritime-sector-legislations.

Government of Papua New Guinea, Department of Transport. *Ports Landings*. http://www.transport.gov.pg/maritime-transport/ports-landings.

Government of Papua New Guinea, Department of Transport. *Road Projects*. http://www.transport.gov.pg/projects/road-projects.

Government of Papua New Guinea, Department of Treasury. 2014. *National PPP Policy 2014*. https://www.treasury.gov.pg/html/misc/Special%20Projects/PPP/PNG%20National%20PPP%20Policy%202014.pdf.

Government of Papua New Guinea, Department of Treasury. 2014. *Public–Private Partnership Act 2014*. https://www.treasury.gov.pg/html/legislation/files/acts/2014/Public.Private.Partnership.(PPP).Act.2014.pdf.

Government of Papua New Guinea, Department of Treasury. 2019. *Infrastructure Financing and Public–Private Partnership Network of Asia and the Pacific*. Presentation for the United Nations Economic and Social Commission for Asia and the Pacific. Ningbo, People's Republic of China. 2–3 September. https://www.unescap.org/sites/default/files/Session%202%20-%20Panelist%20-%202Mr.%20Martin%20Teine_PNG.pdf.

Government of Papua New Guinea, Ministry of Health. *Acts and Policies*. https://www.health.gov.pg/subindex.php?acts=1.

Government of Papua New Guinea, National Executive Council. 2009. *Universal Basic Education Plan 2010–2019*. Port Moresby. https://planipolis.iiep.unesco.org/sites/planipolis/files/ressources/papua_new_guinea_ube_2010-2019.pdf.

Government of Papua New Guinea, Road Traffic Authority. 2014. *Road Traffic Act 2014*. Port Moresby. http://rta.gov.pg/pdfs/RoadTrafficAct2014.pdf.

Government of Papua New Guinea, Road Transport Authority. *Acts of Parliament*. http://www.rta.gov.pg/legislation/acts-of-parliament/.

Government of Papua New Guinea. 1981. *Land Registration Act 1981*. http://extwprlegs1.fao.org/docs/pdf/png24837.pdf.

Government of Papua New Guinea. 1983. *Education Act 1983*. https://www.education.gov.pg/TISER/documents/legislation/ea1983104.pdf.

Government of Papua New Guinea. 1992. *Investment Promotion Act 1992*. https://www.italaw.com/sites/default/files/laws/italaw6297.pdf.

Government of Papua New Guinea. 1992. *Mining Act*. https://www.ilo.org/dyn/natlex/docs/ELECTRONIC/82401/90191/F973763837/PNG82401.pdf.

Government of Papua New Guinea. 1996. *Land Act 1996*. http://extwprlegs1.fao.org/docs/pdf/png20843.pdf.

Government of Papua New Guinea. 1997. *Local-level Administration Act 1997*. http://www.paclii.org/pg/legis/consol_act/lgaa1997403/#:~:text=Local%2Dlevel%20Governments%20Administration%20Act%201997%2C,Governments%20and%20for%20their%20administration.

Government of Papua New Guinea. 1998. *Oil and Gas Act*. http://www.paclii.org/pg/legis/consol_act/oaga199894.pdf.

Government of Papua New Guinea. 1998. *Organic Law on Provincial Governments and Local-level Governments*. https://www.ilo.org/dyn/natlex/docs/ELECTRONIC/88035/100550/F518409/PNG88035.pdf.

Government of Papua New Guinea. 2002. *Electricity Industry Act*. http://prdrse4all.spc.int/system/files/electricity_industry_act_chapter_78_consolidated_to_no_10_of_2002.pdf.

Government of Papua New Guinea. 2002. *Independent Consumer and Competition Commission Act 2002*. http://www.paclii.org/pg/legis/consol_act/icacca2002483.pdf.

Government of Papua New Guinea. 2011. *National Health Service Standards for Papua New Guinea 2011–2020*. https://hwfsmspng.net/publications/NHSS_PNG_2011-2020_Vol1&2/national_health_service_standards_for_png_2011-2020_Vol1.pdf.

Government of Papua New Guinea. 2015. *WASH Policy 2015–2030*. https://png-data.sprep.org/system/files/WaSH_POLICY04.03.2015.pdf.

Government of Papua New Guinea. 2016. *National Water Supply and Sanitation Act 2016*. http://extwprlegs1.fao.org/docs/pdf/png177402.pdf.

Government of Papua New Guinea. 2018. *Final Budget Outcome 2018*. https://www.treasury.gov.pg/html/national_budget/files/2013/budget_documents/Related%20Budget%20Documents/2018%20Final%20Budget%20Outcome.pdf.

Inframation News. Australia and Papua New Guinea Plan—A$250 Million Energy Project Spending. https://www.inframationnews.com/news/3748526/australia-and-papua-plan-aud-250m-energy-project-spending.thtml.

Inframation News. Governments to Consider PPP for Papua New Guinea Electrification. https://www.inframationnews.com/news/3213251/governments-to-consider-ppp-for-papua-new-guinea-electrification.thtml.

International Labour Organization. *Papua New Guinea*. https://www.ilo.org/dyn/natlex/natlex4.detail?p_lang=en&p_isn=88036.

International Monetary Fund. 2015. *Public Expenditure and Financial Accountability Assessment—Papua New Guinea*. Washington, DC. https://www.pefa.org/sites/pefa/files/assessments/reports/PNG-Aug15-PFMPR-Testing-version-Public-with-PEFA-Check.PDF.

J. Grundy et al. 2019. *Independent State of Papua New Guinea Health System Review*. 9 (1). New Delhi: World Health Organization, Regional Office for South-East Asia. https://apps.who.int/iris/bitstream/handle/10665/280088/9789290226741-eng.pdf?sequence=5&isAllowed=y.

J. Quan-Sing et al. 2020. PNG Proposes a New Regime for Arbitration. *Allens Insights & News*. 26 February. https://www.allens.com.au/insights-news/insights/2020/02/png-proposes-a-new-regime-for-arbitration/.

Kumul. *What We Do*. https://www.kch.com.pg/what-we-do/our-portfolio/national-development-bank/.

National Airports Corporation. *About Us*. https://www.nac.com.pg/about-us/services/.

National Airports Corporation. *Airports*. https://www.nac.com.pg/airports/pmia-ppp/.

National Economic and Fiscal Commission. 2018. *2018 Budget Fiscal Report*. Port Moresby. https://www.nefc.gov.pg/documents/publications/fiscalReports/2018Fiscal_Report.pdf.

National Information and Communications Technology Authority. *Acts*. https://www.nicta.gov.pg/legislative/acts/.

National Maritime Safety Authority. 2013. *Separation of PNG Ports Corporation's Regulated and Unregulated Businesses*. Port Moresby. http://www.pngports.com.pg/docs/Public-notices/Issues-Paper_Seperation-of-Regulated-and-Unregulated-Buinesses.pdf.

Oil Search. 2019. NiuPower and PNG Power Limited Sign Historic Power Purchase Agreement. https://www.oilsearch.com/__data/assets/pdf_file/0006/34557/190428-NiuPower-and-PNG-Power-Limited-sign-historic-Power-Purchase-Agreement.pdf.

Oxford Business Group. *Overview*. https://oxfordbusinessgroup.com/overview/beaten-track-investing-infrastructure-key-unlocking-potential.

Pacific Islands Treaty Series PACLII. *Arbitration Act 1951*. http://www.paclii.org/pg/legis/consol_act/aa1951137/.

Pacific Islands Treaty Series PACLII. *Environment Act 2000*. http://www.paclii.org/pg/legis/consol_act/ea2000159/.

Papua New Guinea Ports. 2020. *2020 Essential Port Services Tariff Schedule*. Port Moresby. http://www.pngports.com.pg/docs/tariff/2020/2020-Essential-Port-Services-Tariff-Schedule.pdf.

Papua New Guinea Power Limited News. PNG Power Complies with Third Party Access Code. http://www.pngpower.com.pg/index.php/news/view/png-power-complies-with-third-party-access-code.

Port Strategy News. Close Collaboration Underpins PNG Port Reforms. https://www.portstrategy.com/news101/world/asia/close-collaboration-underpins-png-port-reforms.

Post-Courier. 2018. PPP Act in Operation. 18 April. https://postcourier.com.pg/ppp-act-operation/.

Post-Courier. 2018. Ramu 2 Set to Flood the Country with Energy. 26 September. https://postcourier.com.pg/ramu-2-set-flood-country-energy/.

Post-Courier. 2019. US2B Ramu 2 Hydro Power Project Stalled. 1 August. https://postcourier.com.pg/us2b-ramu-2-hydro-power-project-stalled/; https://www.thenational.com.pg/k3-31bil-hydro-project-to-start/.

S. Kuman. 2018. New Formal Framework to Help Develop Infrastructure within PNG. *Allens Insights & News*. 26 February. https://www.allens.com.au/insights-news/insights/2018/02/new-formal-framework-to-help-develop-infrastructure-within/#Footnotes.

S. Kuman et al. 2019. PNG Accedes to the New York Convention—What Will Change. *Allens Insights & News*. 7 August. https://www.allens.com.au/insights-news/insights/2019/08/png-accedes-to-the-new-york-convention-what-will-change/.

The Constructor. *PPP Construction Projects – Types and Benefits*. https://theconstructor.org/construction/public-private-partnership-ppp-construction-projects-types-benefits/1319/#12_Rehabilitate_Operate_and_Transfer_ROT.

The Economist Intelligence Unit. *Papua New Guinea*. https://infrascope.eiu.com/.

The National Research Institute, Papua New Guinea. 2018. *Potential Public–Private Partnership Strategy For Promoting Effective Housing Delivery in Papua New Guinea*. Discussion Paper No.165. Port Moresby. https://pngnri.org/images/Publications/DP165.pdf.

United Nations Development Programme. 2016. *Community Development in Papua New Guinea*. Port Moresby. https://www.pg.undp.org/content/dam/papua_new_guinea/docs/MDG/MDG%20high%20res/019UNDP%20CDM_DIGITAL%20(3).pdf.

United Nations Educational, Scientific and Cultural Organization. 2016. *Papua New Guinea National Education Plan 2015–2019*. Port Moresby. https://planipolis.iiep.unesco.org/sites/planipolis/files/ressources/papua_new_guinea_nep_2015-2019_doe.pdf.

United States Department of State. 2019. *2019 Investment Climate Statements: Papua New Guinea*. Washington, DC. https://www.state.gov/reports/2019-investment-climate-statements/papua-new-guinea/.

Universal Postal Union. 2018. *Guide to PPP for eServices in Postal Sector, Papua New Guinea*.

Wiley. The Political Economy of Road Management Reform: Papua New Guinea's National Road Fund. https://onlinelibrary.wiley.com/doi/full/10.1002/app5.142.

World Bank. 2017. *Benchmarking PPP Procurement 2017 in Papua New Guinea*. Washington, DC. https://www.procurementinet.org/wp-content/uploads/2017/02/Papua-New-Guinea.pdf.

World Bank. 2017. *Water Supply and Sanitation Development Project*. Washington, DC. http://documents.worldbank.org/curated/en/591931485443649141/pdf/PAD1746-PNG-Water-Supply-PAD-01232017.pdf.

World Bank. *Benchmarking Infrastructure Development*. https://bpp.worldbank.org/.

World Bank. Infrastructure Finance, PPPs and Guarantees. Country Snapshots. *Papua New Guinea*. https://ppi.worldbank.org/en/snapshots/country/papua-new-guinea (accessed 30 June 2020).

www.ingramcontent.com/pod-product-compliance
Lightning Source LLC
Chambersburg PA
CBHW061234270326
41929CB00031B/3490
9789292621124